Love Fat

Tabitha Farrar

Cover art by Bethany Alderson

Before we get stuck in . . .

This book describes two different complications and the combined effect that they had on my health and wellness, both mentally and physically.

The first factor was Anorexia—a genetic, brain-based disorder that caused me to suffer severe weight loss and a devastating fear of food.

The second factor was the impact that the low-fat diet culture had on me. This, first of all, was not helpful in helping me overcome my eating disorder, but it also really tampered with my ability to listen to the nutritional needs of my own body, rather than that dictated to me by scientists, the media, and "health gurus."

It's a long account, and somewhat of a ramble, as most true stories are. If you cannot be fagged to read it all, here are the key take-away points:

<u>About Eating Disorders:</u>

Eating disorders can affect any person, regardless of age, race, and gender.

Eating disorders have a genetic base; they are not chosen by the sufferer, nor are they simply instances of extreme dieting.

Calorie restriction can act as an environmental cue in a person who is genetically predisposed to having an eating disorder. Dieting does not cause eating disorders unless that person is already susceptible to developing one due to their genetic makeup.

Negative Body Image is often a symptom, often a complication, often a detriment to recovery, but never a *cause* of an eating disorder.

Likewise parents—good, bad or indifferent as they may be—cannot *cause* a clinical eating disorder.

Eating disorders can be deadly, very deadly: they have the highest mortality rate of any psychological disorder.

Eating disorders are treatable.

On Diet Culture:

Do not believe anything that you read; instead, believe what you feel. You read with your head, but you feel with your body. Let your body dictate what you eat rather than your brain.

Eat things that feel good to eat regardless of what your brain tells you about their nutrient content. When it comes to nutrition, your gut knows what is good for you. Trust your tummy over your stressed-out swede.

Do not believe anyone who calls themselves a health or diet guru. This is all the more true if they are trying to sell you something. You have a high-functioning diet guru built in to your stomach—start listening to that one instead of the prat shoving coffee up his arse or pretending she knows what cavemen liked for elevenses.

Do not believe anyone who tells you that you need to cleanse your liver. Mind your own business, tell them to mind theirs, and leave your liver to do what it does best: clean.

Likewise, do not believe anyone who tells you that you need to cleanse your colon. Your colon is not a shit hoarder. Leave it alone.

You do not need to join a Food Tribe or seek out others who share the same self-destructing-gut syndrome that you *think* you have. You do not need a dietary label to box yourself into, nor do you have to be vegan to find like-minded people. Just be yourself, and eat food that your body likes.

Fat is your friend. Low-fat is old, erroneous news—get over it and move along.

The vast majority of the population do not need to restrict food of any category and can eat any type of food as part of a balanced diet. The chances are, there is nothing wrong or "special" about you that means your body will be annihilated if you enjoy a moderate amount of gluten, dairy or meat.

Unless you have a medical condition that calls for them, you do not need to take supplements. You just need to eat real food and eat food that makes you happy.

There is no single dietary life-choice or supplemental pill that will solve all your problems, make you better in bed, clear up your skin, put a shine on your hair, rid you of disease, or

4

get you a job promotion. Your best bet for achieving all of these things is to eat real food, and eat food that makes you happy.

Whether you like it or not, you are at the top of the food chain. Our ancestors did not get us here by worrying about what they ate or fretting over what their gut microbes were doing; show them due respect by eating real food and eating food that tastes good.

Bottom line: eat food and enjoy doing so.

Chapter One

I was going to start this story at the beginning, but I realised I have no idea where that is. Then, I thought I would start it at the end, but I don't know where that is either. So, I settled with starting it smack-bang in the middle.

June 2010

I heard someone approach me softly from behind and felt a hand on my left shoulder. I was standing in the middle of my parent's garden in the South of England, trying to look as if I was invested in the conversation that I was having with the mother of some child who, apparently, I used to babysit for. I tilted my head to the left in order to listen to whatever it was the person behind me had to say.

It was my mother. "Honey, we will do speeches in about ten minutes," she informed me.

I nodded to let her know I had understood and returned my gaze to the face of the woman in front of me. I could not remember her name. *Was it Alice? Audrey?*

Yes; it was Audrey. What was the name of that bleeding child of hers?

I tried to remember the snotty nosed brat that I had been entrusted with on the odd occasion when her parents had wanted to escape for a dinner date. That child had been a thorn. She had never wanted to go to bed when I told her to and cried as soon as her parents left the house.

Audrey's lips were still moving and Matt, standing on my right hand side holding my hand, gave my fingers a squeeze. In a shared glance we secretly commiserated with one another; this was our duty as the newlyweds at our wedding reception: to stand and accept congratulations from every person in attendance—even if we did not have a clue who they were. Someone's great aunt or so-and-so's ex-husband's niece who apparently fed me jelly from a spoon on a trip to London Zoo when I was three. It didn't matter; just stand and nod and be polite. I could do that.

"Tabby?" My mother was at my left shoulder again.

"Yes Mum . . . I heard you . . . speeches in ten." I felt irritated now, not because she was distracting me from what Audrey was saying—that was welcome—but because she kept placing her hand on my shoulder, which I hated.

I did not like to feel her fingers make contact with the bony topside of my shoulder blade, which protruded despite my attempt to hide it under the beautiful silken shawl that my mother-in-law had made for me. I knew that each time Mum touched me, both she and I would be reminded about how dreadfully thin I was. Her fingers on my shoulder brought

6

back the conversations from a year ago, when she had begged me to put on some weight for my wedding day. I had promised that I would, and I had failed.

I shrugged her hand off me roughly then immediately felt guilty in case I had hurt her feelings. It was not *her* fault I was so thin. It was not *her* fault I had been unable to gain even a couple of pounds in a year. It was not *her* fault that standing here on a midsummer's evening I was cold already whilst everyone else sweltered in formal wear. It was certainly not *her* fault that I hated for her to touch me because I was paranoid that it would remind her of my thinness.

"I just wanted to let you know that we will do the cake after that, that's all Sweetie."

The cake. *Shit.* I nodded silently.

My stomach knotted as I turned my eyes back to Audrey, who was still prattling on to Matt about her godforsaken child. *The cake.* I suddenly felt hot, really hot. I wondered if I could excuse myself for a second. I wanted a glass of water. There were so many people in the small garden that, despite being outdoors, I felt suffocated. I wiggled my fingers out of Matt's hand and ignored his questioning glance. My hands were hot. *The fucking cake.*

The cake was something else that had been the subject of many discussions in the last year. I had never wanted a wedding cake, just like I had never wanted a wedding dress. The dress I had felt opposed to having because I did not think that my skinny frame deserved one. I was embarrassed of my figure and wanted as little attention drawn to it as possible. That's not what I told everyone else. No, instead I told them that I was just not "into" the traditional "wedding stuff" or that I was not a "girly girl," nor did I care at all for "expensive dresses." Half of that was true, but there was a part of me that wanted that wedding dress. Unfortunately for me however, I knew I would look ridiculous in any dress, and that getting something to fit me would be impossible. I was six foot tall and had no curves for a dress to hold on to—no boobs, no bottom—just skin and bones. The thought of dress shopping made me shudder. I would have had to emerge from changing rooms to the plastered-on fake smiles of my sisters and soon-to-be sisters-in-laws who would try and tell me I was beautiful. I was not beautiful. I was emaciated. It was a joke—me trying to look pretty. An expensive dress would have been an inexcusable waste of money.

Then, my mother-in-law, an expert seamstress, had offered to make me a dress. This had seemed like a compromise of sorts; no shopping trips, no huge amount of money spent on attempting to dress up a skeleton, plus, whatever she made for me would fit.

She had done a wonderful job: a long cream gown that fell to the floor, covering my thin pins. The shawl had been a great addition, because I could hide my shoulders too and, therefore, stay both warm and concealed.

Now the shawl was choking me. I felt hot for the first time all day at the thought of that cake.

Initially, when the wedding plans had begun in earnest, I told them—the mothers—that I did not want a cake. That little revelation had not gone down well. In fact it had not gone down at all; it were as if they had not heard me, as they had just continued to discuss the type of sponge, icing decorations and number of tiers regardless. Then there had been all these questions about the type of cake that "I" wanted. "I" did not want any cake at all. "I" did not want a Victoria sponge, or a chocolate sponge, or an angel sponge. "I" did not want icing or ganaché. "I" did not want bows or flowers on top.

I did not want a bloody wedding cake.

I did not want a wedding cake because I did not want the wedding attendees looking at me expecting me to eat a slice of that wedding cake at my wedding reception.

I could feel my heart-rate rising. I realised that I had been staring at Audrey's lips, and that she must have said something to me that required a response on my part, because all the faces in the small circle of people around us were now looking to me. Matt came to my rescue, saying something on behalf of the both of us—probably a thank you—and my mind slipped back into itself.

The cake had ended up, like the wedding dress, being home-made. One of the ladies in my parents' village just so happened to be a master baker. Mrs. Carrington was the reigning champion in the annual village fête cake baking competition. Her victory that past Spring had seen her undefeated for the fifth year in a row. Not only had she won the sponge section, but she had also been awarded first prize for her cherry pie in the pastry category. Her strawberry jam had come second by a whisper to the blueberry jam made by her neighbour and arch-enemy, Mrs. Hobbins.

Mrs. Carrington had very generously insisted that we allow her to make my wedding cake. She, like every other resident in the Wiltshire village that I had grown up in, had known me from the day that my mother and father returned with a newborn baby from the hospital. Mrs. Carrington had told my mother that it would be an honour to make the wedding cake. Unfortunately, Mrs. Hobbins had also requested cake making duties, and fearing a village feud, my mother had tactfully negotiated a way to let them both contribute: Mrs. Carrington had made the cake, but it was filled with Mrs. Hobbins's blueberry jam.

That cake had sat now for two days on the Welsh dresser in my parents' kitchen. Three tiers of white pearly glory decorated today with fresh cut flowers and bows. It was perfect. Each time I had walked past it I had admired its beauty and felt a wealth of gratitude to the women that had created it. Then, I had said a prayer that someone might accidentally knock it off the side of the wooden dresser that it sat displayed on, sending it smashing onto the kitchen floor.

That's what happens in films and comedy sketches: the wedding cake gets wrecked.

I should be so lucky.

That cake terrified me. It would have been baked with ample amounts of butter, sugar and eggs. Covered in a thick layer of calorie-laden icing, undoubtedly there was also buttercream under Mrs. Hobbins's blueberry jam in the center. Thousands of calories, most of which would be from fat.

For the past two days I had been contemplating ways that I could excuse myself from eating any. I had considered feigning sickness, a food allergy, even criminally destroying the thing. Now the time was upon me and I felt trapped in a garden full of people, all of whom would soon be looking at me expecting me to eat a slice of this delicious, fat-laden, ceremonial cake.

A sharp dinging noise cut through my thoughts. My sister Beth was standing on a chair, looking fabulous in her bright orange designer dress, knocking a knife onto the side of her champagne glass and hollering for everyone to quieten down. The speeches were about to start.

The babble of voices simmered to a watery murmur as my father began to talk. Another hand on my shoulder, this time it was Simon, Beth's photographer boyfriend, who had generously offered his professional shooting skills as his contribution to our big day. I had spent the best part of the afternoon slinking shy of his camera. I had no desire to look at pictures of myself; no good ever came of doing that. Unfortunately for me, at weddings, the bride is usually the focus of the camera lens.

"So . . ."

I couldn't help rolling my eyes as he began to talk to me; it all seemed so very trite. Luckily, Simon was shifting through the thousands of photographs he had already taken as he addressed me, so he failed to notice my attitude slip and carried on, "after you've cut the cake, I want to get a shot of the two of you crossing arms and feeding each other a slice."

Simon shot a couple of weddings a week at least. Clients flew him all over the world so that he could take pictures of them because he knew exactly what he wanted to capture; the precious moments that a person might look back on in five years time of such a grand day. I should have been honoured to have him behind the camera working as hard as he was, but instead I felt a growing irritation. I was tired of being told what to do and where to look. I was cross that he was going to insist on the cake-eating tradition. I wondered if I could refuse. Was there an excuse?

Maybe I could tell him I was worried in case I spilt cake on the wedding dress.

Maybe I could tell him I had suddenly developed a headache.

I realised that there was no rational excuse for not wanting to take a small bite of cake for the purposes of a once-in-a-lifetime photograph on my wedding day. In that moment I wanted to tell Simon the truth. I wanted to tell all of them the truth. I especially wanted to tell Matt—my best friend in the world—the truth. I wanted to tell him that I was shit-scared of eating a mouthful of wedding cake because it had fat in it.

The speeches, the toasts, and the cheers had blurred into a haze of colour and sound as the cake cutting approached. I sat, outwardly serene, whilst the inner chaos raged. I was used to hiding my emotions because in all honestly I understood how very irrational and insane they were. Who would understand my fear of food?

Nobody could possibly comprehend how terrified I was of eating fat, especially if they knew that I simultaneously hated my thinness. I wanted desperately to gain weight and to look "normal" enough to be able to wear a dress without having people stare at my legs and arms with tight lips and furrowed brows. I wanted my body back. I wanted to be able to enjoy my wedding day without constantly feeling that slap of adrenaline that came whenever I looked over at the buffet table, or saw someone walk past with a plate of food.

Who could ever understand my fear of fat and hate of thin?

Admitting to it would wind me up in an institute; so, I did the same thing that I did every day: I smiled, blinked back tears, and pretended everything was just fine. When the time came to stand up and cut the cake, I did. I posed with Matt's hand holding a slice an inch from my nose, then I bit into it for the cameras. I pushed the mouthful of sweet sponge to the corner of my mouth and held it in between my molars and the flesh of my cheek until there was opportunity for me to carefully fake a sneeze and spit into a handkerchief minutes later. And nobody knew that I did that, nobody knew because I had over eight years experience in the fine art of feigning food consumption. If there was one thing I was good at, it was pretending to eat.

The irony struck me later that night, as I left Matt sleeping in the spare bedroom of my parent's house and tiptoed down the carpeted stairs, along the stone floored corridor, and into the kitchen. I went over to the fridge, opened the door and silently removed the airtight box that my mother had so diligently used to save the remains of the blasted wedding cake into. I gingerly moved dirty glasses aside on the countertop, and placed the box in the empty space I had created for it.

I opened the box and started eating.

I barely tasted the cake that was entering my mouth by the handful. Frenzied, I fed myself until my stomach was so full that I gagged. At that point, I pushed the cake box away and turned around to sit on the kitchen floor with my back against the fridge. Too full to move, I felt nauseous and suffocated. I resorted to lying down on my side in an attempt to ease the pressure on my stomach.

I lay on my back and stared blankly at the ceiling, waiting patiently for the nausea to subside enough to allow me to creep back upstairs and return to bed. A couple of hours earlier, I had been utterly unable to ingest even a small bite of wedding cake, yet here I was now, a puddle of cake on the floor, brazen and used by my uncontrollable desire to eat.

My tired eyes wandered over the items on top of the kitchen table: leftover paper plates and glasses from the party littered the surface. My mother, who had retired to bed before the last stragglers had left that evening, had asked my sisters to make sure everything got put in the dishwasher. Fat chance.

For the wedding party weekend, Beth and Candy had returned to my parents' house in the Wiltshire countryside, leaving the depths of London to celebrate with us. Fun as they were, my sisters were not very skilled when it came to cleaning up; that had always been my forté. The cleaner-upper: that was me.

Beth was only twenty-one months younger than me; as children, we had liked to do the same things, like colouring in pictures and doing the dot-to-dots. I smiled as memories of the mischief that we had achieved flooded my inner eye. Sniggering through church services; building dens in the woods; hiding behind trees and trying to scare Candy. We had been scallywag children, and we were always bickering.

The chiming of the grandfather clock in the hallway snatched me out of my memories. Oh, yeah, here I was, on the kitchen floor, bloated and disgusting.

I would run in the morning. I would run to make it alright. I would restore the balance at dawn when I would again creep out of my bedroom and down the stairs. This time I would not stop at the fridge, I would pull on my trainers and run until the cake was gone, negated. That would make it okay. I despised running, but that was beside the point. When it came to food and exercise I was a passenger to my actions and rarely could my personal preferences influence them. My feelings on such matters were irrelevant.

What would it have been like to have been able to eat a slice of cake when everyone else did at the reception?

Only at night was my fear of fat overcome with a different fear. At night came a deviant fear from a disparate place. In the day, the fear of food came from my brain, my mind. The daytime fear would not allow me to eat a morsel.

The night fear came from my body. At night, my emaciated being screamed for food. At night, expiration threatened and the survival instinct to eat took control.

I wondered what it would have been like to have lived though my wedding day without fear. I wondered if I would have heard the words of my father's speech? Would I have been present in the conversations that I had been having with relatives and friends? Would I have known what today should have felt like?

Tears percolated behind my eyes as I contemplated my loss. I had just lived through my own wedding day without feeling it. This had just been another day stolen from me by something that I had no control over. Just another day to add to the years upon years that I had existed in this shack of a body consumed and strangled by disinterest and numbness.

It had not always been this way. I had loved food once. I had loved fat once. As I lay on the kitchen floor, I tried to remember what life had been like before.

So, that was my wedding reception. Rather sad, isn't it?

I know that weddings are usually more stress than they are fun for the bride and groom, but if you spent your own worrying about more traditional elements—will your beloved actually show up? Was there enough booze ordered? Is the DJ going to play ABBA all night? Will your mother-in-law get legless and try to hit on the vicar?—then I envy you: at least you were fretting over things that were relevant to your actual wedding.

If you are wondering why I, on my big day, spent the entire time agonising over taking a single bite of wedding cake: welcome to the world of eating disorders.

Chapter Two

The worst thing about my eating disorder was that I had no idea that it was there. Oh, I knew that I was messed up, but I did not know with *what*. We'll cover why a person such as myself can have Anorexia Nervosa and not know it later on, but right now: you, dear reader, are savvier than I was to the crux of my problem. Let's pick me up off the kitchen floor at least though:

I got up off the red-tiled floor and made my way over to the kitchen table. My stomach and my mind full of food, I felt uneasy and tired, yet not ready to return to bed. Looking for something to distract me from thinking about all the wedding cake that I had just eaten, I searched through the magazine rack under the table. An old copy of *Horse and Hound* caught my eye and I pulled it out of the pile. The picture on the front was of a group of teenagers hacking over a plain. The bay Thoroughbred horse leading the group reminded me of one of the horses that I used to ride; the scene on the front of the magazine cover was like a snapshot of my youth. It could have been taken on any one of many days that I had spent astride a horse, hacking out with friends.

In my food-coma state, I relaxed a little more into my seat and allowed the memories to flow: The Thoroughbred pictured on the front of the magazine had transported me back to late-March in the spring of 1998; Spring, when the daylight hours were just beginning to get longer and the grass a bit brighter. I was riding with friends; friends who had been friends since we had met six years earlier in the local Pony Club. Back then, at Pony Club, you would have seen a group of eleven-year-old kids bouncing about on the backs of tiny ponies; full of giggles and pigtails in hair. Those kids on ponies were now young women astride strapping warmbloods tearing up the English countryside. We were all good riders; most of us competed professionally on the British Eventing circuit. But, every now and then we would get together and just ride out for fun.

A typical day in England meant rain, and raining it was. I was aboard a bay, sixteen-hand, five-year-old part-bred Arab called Shai. I did not own Shai of course. He, like all the other horses I rode, had been given to me to ride for the purpose of training; I was teaching him the things that he needed to know about being a good riding horse so that he could eventually be sold. I liked Shai. He demonstrated a strong desire to please and listened to my instructions well; because of this he was making fast progress and I expected him to find another home soon. This was how the stud business worked for me: I would train the young horses up until the time that the right buyer came onto the scene. Shai was a sweet horse, through rather tall and gangly; like an awkward teenage boy, he had not yet grown into his body.

The track that we rode that day took us way out through the woods and onto Salisbury Plain. (If you have never been to this part of England it is rather lovely—fields interspersed with woodland copses and undulating hills.) We covered the rolling and open space sprinkled with dense thickets of bushes and trees. Most of the landscape was utterly sodden that day due to the rain having drenched the countryside for the past week. Shai and I brought up the rear as we followed the other seven horses along the muddy tracks. As the path wound up the steep edge of a hill and into some woods, we slowed our pace to a walk and organised ourselves into single file. And as the muddy track scaled the rising ground, I noticed a sharp drop on the right hand side of us.

We all rode the very same path that day, every horse in front of me treading the same ground as Shai did, each rider taking the same caution that I had to guide her horse safely up the boggy incline. I held Shai back a little as we started up the embankment; Jen, a good friend and excellent horsewoman, was about fifty yards in front of me on a stocky little Irish Draft called George. I tightened my rein to give my horse some more guidance and pressed my right leg firmly into his side to remind him to keep his body to the left. As Shai struggled on up the slope I felt his hindquarters give to the right a little more than I knew was safe. I shifted my own body left to try and encourage him over onto the more solid ground. Despite my efforts to straighten him, Shai's right hind foot misplaced itself too far to the outside of the path. He lurched forward in an attempt to correct himself, but the rest of his body followed his sliding hind foot. Shai tumbled and slid down the steep bank and I went with him. Coming out of the saddle, I slid alongside my horse, out of control, faster and faster, with mud in my face, my ears, and my mouth.

When the mudslide finally turned to level ground, I found myself with Shai, in a deep puddle of slimy, silty mud at the bottom of the steep slope that we had been riding up. There were thick bushes to my left and some sparser trees to my right, but, for the most part, all I could see was mud and water. Winded as I had been from hitting the ground when my body first parted from the saddle, the cold of the bog shocked me into breath. The pain along the outside of my knee told me that my left leg had been squashed between Shai's body and the embankment during the fall. *Jesus Christ I hope I can still walk on it.*

With one hand groping for a hold in the slippery mud that lined the banks of the ten-foot-wide puddle and the other supporting my protesting knee, I eventually clambered to my feet and looked over at my horse. With a grunt and a forward lurch, he pulled himself back onto all four feet and leapt out of the bog. Neighing for his friends, he crashed through the trees to the right of me, then galloped off.

That day on the moors, my body aching from the fall, with the sharp, cold March air biting at my sodden skin, I stood and watched Shai disappear into the distance. Notwithstanding my relief in seeing him stand up unhurt, I groaned audibly at the thought of the feat that lay ahead of me now. I imagined that catching Shai on Salisbury Plain would take hours of trailing over the miles of land on foot. If the horse had not managed to damage himself when he fell down the bank, chances were he would do somehow in tearing about riderless over the plain. There were all sorts of bogs, ditches, and barbed wire fences for him to potentially tangle himself up in. I was cold, I was wet, my body hurt and right then all I wanted to do was sit back down in the puddle that I was standing in and wail.

The thing about horse riding is that when it is fun, it's really fun, but when it goes to shit, it really goes two bob bit.

Pony Club girls do not wail. Instead, I staggered my way out of the puddle; slipping and sliding I made it up over the bank, and slowly began trudging along in the direction that my horse had run off in. I stumbled in my waterlogged boots over the chilly plain following the trail of broken turf that Shai's galloping hooves had left. In an attempt to see where I was going, I began wiping the mud off my face. I did my best, but my muddy fingers were probably just smearing and repositioning the dirt that was clinging to my eyelids and my eyelashes to join the dirt on my cheeks.

As I walked, I tried to get my head around what had just happened. None of it made sense. All the horses in front of us had climbed that ridge and made it safely over. It seemed so bizarre that an otherwise surefooted horse would fall like that. Nobody else's horse had slipped.

I was a mess. Ashamed. My clothes were ruined, my leather boots also trashed. But, a good rider just gets back on and continues regardless; one must always get back in the saddle after a fall. After two hours of looking for him, I eventually found my horse. A miserable blob of mud, I got back in the saddle and I rode home.

We had all ridden the same path that day, but only my horse had fallen.

Now I bet you are wondering why I chose to tell you that particular memory? Mostly I did so because I distinctly remember sitting at my parents' kitchen table and lusting for days-gone-by—or at least the days before I binged every evening—and my horsey days cropped up as those were certainly pre-food-problem. But this particular story draws a parallel to my misfortune of being the one—for what seems like no good reason at all—to develop an eating disorder. I've pondered, wondered, and "why me'd" this reality many times in the past five years, and the only conclusion that I have drawn thus far, is that shit happens.

Unfortunately, it happened to me.

Back to the horses:

Horses were a huge part of my life in my early to late teens. As I grew older I competed more and began to work in professional yards. I was at the stables any time that I was not at school. I was constantly being scolded by my teachers for filling my workbooks and notepads with doodles of horses instead of mathematical equations or English prose. I know that sounds like some corny English-girl cliché, but it is true. I ate, slept and dreamt horses.

The night after my wedding party, as I flicked through the pages of *Horse and Hound* I revisited those glorious weekends in my mind. Before my muscles had been stripped from my body by my fear of food, I had been a strong rider. If I do say so myself: I was pretty good. I was also very competitive, and I wanted to be the best. This drive and passion was by no means responsible for my eating disorder, but in a roundabout way, it was instrumental in kicking it off.

3rd March, 1998

"Look at that!" Jen chortled as I bent down to fasten my shoelace against a pile of horse feed, "you're filling out!"

"Huh?" I looked up at her in confusion. *What is she on about now?*

I was flustered because the laces on the pair of yard boots I was wearing kept coming undone and my long blonde hair was falling into my eyes each time I had to bend down and retie them. We were in a local feed store picking up a couple of sacks of oats after having spent the morning mucking out the horses. It was noon and, having not eaten anything since our mid-morning tea and biscuit break, I was hungry.

"You're filling out!" She gestured towards my stomach, which had poked out over my jeans as I had bent down to fix my shoe. "Finally!" She pressed the palms of her hands together and looked up, mimicking a prayer of thanks towards the Gods for my protruding tummy. With a playful wink, she turned her gaze back to where I was still fiddling with my bootlace on the ground.

"About time you stopped looking like such a string bean . . . I knew all those chocolate bars that you eat would begin to catch up with you one day."

Jen was right, I did eat a lot of chocolate; at least a couple of Mars or Snickers bars a day.

Being slightly pudgy herself, she had always teased me for being too skinny. In fact, Jen would tease me for anything and everything. We were old friends and that was how things were with us; affection via insult.

"Stop at McD's on the way back to the stables?" I asked as we wandered towards the checkout.

"You bet, fatty!"

I had thought little of Jen's comments that day, it certainly did not stop me ordering a Big Mac, chocolate milkshake and large fries for lunch, but that evening as I cleaned myself up before heading out to the pub, I pulled on my favorite old pair of jeans and the zip got stuck halfway up. That had never happened to me before. *Humph*, I thought, *Jen was right.*

I had put on weight; my clothes were getting tighter, and a couple of pairs of my jeans did not fit me. However at six foot tall I was realistically just "filling out" as Jen had put it, and when I looked in the mirror I was somewhat thrilled to see that I was finally developing breasts. The "fried egg tits" taunt that the boys at school used to tease me with still played in my ears every now and then. I was quite happy to have a bit more of a cleavage if one wanted to appear.

I felt rather nonchalant about my weight gain; there was absolutely no way that it was going to influence any change in what I ate. No way at all. I loved eating food almost as much as I loved riding horses.

As a teenager I had no problems with low self-esteem or negative body image. In fact, I was secretly rather self-confident.

I loved my height; the very thing that had been the cause of the "Tabby Long Legs" taunts in primary school was now considered an asset. I had long, blonde hair and clear skin. I liked my body a lot, but thought of it in a rather pragmatic and unemotional way. I had even grown to like my small chest because it was so useful in terms of sport. The big breasts some girls had that I had envied for a while at high school were no longer something I desired. Breasts would have got in the way and bounced about all over the place when I was riding. I was very thankful for my B-cups that stayed neatly in place.

Apparently, I was not the only person who thought I was hot. My friends often told me so, but I never really considered their opinions as counting for much as it was their job to tell me such things—just like it was my job to tell them the same. My mother was constantly telling me I was beautiful, but that did not count either as she was obviously biased.

What did count was the turning heads from the men that I passed in the local high street, and the ones that would cluster behind me if I went out dancing. Or the guys that would offer to buy me a drink if I was in a local bar. I was not naive enough to think that they were making judgements about my stunning intellect on first sight; I knew they just wanted to get into my pants. I had no intentions around letting that happen whatsoever. From what I witnessed in my friends, sex spelled stress. I could do without all of that. Public attention from other people regarding my looks made me feel embarrassed and uncomfortable and quite frankly, I did not welcome it at all.

When I was seventeen, I had never had a boyfriend and I did not intend on having one anytime soon. There were times when this self-inflicted celibacy got to me, when my friends were on date nights with their boyfriends or Valentine's Day. There were times when I really longed for some physical contact other than a horse's muzzle in my ear. There were evenings when I would sit on my bedroom floor rubbing polish into my riding boots and feel like I was rotting away unseen. There were nights when I would wish that there was someone in the room other than Tiffy, our doting springer spaniel, to look at me lovingly. Then I'd get a phone call from a friend in tears because she'd been dumped and it would all come back into perspective.

Despite the odd bout of loneliness, I knew that I was being smart in staying single. From what I observed in my friends escapades with men, it always quite literally ended in tears. I could do without all that. After all, I couldn't go getting all upset and heartbroken because I had my horse riding career to think about; riding was my number one priority.

At that age, seventeen, I lived to eat. A typical day would start with two or three pieces of toast with lashings of butter topped with a thin layer of Marmite. If Mother were watching, I would eat some fruit too. Tea would always accompany breakfast. I preferred to drink PG Tips or Tetley with milk; no sugar.

I'd typically snack on a Mars or Snickers bar during the college mid-morning break. Lunch might be a chicken burger from the canteen and a chocolate muffin or a slice of pizza. After classes, I'd head straight to the stables to ride a couple of horses before dusk. On the way there I would grab another chocolate bar, a packet of crisps, or both. When I returned home after riding, Mum would have a home-cooked meal ready. In the evening I would snack on chocolate, crisps and Greek yoghurt.

I loved to eat, and I was happy with my weight so no reason to stop eating or try and diet even if it meant that Jen would have more reason to poke fun at me. All more the shame that less than a year later, the very thought of a chocolate bar brought with it a spike of adrenaline.

April 1998

I got a job at the local racing yard, Harringdon Stables. The summer holidays were on the horizon, college was just about out, and I had this wide open space of a summer before going to university in the autumn. I loved the idea of getting up before sunrise and setting out onto the mile of specially conditioned turf known as "the gallops" to exercise thoroughbreds.

And it was glorious. The mornings were the peak time for me now, I would be at the yard by a quarter past five and up on the first ride of my day fifteen minutes later. The yard consisted of three long barns joined end on end with a gutter down the middle and loose boxes either side. The tack room was a converted shed tacked on to the end barn, and inside there was a large, faded blackboard.

The head trainer was a cantankerous fellow called Thomas. Each morning, he would allocate horses to exercise jockeys for the day, and chalk the list up on the tack room blackboard. As soon as I got to the yard I'd excitedly totter in and check out which horses my name had been chalked up next to. Then, I would tack up my first horse and clip-clop my way along the lane toward the gallops with the other jockeys.

Those mornings were splendid. The sun would crest the hills as we walked the horses the half-mile down the lane and out to the track. Now, many people assume that when exercising racehorses, one would just arrive at the bottom of the gallop and let rip. Not the case. In fact, the horses only really get to go full whack when they are in a race; the exercising canters as just that: a canter. A controlled canter.

There is a lot of conditioning involved in exercising racehorses to get them fit for the track; most of the work is done at a strong canter in groups rather than a flat out sprint. We would hack the horses leisurely over to the gallop in a haphazard gang, taking advantage of the lack of cars on the roads that early in the morning. Then, at the bottom of the gallop strip, we would organise ourselves; pairing up so that we could canter the horses up the strip in a double file line. The riders at the front set the pace, which should be strong, yet civil.

Up the gallop we would canter, then down we would walk before turning and setting off up it again— rather like interval training. After three or four runs up and down we would hack the horses back to the stables to wash them down before going again with the next group. The turnovers were fast, tack off one and onto the next, so before nine o'clock, we could have had every horse in the yard of thirty exercised, washed, groomed and fed breakfast.

I would get an average of four rides per morning and for the first couple of weeks, because I was new to the tiny saddles and short stirrups, I was getting my name chalked up next to the more experienced, steadier, and easier to control racehorses. As I got more comfortable in my new role, my competitive nature began to kick in. I never had any interest in racing on the track—I was an exercise jockey and that was all that I wanted to be—but within the race yard my ambition got the better of me. I wanted to be the best exercise jockey in the yard even if I could not be the most experienced.

A couple of weeks after I started at Harringdon a pretty and petite thoroughbred mare called KitKat came in for training. She was a striking chestnut with two white front feet and a wide blaze on her face. She had a graceful, slender neck with a soft flaxen mane that whispered around her withers when she cantered up the gallop.

KitKat was amongst the fastest horses in the yard and was also the most difficult to handle.

Thomas told me that she had come from a yard in Ireland where "they give 'em an 'ard time," which I took to mean that a lot of her kicking and biting behaviour was due to having been knocked about.

There was certainly a lot of fear in KitKat; she pinned her ears and snapped at me the first time I entered her stall to feed her. Whenever she had the chance to do so, she would swing her hindquarters on me and threaten to kick. I knew that her fear was not indicative of her disliking me, but rather a product of a learned behaviour. I recalled that earlier that year, I had been learning about fear conditioning in psychology classes at college. KitKat had been taught that humans meant pain and this was her response. The second morning that I fed her she bit me on the arm as I emptied her grain into her manger. Luckily, due to the cold early-morn chill in the air, I was wearing my thicker jacket. The bite that mare gave me that day did not manage to break the skin, but it hurt all the same.

I wanted it to be known that I could ride any of the horses on the gallops, including KitKat, whom I was working with on the ground every day in an attempt to teach her to trust me. I spent a lot more time with her than any of the other horses. Standing outside the mare's stall speaking to her softly, going in and stroking her long neck should she let me. Gradually her ears stopped flattening back at the sight of me, and one morning she even nickered when I entered her stable.

I adored that mare. Every morning I walked into the tack room hoping to see my name chalked up next to hers for the morning exercise. I was always disappointed when I saw that one of the other jockeys had been chosen to ride her despite it being obvious that she trusted me more than anyone else on staff.

Thomas was a man of little words; if he did utter anything it was usually critical. If there were to be any measure I was riding well, it came from seeing that he had chalked my name up next to one of his favourite or fastest horses. Within a couple of weeks it became clear that my height and my weight were the restricting factor for me as he was only ever putting me down for the bigger horses in the yard. I was taller than all the other exercise jockeys by almost a foot, and much heavier and it dawned on me that because of this, I was not going to get that ride on the chestnut mare I adored so. My height I could do nothing about . . . but my weight I could.

Three weeks into my job at the race yard I went on my first ever diet.

21

Chapter Three

I hated dieting.

It astounded me how anyone could do it at all. Most of my friends at school had been on diets at some point; some of them were constantly worrying about what they ate and the number of calories in their food. Donna, a girl I often sat next to in mathematics, seemed particularly preoccupied with how she looked. She was constantly comparing herself to pictures of other women in the magazines that she read. In class, she always had some issue of *Just Seventeen* or *Bliss* stashed on her lap so that the teacher could not see it. Her mithering on the subject bored me.

"Do you like Jennifer Aniston's hair? Do you think I should put layers in mine like hers?" Donna questioned me one afternoon whilst flicking through a rag in maths class. The teacher, Mr Woodford, was one of these highly intelligent creatures without an ounce of street sense. One could put one's feet on the desk and he would not notice. For this reason I had my feet on the desk and was reading *Horse and Hound*; a highly preferable alternative to listening to him passionately rave on about fractions.

I rolled my eyes. *Why are people always so obsessed with hair.*

"The one from Friends right? I don't know, did she change it?" I answered curtly.

I could not remember which *friend* Jennifer Aniston was, and honestly I did not care to. As soon as I asked the question I winced, I should have just nodded and agreed with whatever it was Donna was harping on about, questions might give her the wrong impression. She might think I gave a rat's arse.

But Donna was already on the next page, musing over a picture of *Destiny's Child*. "What do you think about Beyonce's butt? Do you think it's bigger than mine?"

Oh Jesus, I thought. *Here we go.* I pretended to be very consumed with what I was reading about the correct way to store hay.

Two minutes later, Donna was at it again. "I wish I were thin like Kate Moss, don't you think she is just perfect?"

"Good grief Donna . . . who cares?" I asked her in desperation.

And that is a very good question.

What I learnt years later, as I studied into the concept of negative body image in Psychology class, is that lots of people care. Studies I read then claimed that up to forty percent of school age girls perceive themselves as too fat. Researchers have relayed that most students, when questioned, admit attempting to lose weight at some point in their lives. Social and environmental influences are regarded to be the most influential factor on a person's self esteem. Thin models, ridiculously photoshopped cover girls, and slim figured television stars set an unachievable and often utterly unrealistic goal for the teenagers that are their target audiences.

But I did not know that when I was seventeen, and even if I had, I would not have cared. I did not give two hoots for popular teen magazines, or who looked like what on television shows, and I certainly paid no attention to fashion models. The only magazine I felt was worth reading was *Horse and Hound,* and I had no idols. People look at me like I am kidding when I admit that I have no heros, heroines or idols, but it is true. I do not now and I never have. That's weird isn't it?

Despite my own lack of interest in fashion and looking good, I knew that most of my friends did not feel the same as me about their own bodies.

For the most part I steered clear of body-related discussions at school. Nurturing damaged egos did not come naturally to me and I always felt clumsy when I tried. I was not very good at the heart-to-heart conversations that my girlfriends were so invested in having about looks, boys and clothes; I often felt as if I simply did not possess whatever it was that they had which enabled them to care deeply about such things.

So imagine how I, of all people, felt about embarking on a diet. I was embarrassed. I told nobody; I did not want anyone thinking that I was dieting because I'd suddenly got all self-conscious about my looks. I would have hated anyone to assume that I did not like myself the way that I was; because I did, I just needed to get that ride on KitKat.

The first week of my "diet" I gave up eating chocolate and crisps. It was easy. I have always had a lot of willpower, and am good at making myself do things that I do not want to. If I set myself a goal of not eating chocolate then I would not eat chocolate. No ifs, no buts, and no maybes. I certainly had the willpower that others complained that they lacked.

Donna would often whine about thinking she were fat and tell me she was on a diet, then buy herself a chocolate bar from the vending machine in the corridor when we passed it on our way out of class. This struck me as bizarre, but apparently it was more normal that people should have problems sticking to a diet than not. I chalked that down as just another way that I was different to most of the girls at my school.

I remember very well the first time that I weighed myself after a week of dieting. I had felt pretty excited about getting on the scales as I was sure that the needle would show a decent drop. A whole seven days without chocolate and crisps would surely reward me with a sizable shedding of bodyweight, right?

Nope. Regardless of my careful avoidance of what felt like *all* of my favorite foods, there was only a tiny movement downwards of that blasted needle. I got on and off the scale three times, but each time it gave me the same dratted information: I had only lost a measly couple of pounds. I was disappointed. I felt depressed at the thought of going without Cadbury's for much longer. At this rate it was going to take weeks.

My aim had been to lose about eight pounds, which would render me light enough to ride KitKat. I had heard some of my girlfriends talk about "fasts" and "cleanses" before; I

23

figured that I would just do one of these and get the whole weight-loss thing over and done with as quickly as possible.

Lots of girls at college say that fasting is a safe and effective way of losing weight . . . plus there is that ad on the telly that said so, too.

It seems like the most efficient idea.

Later that afternoon, I spent a couple of hours in a bookstore in Andover town centre browsing for a cleanse book that my friend Sally had been telling me about, called *The Master Cleanse*. Sally had been on it for ten days or something ridiculous; she had told me that it meant she was in *kee-toe-sis* or something that sounded like a Chinese food.

I had no desire to go as long without food as Sally had done, but I did want to know if it would help me lose half a stone faster. I could not imagine going without food for ten days; that seemed like a purely ridiculous thing to do. I set a plan for a moderate, five-day fast—with the option to abandon ship if I felt weak or giddy. I didn't want to fall off a horse or something stupid just because I was not eating. I remembered reading about a girl in the local paper who had fainted because she had not eaten enough. *What a dumb twat she must have been! How silly and vain.* Nowadays I'd have a lot more sympathy, but as a teenager I was pretty petulant.

I had always thought girls were silly, and the sheer volume of diet books in front of me in this small town bookstore seemed testament to that. Apart from girls who rode horses or were serious about sport, most of the ones that I sat with in classes at school drove me crazy. Girls who were not fussed about whatever their hair looked like were okay, but most of them were obsessed with mindless things like make up and dresses.

I certainly had no time for the silly type of girl who went on a diet. I felt sheepishly embarrassed at the thought that someone might see me even looking at the diet section of the bookstore; so much so that I frequently checked over my shoulder to make sure that nobody I knew might see me standing there.

As I scanned the titles in front of me, the brightly coloured covers jumped out off the shelves. I had never have imagined that there could be this many books on a subject as tedious as *diet*.

There was one thing that really stood out to me, one thing that all the covers seemed to have in common: low fat. All the books I could see were touting those two words.

"Low-Fat Diet"

"How to lower your fat intake for a slimmer you!"

"Eat low-fat foods to drop a dress size!"

Low Fat. Huh.

I had never really made that correlation before. Honestly, until that point I'd had my head firmly into dressage, eventing, and mucking out stables, so in my whole seventeen years of living it had never dawned on me that it was the fat in my diet that had been responsible for my "filling out". I had heard other people talk about eating *low fat* before, and that they were doing that to lose weight, but I had also heard people talk about getting boob jobs and two-hundred-pound hair cuts. I had put discussions on things like avoiding fat into the *rubbish-things-silly-girls-do* section of my head. I had never paid any attention to the foods that are high in fat before.

I picked up a book titled *Lower fat = Lower weight!* and flicked through the first couple of pages. The opening chapter had a chart in it with the number of calories per gram of what were called *macronutrients* in. Until that day, the only *macro* that I'd thought much about was that pertaining to *macro*economics, but it made more sense when I recognised the *macro*nutrients that the chart was referring to: fat, protein, and carbohydrates.

In those first couple of chapters I saw that, while protein and carbohydrates were both four calories per gram, fat was nine calories per gram. With that little golden nug of information, I understood the reason that so many people were talking about *low fat*, because, gram-for-gram, fat is higher in calories.

Huh.

I checked the book out.

That was my first mistake.

My fast lasted five days, which, with the amount of riding I did, was long enough for me to lose a considerable amount of weight. Being tall and very physically active, the pounds dropped off me. I felt pleased about that, and I was looking forward to going back to eating again. I thought it would be easy. In fact, I did not really think anything of it at all.

Up until now, things had taken what I consider to be a relatively run-of-the-mill course for a teenager who goes on a diet: stop eating; lose weight. It is what happened next that should have been my first clue that my body's response to calorie restriction had been far from ordinary. In fact, the problem was within my brain, but it took a long time for me realise this.

It started normally enough: from day one of my fast I was looking forward to day five and I wanted to be done already. I was drinking tea, coffee, and lots of water to fill my stomach and stop it grumbling at me. I could barely think of anything other than how good life would be when day five came and I could eat again. It was day six that the trouble began.

Chapter Four

Finally, day five of my fast came and went. I woke up on the sixth day excited that I would be able to eat again and fully intending to have a big breakfast. I bounded downstairs from my bedroom at such a speed that the dog jumped up excitedly from her place on the couch and barked at me as I headed to the kitchen. Ignoring her jumping around my heels, I tore open the fridge door.

Usually when I open the fridge I feel as if I have opened the door to a treasure trove of possibilities. Standing in front of an open fridge is somewhat of a pastime of mine that greatly annoys my parents.

"Tabby shut the fridge door, you are letting all the cold out!"

My father would often tell me off for my listless musing over what to eat, usually my pondering came as a result of seeing too many delicious things and not knowing what to choose, but that day I felt disturbingly not attracted to any of it.

Well, that was a turn up for the books.

I deserved to be *really* hungry. Here I was, after five whole days of no food, and when I opened the fridge all I felt was blank.

Nothing. I was looking at all my favourite foods: cheese, ham, eggs, Greek yoghurt and more. There was even some leftover homemade apple crumble in there. I may as well have been looking at pieces of stone sitting on the fridge shelves for all the excitement that I felt.

Why had my hunger disappeared when I'd opened the fridge?

Oh, well. No big deal.

I decided that until I felt the desire to eat again it would probably be a good thing for me not to; if I was not feeling hungry there was no point in eating, especially seeing as I had a chance to lose a bit more weight. It was odd, but I felt that if I ate when I was feeling so nonchalant towards food that I would be wasting an opportunity to lose another couple of pounds. If I lost another couple of pounds then I would have a buffer zone, because I would have lost more weight than I needed to. That would be a good thing, right?

For the majority of the population, yes, not eating when one is not hungry is probably harmless enough. Not for me it turns out.

I happened to have plans to pop over and see Sally that afternoon when I was finished with the horses. Sitting in her kitchen cradling a mug of tea, I casually quizzed her about coming off her fast.

"So, um, you know that you were telling me that you did that silly fasting thing a while back?"

"Uh huh."

"Were you hungrier than usual when you finished it?"

Sally didn't answer immediately, so I looked up at her. Following her gaze I noticed that I had been absentmindedly fiddling with the crocheted doily in the center of the kitchen table. Sally's Mum hated it when we moved her stuff about. I dropped the doily. Sally relaxed and gave my question some thought.

"Yes."

Pushing back her chair, she walked over to the snacks cupboard above the microwave, and pulled out a packet of chocolate McVitie's Hob Nobs. She opened it and took one out for herself, then offered me the packet. I waved it away, and she placed it on the wooden table between us.

"I probably ate back anything that I might have lost on that week long fast within the first ten minutes being off it," she laughed. "Why's that?"

"Because I went on a five day fast so I would be light enough to ride this new horse at the yard and now I'm not hungry." I shrugged.

"*You* . . . not hungry!" she coughed, "Now, that's a joke, I've never known anyone with an appetite like yours!"

"Yeah, it will come back, no doubt," I smiled at her

But it didn't.

Mum had wanted a family dinner that evening. When I sat down to a meal of homemade pasta and tomato sauce I found myself pushing pieces of penne around my plate. The pieces of pasta might as well have been lego, because I felt more inclined to play with them than eat them. I felt as if the food no longer held any value to me.

"What's wrong, Tabby?" Mum noticed me playing with my food. "Don't you like it?"

"No, no, it's fine," I insisted. "I'm just not that hungry."

"Well, I haven't seen you eat anything all week, Honey. That's not like you, are you sure you are ok?" she asked.

I could feel myself getting flustered and I was not entirely sure why. I did not like the way that Mum was correlating me not eating with something being *wrong*. There was nothing wrong with me; I just did not want to eat. Why was that such a big deal?

"She's on a diet." Beth, who must have been about fifteen at the time, chirped from where she was sat at the far end of the table.

"No I'm not!" I snapped as I attempted to kick her under the table.

"Yes you are too, I saw that diet book in your room." She dodged my foot and smiled smugly.

"Now, Tabby, why would you be on a diet Sweetie? You are perfect as you are." Mum looked concerned.

Great, that was all that I needed. Thanks Beth. I scowled at my little sister who grinned back at me.

I scraped my chair on the kitchen floor as I pushed it back and left the table.

Finally, the following day, I felt hungry. I was pleased to feel my stomach grow restless and I welcomed the gnawing hunger pangs. Unfortunately, the timing was bad, as it was right in the middle of morning exercise at Harringdon and I was up on one of the racehorses. Unable to eat right then and there, instead, I enjoyed crafting in my head what I was going to eat when I got home. I settled on a toasted cheese and ham sandwich. I would use the Breville sandwich machine—one of my favourite contraptions for creating cheesy gooey goodness with. My mind wandered to cheese and ham and constructing the perfect toasted sandwich as I rode back towards the stables with Terry and Tony—the other two exercise jockeys with whom I was riding that morning—whose chatter dimmed into the background. I could practically smell that sandwich already and see the melted cheddar cheese dribbling off the side of the plate.

"Tabby, what's going on, you in some kind of dreamland this morning!" Terry, riding a large dark bay horse called Sinbad a couple of feet behind, heckled me, and I realised that I had just ridden right past the entrance to the race yard.

"Yes actually," I laughed as I turned the filly that I was on back toward the gate, "I'm dreaming of a cheese toastie."

"Good for you girl," Terry smiled at me. "You're getting a little on the skinny side."

I was hungry. Well, at least, I thought I was. Until I actually got home.

I hurried in the front door.

"Get your muddy boots off before you come in here!" Dad warned me without looking up from the paper. It was late-morning, and his coffee mug was painting a dark rim on the morning paper he was using as a coaster.

I sighed audibly and rolled my eyes, but reluctantly stepped back into the porch where I yanked my boots off. Barefooted, I made a beeline for the kitchen. I pulled out the Breville machine from its place in the Welsh Dresser and turned it on to warm up. Just the smell of one of those things warming up is delicious—they smell like grilled cheese. I stuck my arm into the bread bin and hauled out a couple of slices of white bread (I am of the opinion that, for grilled cheese toasties, white bread tastes better than brown). Then, after arranging the bread on the cutting board, I opened the fridge door and found the Cheddar and sliced deli ham.

As I busied myself getting the elements of my sandwich in place, my rush ebbed away; I paused for a second and studied the cheese that I was holding in my hands. I turned the packet over to the nutrition information on the back.

Cheese is very high in fat.

I felt my heart rate rise slightly; I could hear it beating in my ears. A shot of adrenaline gave me a headrush, so I reached over to the sink for a glass of water, putting the cheese back down on the chopping board. I turned my back to it and leant against the kitchen counter, as I drank.

Why do I feel sick?

Why do I feel stressed?

As I gazed down at the empty water glass in my hands I recognised that I felt the way that I usually did before an important horse event or competition: anxious. I was not competing that weekend, so why should I feel anxious?

Why do I feel so giddy?

And thirsty. I'm really thirsty.

I poured another glass of water. As I sipped it down, I wondered if eating such a high-fat food as cheese was stupid. Maybe cheese and ham was not a good choice for me? Maybe I should be eating something slightly less fatty, with fewer calories?

The thought of saving calories felt great. It felt right. Pleasing. My heartbeat slowed down and my nerves turned to excitement. Until that point I had never considered that anything could feel better than eating cheese did. Yet here I was, discovering that I felt really good if I did *not* eat cheese. When I wanted to eat cheese, not eating it actually felt incredible, and I had no idea why.

I put the Cheddar back in the fridge and unplugged the Breville. I took the bread and put it in the toaster; I would just have some toast and jam. That was the right thing to do, I knew if because I felt it.

That's one of the (myriad) reasons that Anorexia is such a bitch of a disease. It makes the sufferer feel as if its choices are one's own. It convinces the sufferer that he or she is following what feels right, or intelligent, or correct, when really they have been duped by a very fraudulent impostor.

I think that was the day that what *I* wanted didn't matter anymore. The disease was in the cockpit now.

There was this blissful slither of time where I was the perfect weight to be an exercise jockey, and in that time I got all the rides that I wanted. So, at least in that sense my original plan had worked.

Was it worth it? Was a couple of months riding all the horses that I wanted to ride worth what turned into twelve years of perdition? No.

All the same, for about a month I was the most versatile exercise jockey at Harringdon Stables because I was strong, light, and had the ability to stick a buck. After time, however, I noticed—as did everyone else—that I was beginning to have trouble holding the horses. I was getting weak, which is a common side effect of malnutrition.

One midsummer morning, I was up on KitKat—who conversely had been growing stronger over the summer. That morning, as usual, we were instructed to go up the gallop at a canter in a civilized string of four paired horses. KitKat, excited to be out, started too fast. She pulled the reins from my hands and took off. I was simply unable to find the strength to pull her up.

We shot right through the middle of the neatly cantering pairs of horses in front of us at a flat out gallop. Leaving the rest of the horses scattered behind us, she took me right up the strip, past the pull-up area, and through the gate at the of the top of the field. I finally managed to pull her up somewhere in a corn field about three-hundred yards later.

Red faced and panting, I had to turn around and ride her back down the gallop to where the other jockeys had all pulled their horses to a halt. That was an embarrassing ride to say the least.

"Steady on there girl, you lose your rein?" asked Terry, who was on board a leggy bay thoroughbred.

"Yeah," I panted, "I dunno what happened." I was still catching my breath, my red cheeks telling not only of the struggle that I had experienced in pulling the mare up at all, but also of my embarrassment.

"Ah, never you mind Lass. It 'appens to the best 'e us." Terry was kind, but that did not console me. I put on a smile and pretended to shrug the incident off, but the truth was I was devastated.

Thomas said nothing of the incident, so at least I avoided a scolding, but the next day it was Terry's name chalked up to ride KitKat, not mine. I pretended not to notice when Terry pulled KitKat out of her stall and yelled at her as she nipped his arm. I bit my tongue when I wanted to tell him off for jabbing her in the ribs with his heels as she skittered from side to side when we rode down the lane. That was not my horse, and I had no business getting attached or jealous. My emotions were my problem, not his.

Towards the end of the summer, Kit-Kat won a race by a good margin, and to celebrate a good season overall, Thomas organised us a breakfast to be held after the morning exercise on the following Sunday. We were to finish up with the horses and then gather in the cottage that he lived in on site for brunch.

The other jockeys and stable hands were all a clamour about our upcoming Sunday social, planning Bloody Marys and bacon baps. A couple of the stable girls wanted to bake brownies and cakes, and someone even offered to bring bucks Fizz. It had been a long summer of hard work, and the yard was looking forward to a celebration of sorts.

Sunday approached and I was relieved to see that I had been chalked up to ride a sweet little horse called Timmy in the the last ride of the day. I had hoped that this would be the case; that way I could still be untacking and grooming when the brunch party began. This shows how much I had changed in a very short time, as only a few months earlier I would have been annoyed at this inconvenience. Oh, yes, at the start of the summer I would have wanted to be the first in the line for a bacon butty as soon as the grill had been fired up.

I sponged Timmy off slowly while the other jockeys fought over the water buckets and hose in their haste to be finished. He was not actually very sweaty by the time we had walked back from the gallop to the stableyard, but I bathed him thoroughly anyway in a bid to kill more time. As I rinsed the soap suds out of his tail, I could hear the sizzle of meat on the outdoor grill. As I picked out his feet and polished his hooves, the bacon smell wafting through the stableyard was enough to make the other riders clamber to fling their tack into the tack room and hurry across the gravel courtyard towards the little flint cottage where the food was being cooked.

I should have hurried with them, because didn't I love bacon and eggs washed down with mugs of hot tea? Not to mention that even Thomas had told me I was getting too thin. Most of all, though, I should have been there because, usually, if there was going to be any kind of social gathering, I was the wit and the fun at the centre.

The longer I stood with Timmy in his stable, the more my feet felt rooted to the straw that I was standing in. The louder the chatter became from the garden fence of the trainer's cottage, the tighter my hands gripped the brush that I was working gently though Timmy's mane. I hoped that nobody would notice if I stayed here. I listened to the prattle of the Irish lads, the bellowing Scottish braw of Sarah the head groom, the bustle and the banter that I should have been a part of. I heard Terry asking where I was and Sarah answering that she thought I had already come in. "Is Tabby still in the yard?" she asked Tony as he walked into the garden where they were all sitting and eating.

I silently closed Timmy's stable door behind me as I skipped out into the corridor in the middle of the stable barn. Checking that nobody was about, I crept out of the sliding double doors at the end of the line of stalls and tiptoed over to my car, which was parked on the grass to the side.

I felt alone as I drove home. I was confused and sad that I had not wanted to relax and spend time with my stablemates celebrating our summer. I felt all of those things, but I felt none of them as strongly as the sweeping relief that floated through every cell in my body. I felt none of those things as much as I felt victorious and clean. I understood then that eating was the problem, and that when I avoided eating I felt like this. I felt good.

The cream that I used to love to taste had turned sour.

"You know, your BMI is very . . ." Doctor Watkins looked up at me over the rim of his spectacles for increased effect, " . . . very" then looked back down at his notes, " . . . low."

Gazing intently at my hands, I said nothing. I was there to talk to him about my periods—or lack of them—and for a proud seventeen-year-old with a male General

Practitioner, that was quite embarrassing enough.

"It's no wonder that your mother is worried about you Young Lady," Watkins's voice was stern: accusatory. That pissed me off; it still does.

I rolled my eyes, not caring if he saw. I hated being called "Young Lady", and I did not need him to remind me that my mother was worried about me. She told me that herself every bloody day.

"Are you aware that you are underweight?" Watkins continued.

I considered not dignifying that with a response. Of course I knew that I was underweight—any idiot could see that. I rolled my eyes again.

"Look, I know that according to your standard Bell curve graph I am underweight, but everyone knows that those things get skewed for the general population, and the general population includes all those overweight Americans, so if you ask me, the graph is wrong." Sure, I was a Smart Alec.

Watkins did not look impressed, nor did he look convinced that I knew what I was talking about, so I elaborated for him, "I study Psychology at college, we cover all this kind of stuff, you know."

"Did you cover Anorexia Nervosa?" Watkins's voice was softer this time.

Good grief, are we really talking about this? I sighed audibly.

Sure, we had covered eating disorders in class. Here is what I learnt:

Anorexia Nervosa is an eating disorder characterised by severe food restriction, ritualistic and inappropriate eating habits, obsession with thinness and an irrational fear of weight gain. Sufferers attempt to lose weight to the point of starvation because they are scared of getting fat. Sufferers also might do this as an attempt to control their lives. Parents and trauma can cause it. Anorexia Nervosa, and the associated malnutrition that results from self-imposed starvation, can cause severe complications in every major organ system in the body.

Yes: we had covered Anorexia Nervosa.

Yes: I knew all about the silly girls that get so obsessed with losing weight because they want to look thin that they starve to death.

Yes: I knew about the 'supermodels' disease.

Yes: I got it that people who have a negative body image get eating disorders.

Additionally, our lecturer had told us that usually eating disorders happen to people whose parents gave them low self esteem. Oh yes, I *thought* I knew all about anorexia, but unfortunately I did not know that everything I had been told was bullshit. So at that time, in Watkins's office, I was pretty pissed at him for even suggesting it.

This guy is such a prat! Everybody knows that people with anorexia want to be thin, and that they have this body dysmorphia thing that makes them think that they are fat

33

when they are not. How can he be asking me if I have anorexia when not two minutes ago I had admitted to him that I knew I was thin? How can he be asking me if I have anorexia when he knows how great my parents are, not to mention how worried my mother is? How could he be asking me if I have anorexia when he knows that I'm a horse rider and don't have time for that sort of vanity crap?

What an asshole.

"Do you want to talk to someone about this?" Watkins was still at it.

Do I heck.

"No I'm fine."

Actually, talking to someone about it was the very last thing that I wanted to do, not him, not some shrink, not my mother, nobody, because there was nothing to talk about, there was nothing wrong with me. Nothing at all.

He paused, noisily sucking the air through his teeth—a feigned pensivity."Well, I think you would have a much better chance of regaining your menstrual cycle if you put on some weight."

This infuriated me, because had he read my notes correctly he would have remembered that the reason that I was seeing him today was not because I had *lost* my menstrual cycle, but because I had never had one in the first place. One cannot regain something that one has never had. I was seventeen and had not yet started my periods. *That* was what I was here to talk about, not my weight, not regaining my cycle, but getting one in the first place. I had not had periods when I was heavier, and I did not have them now, I did not see how my weight change could therefore be an attributing factor to my absent menstrual cycle.

I think that was when I began to lose trust in doctors.

"Since when did you start drinking that nasty diet stuff?" Jen and I were at the local pub.

"Oh, I actually prefer the taste of it." I lied.

"You should drink the full fat mixers, look at you . . . all skinny!" she frowned at my waistline and tut-tutted.

After that I became sneakier about choosing low-calorie drinks. I would wait until everyone else was engaged in conversation to go to the bar and order so that I could not be called out on my request for diet mixers. Any enjoyment that I once got out of relaxing in a pub with my friends was giving way to anxiety.

My life had turned into a continual struggle of stress management that it had not been before. There were some—very few—foods that did not cause me to feel fear, and because of this I opted to eat a lot of these and little of anything else. Fear was a new addition to my daily life. I would happily jump up onto a racehorse or ride an event horse over fences, but here I was with an unexplainable fear about eating. Apples were okay, so they became my biggest staple because they are filling and effective at bulking out an empty stomach. Carrots and other vegetables I enjoyed for the same reasons. The greater the calorific value of a food, the greater the stress. It was a pretty direct and linear relationship.

Any food with fat in it was immediately accompanied by a beating heart and a cold sweat. My weight—or lack of it—was a fringe effect of my fear and abhorrence for calories and fat. As I witnessed my body get thinner and thinner, I felt some sadness about that. But, if it was a necessary side effect for what I needed to do in order to feel safe, then it was a price worth paying. After a while, my eyes felt empty to the shape that my shadow made on the ground or the figure reflected in the mirror. In disconnecting from my body, I was able to remove any stress that compassion for it might have caused me.

Chapter Five

What is particularly sad about my rather long and topsy-turvy story is that as a child, I had loved fatty foods; especially cheese. My favorite cheese always was, and still is, Cheddar: extra-mature, aged Cheddar. The really sharp type. I can feel my taste buds tingling at the very thought of tangy Cheddar cheese. I think I'll take a pause from writing and go eat some; just because, nowadays, I can.

When I wasn't able to eat cheese—which was approximately between September 1998 and June 2011—I still thought about cheese a hell of a lot. My mouth would *ache* for cheese. My taste buds told me that they remembered exactly what cheese tasted like and were constantly asking me why the hell they had not been allowed it for so very, very long.
Because it's full of fat and bad for me! The voices in my head would shout.

Don't be alarmed, dear reader, when I mention the voices in my head; we all have them. Come now, we do. Just in my case, these voices became a little more troublesome as my eating disorder infected them. You'll get to know the voices in my head during this time pretty well later on, as they are a crucial part of this tale.
But for now, back to cheese:

The cheese that my mother used to buy when we were kids would appear in a black plastic packet with gold writing on the front. "Extra Mature Cheddar." Everything that she made for me to eat tasted even more wonderful with cheese in it. Every meal, every family outing, every picnic, every sandwich . . . every day, had been better with cheese.
In those years that I could not eat cheese, I would torture myself by recalling the smell and taste of mature Cheddar on toast; I'd daydream about the way the soft, warm, melty, cheesy topping would droop over the crust of the crispy bread on which it sat. I'd fantasize over cheese to the point that I could almost taste it—which, let's face it, for a long time, is as close as I got.

Cheese is full of fat, which is probably why it tastes so good. As a child, I was blissfully ignorant to the fact that eating fat was considered unfashionable. And even if I had, chances are I would not have cared; my relationship with fat had been innocent and uncomplicated.
What is really sad is that I never, ever, stopped liking things like white bread, butter and cheese. My eating disorder just convinced me that I did not, so for years and years these were all things which I avoided. I think that a lot of the reason I obsessed about these types of foods so much when I had Anorexia was purely because I denied myself them.

I certainly ate enough cheese and bread as a child. Mum would promise cheese on toast for brunch if my sisters and I were good girls on Sunday and did not giggle the whole way through the vicar's sermon in church. It was that sort of irresistible comfort food to me, something that would help me through the tedium of family service.

Church services seemed to last for days when I was a child; a cruel form of torture for a little girl who wanted nothing more than to be outside. I shudder as I remember the mind-numbing sermons and the bottom-numbing pews. The promise of cheese when we got home would give me something to be thankful for. When the vicar asked us to give thanks and praise, I would thank the Lord for making cows. I was very grateful to cows, as I understood that cows were responsible for milk, and milk is what cheese is made out of.

You know what is even better than cheese on toast: Marmite on top of cheese on toast.

Many people do not like Marmite; if you are one of these unfortunate, taste-challenged folks, I pity you: you have no idea how rich the world is. It deeply concerns me when people tell me that they don't like the dark, salty, tongue-spanking spread that I find so irresistible. My husband is one of them. He doesn't like tea either, which is equally as troubling.

A friend of mine, who had recently had a baby, once confided in me that she ate so much Marmite when she was breastfeeding that she became concerned that her milk would taste of it. Lucky kid.

Now, speaking of breast milk:

When I was in my twenties, I embarked on a nutrition course. At the time, I told myself I was doing so because I wanted to be a nutritionist. In reality, I was doing so because I was utterly obsessed with food. Anyway, during that course we touched on breast milk. (I mean that we studied it, not that we actually touched breasts). The lecturer told us that breastmilk is the best food for a baby because it is full of fat and cholesterol—which incidentally, at that time, were both words that I could not help but spit out should the need to punctuate them arise.

Fat, cholesterol. Nasty, evil things!

Our course lecturer had told us that babies need both fat (*yuk!*) and cholesterol (*yak!*) to help their brains and bodies grow. Infants, apparently, are programmed to survive, and fat is in nature's survival kit.

Intrigued by this concept, and somewhat opposed to it, I had taken it upon myself to look further into the science behind breast milk. Maybe my lecturer was wrong—it would not have been the first time. Alas, my independent research told me it seemed that he had been right on that one: breast milk *is* high in fat.

But why? Everyone knows that fat is bad, right?

I studied some more, and learnt that a woman produces breast milk when her body is under the influence of the hormones prolactin and oxytocin; after she has given birth.

Oxytocin?

Prolactin?

What have these got to do with milk?

What have they got to do with fat and cholesterol?

Why did I care?

I cared because I cared about anything that had something to do with fat. I could not help it; I did not *want* to care, but I cared all the same: it was a curiosity that I could not control. When does curiosity cease being curiosity and enroll into the class of an uncontrollable obsession? A long time ago in my case!

I was enslaved by my preoccupation with fat, not just curious. People are curious about questions like: What is the average wage of a porn star? What country is Timbuktu in? I wonder what my dog is thinking? That's curiosity. Me, spending hours and hours in the library researching a snippet of information a course lecturer had given me just because the word "fat" had been mentioned in a good way was more than simple inquisitiveness. Me, at the age of twenty-one, keeping a secret little-black-book, in which I recorded every single ounce of fat that I had eaten for the past three years—including that which I may or may not have accidentally eaten unwittingly— rather than the names and numbers of men who I fancied, was much more than passing interest. Me, researching into the amount of fat in horse or dog food and seeing if it was comparable to that in the average human diet, was beyond what could be considered a nice, sane, intelligent, inquiring mind.

Oh yes! I was well past being curious about fat. I was thinking-of-you-a-hundred-times-a-day obsessed with it.

Anyway, long story short: I know a bit about breastfeeding and things like oxytocin and prolactin because I came across them in my years of fat-stalking. For those of you who are interested, I learnt that oxytocin is a prerequisite to breast milk and is involved in breast milk production, and breast milk is high in fat, and when I had been a child I had consumed breast milk, therefore I considered it my business to know what the hell it was that inspired the human breast to do such as curious thing as give a baby fat.

I learnt the first thing that oxytocin—often quaintly referred to as "the trust hormone" or "the cuddle hormone"—makes childbirth a smoother process by relaxing specific parts of a woman's body enough to allow a baby out. Not something that I will ever have to worry about because I'm never going to have children, but interesting all the same.

Oxytocin then floods the mother's brain, seducing her into believing that the red-faced, wrinkled child she has produced is the most beautiful thing she has ever seen. Nature can be quite underhanded can it not? This is the part where the oxytocin-effect stops the poor woman coming to her senses after hours of painful labour and screaming, "Enough is enough! Take that squawking baby away from me, I need to sleep dammit!"

I would not have blamed my mother if she hadn't wanted anything do with me following giving birth, because, apparently, I had taken my time emerging. She hadn't held that against me, though. Instead, she had pulled me to her chest and kissed me on my hot little forehead; I have the pictures to prove it. *Good Old Mum eh?*

More like good old birth hormones.

Thanks to oxytocin, a smile formed on my mother's lips when she first saw my bald, angry, yelling, scrunched-up little face. I am particularly thankful for this nugget of assistance, as looking back on photographs of myself at this time, it is indisputable that I was a very ugly baby. I had this weird lump on my forehead—which, thankfully, disappeared as the weeks went by. I was as red as a beet with a ridiculously large head in comparison to the rest of me. I had no hair to speak of. Oxytocin is dressing on the windows that we see one another through, and an aptly hung curtain can make even the ugliest of views more scenic. Even that wizened baby face of mine looked beautiful to the oxytocin-drenched eyes of my parents. And, yes, it also prompts the production of breast milk.

I love milk; always have. I should clarify that I mean cow's milk—not breast milk. I stopped drinking breast milk a very long time ago.

At least, nowadays I can admit to liking the taste of cow's milk. I'll go even further and declare that I prefer cow's milk to any other type. Cow's milk has fallen rather out of fashion, having been ousted somewhat by trendy soy and almond variations; shame, as it really is very nutritious.

When I suffered from Anorexia, I drank nothing but skimmed milk for years, and even then it was only the teeny-tiniest amount in my tea. I had stopped using milk altogether in things like cereal in an attempt to avoid the additional calories from fat. There had been a brief phase at university where I had been trying to eat muesli with orange juice on it instead, which tasted foul, but would have been lower in fat than skimmed milk.

Another thing that I had been told by the lecturer running my nutrition course was that a growing body needs fat. According to him, when I had been a child, things like eating cheese and butter were important. Children need saturated fat. He had insisted, "Saturated fat cells are like the bricks of the fat world . . . they are sturdy and work very well as a foundation to build a growing body on."

Well, he would say that, wouldn't he?

If what the fat-nutrition lecturer had said was true, then the milk and the cheese that I was guiltlessly eating as a toddler were providing my body with saturated fats which it could use to build with. "Unsaturated fats help build the cells of the growing body as they will then be used to form the cell membranes," nutrition guy had said. "We get these from the meat and dairy in our diets." Y*our diet maybe, not mine!* I had thought at the time. More fool me, so it turns out.

We are almost done with the *childhood* section of this tale, and really, what I am trying to illustrate with all this, is that my fear of fat certainly was not present when I was a nipper, nor did it evolve out of a fat-shaming household: quite the opposite.

"Mummy?"

"Yes Darling."

"Mummy . . . how do we have cheese?"

"Cheese comes from the cows in the meadow Darling."

"Mummy?"

"Yes Darling."

"Mummy . . . why do the cows give us cheese? Don't they need it for themselves?"

"The cows don't need cheese, we make it from their milk Darling."

"Mummy?"

"Yes Darling."

"Mummy . . . how does the cow make milk?"

"She makes it in her udder Darling."

"Mummy?"

"Yes Darling."

'Mummy . . . how does the milk get into her udder?"

"The cow eats grass and . . . well, it makes milk, which, er . . . comes out of the cow's udder and gets turned into the cheese that you like to eat."

"Mummy?"

"Yes Darling."

"Mummy . . . what happens after I eat cheese?"

Good question.

A question that, by the time I was twenty, sadly, I knew all about the answer to ... .

The years between 1998 and 2010 had witnessed me painstakingly studying all sorts of food-related material from cookbooks to research papers; digestion, and the process of, was something relevant to my interests. I knew, therefore, that when I ate anything—be it the cheese, toast, Marmite or Cadbury's chocolate (*let's not even go there!*) that I had enjoyed prior to 1998, or the ridiculous amount of low-fat foods and vegetables that I had . . . endured . . . thereafter—the morsel would get broken up by my teeth then interact with an enzyme in my saliva called amylase. It would then move from my mouth, down to my stomach. Here, the fat would be further broken down by the gastric juice in my tummy and sent along to my small intestine. There, it would be greeted by bile, which would dissolve it further, so that it could be digested by more enzymes in the pancreatic juice from my pancreas.

From here, the fatty acids and cholesterol move into the mucosal cells of the intestine where they will be turned back into larger fat molecules so that they can be transported through my body by my blood. My bloodstream acts as a transportation system for fat, so that it can be taken to places in my body that needed it, such as tissues.

Basically, I am trying to point out that some of my fat-stalking research taught me about how fat is useful. I got it. Even then, I got it. I understood that my body needed fat. However, my nutrition science books also told me that saturated fat was the enemy for adults, because it causes heart disease and a host of other problems.

Chapter Six

The only *fat* that I was really aware of when I was a kid, was the word that we used to describe overweight people: the adjective form. In the playground at school we would whisper about the *fat* teachers, knowing even at that young age that we should never call them "fat" to their faces; that was rude.

Fat was a bad word, a nasty word.

Fat was a word to describe someone—but never to be used in front of grown ups.

Incidentally—just in case you were wondering why the noun fat is also used as an adjective, whereas protein and carbohydrate are not—the Old English word *fætt* meant: *fat, fatted, plump, obese* and was originally a contracted past participle of *fættian* which meant *to cram, or to stuff.* One might stuff one's face with potato chips, or cram one's mouth full of popcorn. We make our bodies fat when we jam them full of food. Taking a container, be it your own stomach, mouth or something inanimate like a suitcase and ramming it full would be to make it fat.

Mrs. Rodgers had been fat. She was the primary school teacher who taught me writing skills at school in the mornings (so you can blame her if you spot a flaw in this book). I knew that if I dared to call Mrs. Rodgers "fat" in my mother's earshot there would be big trouble. I was not to call people fat because my mother said that it was rude, and I was not allowed to be rude, especially to grown ups. As a child, all these adult rules had seemed disingenuous. If a person was fat, why not call them fat?

Kids don't tend to attach judgement like adults do; they say it as it is.

Regardless of whether I was allowed to say it or not, Mrs. Rodgers was fat. Plump, just like the pigeons that I would watch scavenging for crumbs out in the schoolyard after our lunch break. She was far wider than any of the other teachers, and to a five-year-old she was simply enormous. In the mornings she would shuffle around the miniature desks and chairs in our classroom, peer over our shoulders at the work that we were doing, and beak at mistakes we might be making. I did not like Mrs. Rodgers, but it was not because she was fat. No, it was because she would often grab me by the arm and hoist me to the front of the room to ask me a question in front of the whole class; usually a question that I did not know the answer to. This never failed to make me feel embarrassed and stupid, and as a result I disliked school. That is a sad result, but before you jump ahead to any erroneous conclusions: no, Mrs. Rodgers being a mean old cow did not cause my eating disorder.

What did?

Not so fast, we will get to that all in good time. For now, back to Mrs. Rodgers:

I did not allocate the meanness of Mrs. Rodgers to be a product of her fatness because Mrs. Nelson, our afternoon teacher, was even beastlier, and she was not at all fat. A sparrow of a woman, she would prod and peck at our backs as we hunched over our school desks, squawking at me because I did not know my times tables. The only thing that Mrs. Rodgers and Mrs. Nelson had in common—aside from torturing me—was the spectacles they wore. For a while I was suspicious of any adult who wore glasses.

(Shush. Mrs. Nelson did not cause my eating disorder either.)

Yes, I had hated school, and yes, I had considered most of the teachers to be mean. But that was probably because I was a brat and all I really wanted to do was be outside riding ponies anyway. What we are establishing is that, all-in-all, I had a pretty 'normal' childhood, didn't I?

I had pretty 'normal' friends too. When I was first old enough to go on playdates, I learnt that with each friend's house and each friend's parent came different rules and ways of doing things. Some mothers, like my friend Rhonda's, insisted on making us home cooked meals with vegetables like my own did. Other mothers, like my friend Amy's, let us have sweets all the time. Some mothers read bedtime stories and turned lights out when it was time for us to go to sleep; Amy's mother did not tell us when to go to sleep at all. Being at Amy's house was a whole lot of fun.

Amy was by far my favourite person to stay with; once dropped off outside her front door it were as if I had entered Willy Wonka's Chocolate Factory. Sweets, chocolate, processed and fried foods were a free-for-all in Amy's house. And boy did I love all of those things!

At home we were cruelly subjected to homemade foods and a plethora of vegetables. I liked my mother's cooking but when given the choice, I would choose what she referred to as "junk food" hands down. In my world, a Pot Noodle was a treat for the once in a blue moon days that my mum was not about, and microwave meals were a delight that happened all too rarely.

Even my father knew that we were not allowed junk food very often. I remember one time, when my mother had gone away to visit my grandma, who was sick, she had left the three of us kids with my dad. Because she had to go at such short notice, she was unable to prepare a week's worth of food and leave it in the fridge like she would usually do on the odd occasion that she left us alone with Dad. He only seemed to know how to cook one thing: eggy bread.

What most people call French toast, my father terms "eggy bread." This is how one makes it: Crack some eggs into a bowl and whisk them up. Then, dip pieces of bread into the egg mixture before frying them in butter in a pan on the hob. The bread will go all crispy and fluffy.

We all liked eggy bread enough, but after three days of having it for every meal I was hoping that my mother would return home soon. We were allowed tomato ketchup or brown sauce with our eggy bread, so at least there was a way to vary the taste of it.

Before you ask: eggy bread overwhelm did not cause my eating disorder.

Junk food was the term that Mother used to describe anything that came out of a packet: ready-meals, Pot Noodles, sweets, crisps and chocolate bars. *Junk food* would also be used to describe fast-food chain offerings like Burger King, Kentucky Fried Chicken, McDonald's, and The Wimpy. My father had got himself into big trouble once for taking us for fast-food hamburgers at the local Wimpy instead of heating up the homemade lasagna that my mother had prepared and left in the fridge for our dinner. We were allowed junk food sometimes, but not very often if my mother was around.

At Amy's house, we could eat junk food whenever we wanted to. We could have microwave meals for dinner and follow them up with unrationed chocolate ice cream. We were allowed to top that ice cream with squirty-can whipped cream and sprinkle it all with multi-coloured hundreds-and-thousands. Microwave-warmed chocolate or toffee sauce would be drizzled intensively over everything.

Usually this type of food was only for parties and special occasions: not at Amy's house! Oh no! At Amy's house there were pots of sweets on the counters all year round rather than just at Christmas or Easter. And we never had to ask first. At home asking first was the rule before eating sweets, and the query would often be met with, "only after you've eaten your dinner," or, "have a piece of fruit first." Not at Amy's house, there was no need to ask; just help yourself whenever you feel like it.

Note: My mother never let us eat sweets for dinner. She doggedly stuck to providing us with a nutritious home cooked dinner every night. This abhorrent insistence that we eat proper food is not child abuse and did not cause my eating disorder. Just in case you were wondering.

Some parents let their children eat sweets all day. Some parents do not. Some parents are just plain smart, like Jen's mum:

Jen had ginger hair, which she wore bunched up in pigtails, and freckles that covered her forehead and nose. Jen lived in a large house, and I remember always feeling a little bit intimidated by the size of it. It had those high ceilings and made funny creaking noises. The first time I had gone for a playdate there I had been scared in that big old house.

My fears evaporated when Jen's mum presented us with cheese sandwiches for lunch. I remember wondering why and how Jen's mum knew that I loved cheese; it had not occurred to me at that age that our mothers were in cahoots. To this day I remember the cheese sandwich that I had eaten sitting in Jen's kitchen at the old wooden table. That cheese sandwich had caused me to forget about missing home; about my parents and sisters; and about the scariness of the big and unfamiliar house that I was in. The soft white bread, blanketed by a thin layer of butter, and glorious, sharp, yellow cheddar. There were a couple of leaves of iceberg lettuce in the middle, which added a crisp, fresh crunch to the bite. I guess this was before white bread was considered high glycemic index and therefore the devil of all foods. It was certainly long before I had any concerns regarding things like that anyway.

Before 1998, before Anorexia, I had loved white bread, especially french bread. That soft interior with the crisp outer shell—particularly good when served with an obvious companion: Brie, or Camembert. There is nothing that suits a French loaf better than a ripened soft cheese. Thrifty camping holidays abroad would bring such wonders and delights. Each year my parents booked a Eurocamp tent and packed us all into the Volvo. Off we would adventure to France or Spain for a couple of weeks. I remembered very little of those holidays now, other than the French bread and cheese; especially the ripened Camembert.

How wonderful it must have been to be able to eat everything without an ounce of guilt, because when I was a child, I could do that. All there was to worry about was when my next riding lesson would come about.

When I was seven, there was another girl at my primary school who liked horses, too. Her name was Lucy Tallon and she had moved into the area because her father had changed jobs; she started new at my school halfway through the term.

Lucy Tallon had been the fat kid.

Before Lucy Tallon started at our school I had not had any friends who were fat. I had thought that it was only adults who were affected by protruding bellies and wobbly thighs. Lucy Tallon opened my eyes to the world of fat shaming. She was ridiculed and teased by the older kids. I learnt that the word *fat* could be more than just a bad word to describe someone; *fat* could be a weapon used to hurt.

Lucy kept to herself. Who could blame her? Nobody wanted to be her friend because doing so might leave oneself open for also being called names. Nobody sat with her at lunchtime and nobody waited for her after school. It were as if fat was contagious and the only way to keep it at bay was to humiliate it.

"Lucy Tallon is a fatso! Lucy Tallon is a fat cow!" They would sing as she walked down the corridor.

I was not scared that fat was contagious, or that I would get fat if I spoke to Lucy. When the bullies were otherwise occupied, I would sit with her and talk to her about my favorite pony at the riding stable. His name was Casper and he was a fourteen-hand chestnut gelding. Lucy liked chestnut ponies too.

I liked to talk about ponies with Lucy Tallon, but if the bullies were present I was scared that I myself would become the subject of their taunts. With my gangly long legs I was already a prime target for bullying if I got in their way. They used to call me "Tabby Long Legs," a somewhat humourous play on the layman's term for a crane fly: Daddy long legs.

I hated being called Tabby Long Legs because it brought attention to my height. I was so much taller than everyone else, even all the boys in my class. I was different because of this. I was also different because of my name: Tabitha. There were no other girls called Tabitha in the school that I went to so I got teased for that, too. That was not as bad as Tabby Long Legs though. I hated that nickname.

Because the bullies knew how it upset me, they called me it as often as they could. So for the most part, I too stayed away from Lucy Tallon. Nowadays, with the courage of adulthood and the luxury of hindsight, I feel guilt for not having taken action on her behalf. I know what that feels like now; to be bullied because of one's appearance. I too have been chased down the local high street by the spiteful taunts of schoolkids. I have learnt a compassion for Lucy Tallon that I could not have known at the age of seven.

Chapter Seven

I'll stop going on about cheese soon I promise, but before I do, I need to tell you about my very favourite childhood meal. It's relevant, I promise, as you need to understand that I was never a fat-fearing child; on the contrary, quite the opposite. Are you ready? Can you guess what it was?

Cheese on toast: close, but not the one.

Cheese sandwiches: another very near miss.

Oh go on then, my favourite ever, bestest childhood dinner, was macaroni cheese.

I was nine when I fell in love with macaroni cheese, and my best friend at the time, Rhonda, was in utter agreement with me about this. I was at Rhonda's house once when her mother made it for us and I watched the whole process from the window seat by her kitchen sink. Rhonda was doing her math homework next to me and I was supposed to be working on mine, but I became engrossed by the silky stirrings of the pot on the stove.

Rhonda's house had this funny little kitchen. It had no dishwasher, and this meant that we had to take turns with the washing up after dinner. That was a bore. It was always cold in Rhonda's house; apart from the kitchen as the Rayburn stove managed to keep that room warm all year around. Hence in the winter the kitchen was the place to do homework, to read, to play.

This I liked, as we would be serenaded by the sounds of pots and pans as we did our homework. That day I was watching Rhonda's mother make bechamél. It was a fascinating process. There is a unique sizzle and smell that butter has when it melts in the saucepan, and I think this is what caught my attention in the first place. Looking over at what Rhonda's mum was doing, I watched her rustle open a paper bag of flour and sift a couple of tablespoons into that frothy hot butter, resulting in a thick bright yellow roux as the butter and flour merged.

I remember the clink of the whisk on the side of the saucepan as Rhonda's mother gently added (full-fat) fresh milk to the mixture in her saucepan, turning it a lighter, creamier shade. Next, the turning of the pepper grinder as the sauce thickened, while the rolling boil of the pasta water got louder and louder. Have you noticed that funny still fizz that hisses into silence when pasta is poured into boiling water? I love that sound.

The best thing about watching Rhonda's mum cook, was the satisfaction of knowing that soon—albeit not soon enough—this deliciousness would be mine to eat.

Whenever Rhonda's mother cooked, the inside of the kitchen window would fog up, as would Rhonda's spectacles. This made us giggle. Gloopy, squishy, suction noises came from the far side of the kitchen as the cheese béchamel sauce was churned into the hot pasta. Then, the entire glorious mixture was poured into a large rectangular glass Pyrex dish. Finally the crowning: a sliced tomato carefully arranged over the steaming mass of pasta and cheese, followed by more cheese grated on top for good measure and a crisp crust.

Into the oven it went.

Behind the golden glow of the oven door, the Pyrex dish bubbled and baked. I could see the cheese on the top changing from yellow to gold to light brown. Every now and then I would alert Rhonda's mother to the possibility that it was done.

"The timer will tell us when it is done Tabby!"

There was no need to rally the troops when the timer finally did sound. We were all already there. Me, Rhonda, her brother and her father; all jostling for pole position as we queued in front of the oven. Rhonda's mother, annoyed at our uncouth manners, shooed us all off into the garden, telling us to give her some space to serve up. This was the most torturous part. The wait. Hours seemed to pass until we were allowed back into the kitchen again. Rhonda and her brother would hurry to clear schoolbooks and set the kitchen table. I would fill the water jug and place it in the centre with enough glasses for everyone; that was my job in their household and one that I took great pride in doing well.

Then, finally, we ate, and it was good, it was so good.

This indulgent memory still stirs excitement within me; that beautiful pre-food anticipation of a really tasty meal to come.

There is something beyond wonderful about homemade macaroni cheese. It's the contrast between the crispy crust of the grilled cheese and tomato topping, and the softness of the pasta that lies beneath. Elbow pasta is essential because the hollow tubes fill with the cheesy sauce turning every bite into a miniature, warm, cheddar cheese sandwich.

Due to my macaroni cheese fascination and incessant requests for it, my own mother began to make it for me, too. She would try out new things with the recipe to my delight, and sometimes, my distress. I remember once that she put broccoli in with the pasta before baking it; that was good. Another time she added cooked spinach and mushrooms; that was bad. I thought the mushrooms were too slimy.

Sometimes Mum put mozzarella on top; this was good so long as there was plenty of that tasty sharp cheddar underneath. The variations were interesting, but there was nothing that could top straight up macaroni and cheese. This was by far my favorite meal for years.

Incidentally, I was only properly introduced to the travesty of Mac 'n' Cheese when I moved to the USA in my late twenties. In case you are wondering, this is not macaroni cheese. It is cheap and delicious, but it is not macaroni cheese.

Okay, I'm done with cheese for now. I ate other things too I promise. Actually, as a child I was quite fond of vegetables—but who can get excited or nostalgic about cabbage?

Who could have written thousands of words about broccoli, as I just have about cheese? That's because fats are the delicious element to any meal, and fatty food is extra special.

This was something that around the age of ten. I began to see a correlation between fatty foods and yumminess. I then, innocently, started to use the nutritional analysis panel on the back of food packages to tell me how tasty a food would be. The higher the number of calories, the better food tended to taste. Fat and calories were like a deliciousness score. Seriously.

There was only one person who ever noticed that I was a ten-year-old looking at the nutrient content of food. And that person was confounded by it.

One day, Amy's mum needed to go grocery shopping. Amy and I went along with her because there was nobody else to watch over us at home. As reward for being good girls and not complaining about the tedious process of trailing up and down the aisles of Tescos, we were promised that we could choose whatever microwave meal that we wanted for dinner. An entire meal-for-one each; whatever we wanted!

I felt overwhelmed by the weight of the decision. Should I have lasagna? If so what type? Vegetable, meat, or four cheese? No, maybe I should go with cannelloni: spinach and ricotta, or tomato and mozzarella? Oooh, what about the shepherd's pie? Steak and kidney pie? Chicken curry? Macaroni cheese? Choices, choices—aisles and aisles of choices!

I systematically began moving up the aisle, picking up the handy-sized meal for one packets and turning them over to look at the nutritional content on the back; most specifically, I was looking for the fat content.

We were still where she had left us in the ready meals section by the time Amy's mum was ready to check out her shopping, and she returned to find us. She stood for a minute surveying my orderly approach to comparing the tables on the back of the packets. I remember knowing that she was watching me, and thinking that she would be impressed with my thoughtful and clever method of finding the tastiest meal.

She came and asked me softly what I was looking for on the back of the packets, to which I boldly replied, "The amount of fat."

She stood up straight and asked my why I was worried about looking for the amount of fat in foods.

"Because the amount of fat tells you how good it will taste," was my earnest answer.

She looked at me with disbelief, and then laughed and gave me a hug.

"Yes, yes Tabby, it sure does!"

And that was my system for years: to find and eat the fattiest foods available to me, because these ones were the most satisfying.

Chapter Eight

Ten years on, and that fat-loving child was a fat-fearing freak:

"Tabby, Darling . . . please, talk to me about it." My mother put her hand on my shoulder and tried to get me to look at her. We were at the kitchen table. I was a couple of months shy of eighteen, and skinny.

I shoved her fingers off of me. Irritated. With my eyes firmly locked onto the fabric of the jeans that covered my knees, I returned my hand to my lap and shunted myself another couple of inches away from her.

"What now, Mum?" I seethed. "What do you want to talk about?"

Without waiting for an answer, I pressed my chair back, scratching the feet along the wooden floor beneath me, and got up. I stood there, a simmering mess attempting badly to simulate self-control, nonchalance . . . disdain. *Don't let her know that you are angry*, my head told me, *or she will get suspicious*. I stepped away and looked at her defiantly in the eyes.

"What?"

I felt green of everyone asking me if I needed to talk and if I was ok. *What is wrong with people recently? So I'm a little thinner than before. That's not a crime. I just want some peace and for everyone to leave me alone!*

"You're not eating sweetie," my mother's voice, nervous and cautious, cut through my thoughts. For some reason hearing her trying to mask the sincere worry in her tone had irritated me even more. We had just had a row because she had offered me half of her egg mayonnaise sandwich and I had exploded at her with all sorts of foul language coming out of my mouth. I had felt cornered, panicked and had burst into a flapping mess—just like one of the chickens at the stables would do if I tried to shoo it out of my way when mucking stalls.

Except that to the chicken I was a monster with a pitchfork; the chicken had every right to feel panicked. My mother on the other hand was not a monster; all that she had done had been to offer me a bite of her sandwich.

"I just want to see you eat some . . . "

I interrupted her rudely with an exaggerated sigh. "Bloody Hell Mother!" I rolled my eyes in exasperation. "There is nothing wrong with me. I am fine!"

I had been due to go away to university that autumn. My mother, upset about my drastic and seemingly superfluous weight loss over the summer, had not wanted me to go. Well, that was tough-titty for her as far as I was concerned! I was going! I had been accepted to the university of my choice, I had got myself a loan to pay for fees, and I was going with or without her consent. Her constant mithering over and around my figure had the effect of putting me even more on edge. Well, to be fair, it was not just *her* that was putting me in a snit, everybody and everything seemed to annoy me all of a sudden; I felt fractious and tight.

At that point I was not emaciated and I did not look sick, but I was far too thin. I knew it, my mother knew it, my friends knew it, shit, even the elephant in the room knew it. Nobody spoke of it, because everybody knew that if they did, I would spit venom. If there was one thing guaranteed to turn me into a raging bitch, it was mentioning my bodyweight.

What happened to me? I used to be so laid back! I used to be so . . . fun!

I can pinpoint the shift in my stress levels to that summer in 1998. I had noticed towards the end of August that year; all of a sudden, I had been struggling to crack a smile at the best of times. Jen had even started calling me "snappy turtle" because I was forever biting someone's head off. To my annoyance, my shrewd younger sisters, now fifteen and twelve, had picked up on this nickname with glee and whispered it to one another with a smile whenever I showed them scorn—which was pretty much whenever they were in eyesight.

I came to the supposition that I was simply fed up of the same old scene, bored of village life, and that actually, going to university would do me good. I had hoped that a new crowd would wrench me from the funk I forever seemed to be in; syphon out the agitation and replace it with some . . . *some what? Some me?*

Yes. Some me; that was what I wanted. I wanted my *me* back.

I missed my sense of humour. I missed my wit. I missed my colour.

I also craved space, and time away from the raised eyebrows of the rotund women who tut-tutted at my fleeting fat. So I had lost a little weight, *so what?* Everyone breathing down my neck the whole time was vexing me. It was not helping me find my appetite and only seemed to make me less inclined to eat. I could only assume at this point that my appetite had evaporated due to stress, but exactly what was causing that stress I did not know. I needed some space to work out what was happening to me. I only knew that I felt different somehow. Changed.

I had felt so positive about going off to university, so hopeful. The reality had been somewhat different. Rather than helping me bounce back, university had been influential in my continued decline. Rather than make things better, going away had made everything worse; so much worse.

What a naive idiot I had been to think that leaving would help. I should have known, I should have seen the signs. Heck, even the physical process of getting to university had been hard. I should have known these were hints. Should of, would of, could of, when the reality had been more like: didn't, wouldn't, couldn't.

As my first term had approached in the autumn of 1998, I had felt troubled with the logistics of going away. The most pressing of which, to my surprise, was the eight-hour drive up from the South of England, where I lived with my parents, to Edinburgh in Scotland, where I was going to university. I had always enjoyed road trips as a teenager, but this one I felt remarkably different about. What I had been dreading the most had not been the length of the drive, but rather the inevitable road-stop for lunch. How ridiculous! Of all things to apprehend upon going away to university—workload, finances, making friends, having to wash my own clothes— I had been scared of a lunch-break.

A self-assured, risk-taking, scared-of-nothing seventeen-year-old was allowing something as mediocre as a midday meal act to freak her out; unlikely as that may seem, it was true.

I predicted that my looming lunchtime snub would surely cause a scene with Mother, who had been getting less and less tolerant when I refused to eat. How was I going to get out of the lunch-stop? Devious and desperate, my mind grappled with suggestions. *Could I pretend to be sick? Or nervous about my first term? Motion sickness? That was the ticket! I'd tell them that I had become carsick*; something, anything, to get me out of eating.

Leaving day: my anxiety kicked off first thing in the morning, when Mother tried to make me eat something before getting into the car.

"Honey can I make you an egg on toast?" she called to me up the stairs as I was finishing packing up in my bedroom.

"No thanks Mum. Not hungry." I took out my annoyance on the zipper on my suitcase, yanking it so sharply that the handle broke. Swearing under my breath, I knelt down next to the case to try and figure out how to fix it back on again.

"Darling," Mother persisted, "I won't get to make you brekkie again for months . . . just let me get you something to eat before we leave today?"

I sat back on my heels and threw my hands in the air. *Bloody Hell Mother!*

I resented her for making me feel guilty about not wanting to eat. This was not something that I was able to negotiate; why could nobody understand that? It wasn't like I had the ability to simply decide if I wanted to eat or not. I could not. Not that morning. Not for her. Not for me. Not for anyone.

"Mum will you get off my back?" I snapped as I roughly pushed the suitcase aside. "Why can't you just drop the stupid food thing?"

I had waited then, holding my breath and listening for her to reply, thinking that surely she would, but I was met with silence. I could tell I had hurt her, and knowing that did not make my situation any easier. When I had heard her footsteps slowly return back down the corridor to the kitchen, I felt a strange mixture of victory, guilt, and compassion. *Why had I had to do that to her? Why rob her of one last chance to feed me a good breakfast before I left for university.* I felt sad for my mother; all she had ever wanted to do was look after me, and simply cooking me breakfast would have meant so very much to her. I also felt angry at her; she had caused me this guilt. *Why did she have to do that? Why did she have to make this harder for me?* In the simple act of offering me food, she had made me feel so threatened. My head started to throb and my ears had began to ring. I turned on my stereo; it was all that I could do to quieten the noise.

That journey to Scotland, with a car full of my belongings and my parents, was just as onerous as I had expected it would be. I felt fractious and picked at my nails as we drove. Nervous about the impending first term at university in a city that I had never even visited before, I began questioning my decision to leave the horses, my home, my friends, my family and so many other aspects of my life that I loved.

My mother, mithering me from the back seat, was not helping my anxiety. I tried to tune her out as she prattled on about watching out for this and looking out for that, making sure that I remembered to lock my bedroom door, taking care to put my purse in a zippered pocket, and other priceless gems of wisdom that can only make a teenager wince.

"Yes Mum." I duly responded whenever there was a gap in the dialogue. I considered myself lucky that she was not bothering me about food again. I would prefer to talk about anything other than my eating habits, and with the promise of that roadside lunch-stop impending, I was growing more agitated by the minute. Each time a "Services" sign came up on the motorway indicating that there would be a fuel and food stop station within the next ten miles I held my breath. Would it be this one? I'd feel hot and clammy drifting in the suspense. Would they want to stop and eat here? As we passed by each service station on the M6 without stopping, I would internally sigh with a short lived relief. Safe, but for how long? It had been a very nerve wracking journey.

"Tabby, do you think you will miss riding?" My mother's tone rose, signalling a question, and caught my attention; I snapped back to the conversation, which, apparently, I had been having with her.

"What?" The impatient and angry colour of my voice had been sharp enough to surprise even me. As I listened to myself speak, I wondered why I was always so defensive and petulant. The volume of thoughts in my head in those days had made even the most harmless of questions feel like an attack.

"Tabby! Don't be so irritable!" My father, who had remained quiet as he drove, interjected to scold my tone. "Your Mother was just asking you a question. Why do you have to be so bloody rude to her?"

I had not begrudged him telling me off; it was well deserved. I was being horrid. I was horrid.

"Sorry Mum, what did you say?" I made an effort to soften my voice.

"The horses, will you miss the horses?" Graciously unfazed, Mother carried on with the conversation. "I mean all you do is ride sweetie . . . won't you miss it terribly?"

Good question.

A question that I had been considering for the latter part of that summer. At the stud, my event riding season had not gone particularly well. Shai had been sold earlier than anticipated, leaving me with just the green-broke youngsters to ride. I was tired of trying to sit on some bucking four-year-old. Tired of being bitten by unruly yearlings. Tired of shoveling ceaseless stacks of horse shit.

I had been hurt a couple of times that summer due to a couple of pretty shocking falls. Impromptu dismounts, incidentally, are nothing to bother over for the horsewoman. Coming unstuck is part of riding. In the latter part of that summer however, without the padding I had once owned, falling of smarted more than it had done before.

Then there had been the KitKat thing. A whisper of shame still trickled through me every time I remembered seeing Terry up on her each morning since that day she had run away with me on the gallop; the flavour of abashment that dwells in one's gut and smells like rotten apples. That horse, out of all those that I had ridden in my beloved and blighted equestrian career, had been the most special, the most loved. I had lost that ride, and I could not whine about it because that was the way the business worked. *That's the way the cookie crumbles.* That is what I had signed up for working with those horses; I needed to be steadfast and stop allowing my emotions to get the better of me.

All-in-all, horseriding had presented me with nothing but hurt and heartbreak that year. I had felt sour; tired of the work and the toil and the strife and the struggle. I felt that I had given equestrianism my best shot and all I had received in return was sod, flung from galloping hooves. Mud in my face. Sitting there thinking about it in the car travelling up to Edinburgh had been enough to bring tears to my eyes.

Silly girl getting all upset, I had thought to myself. *Silly stupid girl.*

"You know what Mum, I think I need a break from riding." I had managed to curb the unwelcome wobble threatening to present in my voice and reply cordially.

"We'll stop at the next services." My father's announcement cut through any emotional indulgences I might have been indulging in. "I need something to eat and a cup of tea."

"Yes good idea Honey!" Mother eagerly agreed, "I bet we could all do with some food . . ."

I looked down at my hands. *Perfect, just bloody perfect.*

Chapter Nine

Along with the other freshman freshers at The University of Edinburgh, I was required to stay for the first year in shared digs at The Pollock Halls of Residence. As part of my boarding fee, I was entitled to two meals a day at the dining hall: breakfast and dinner. The dining hall was vast; it needed to be so, because hundreds of first year students swarmed there to nosh on a daily basis. The food offering was adequate: salad bar, pasta bar, baked potato bar, a daily offering of three main hot dishes, desserts, fruit juices and snacks. I never attempted anything more than the salad bar and a couple of select items from the continental breakfast spread; I had gathered that it was all very tasty from the reports that my housemates gave.

The relationship I had with dinnertime was complicated; I feared it, but was strangely spellbound by it. My housemates would gather as a chattering, nattering group outside in the parking lot at six o'clock each evening before walking across campus to the dining hall. I could have chosen to abstain from attending mealtimes of course, but I always opted to go with them. I felt compelled to try and keep up appearances; to show that I was eating. It seemed important to me that people considered me to be normal. Or whatever that means.

I held a fearful fascination with that dining hall. I would analyze the food trays of the other diners out of the corner of my eye. I would watch with wonder what they ate and what they wasted. There was never any form of judgement over what other people were eating on my part, but there had been a curiosity that I had never felt before. That was when I had first noticed that it pleased me very much to observe other people eating.

I was not oblivious to the rumours that circulated about me: anorexic, skinny, gaunt, sick. I was aware that people were talking as if I had an eating disorder. In an attempt to quell these concerns, if I did eat anything, I wanted other people to acknowledge it. I would make a big deal about whatever I consumed, remarking on how terribly tasty it had been in an attempt to draw attention the fact that I had eaten. *Look everyone! Look! I ate! Yes me! The one that you think has an eating disorder! I don't, because I just ate. I hope that you took note? I hope that clears the confusion? I do eat! I do!*

Had Facebook and Pinterest been as popular when I was at university as they are now, I am sure I would have made the most of them. I'd have been the girl who is forever posting pictures of what she has (apparently) eaten.

But I did not have an iPhone then, and Facebook was still not really mainstream. Me picking at salads in the dining hall was not cutting the mustard—people were still talking about me, saying I ate nothing of substance. I had to do better; I began pretending to eat.

I quickly became pretty well practiced at feigning normalcy. I acted, I lied, and I staged. I would leave crisp packets and sweet wrappers out on display in my bedroom. I had once frequently eaten snacks in my room, so setting my stage had not been hard to do. Conversely, I had always been rather tidy, and had never left the litter in place. As a neat person, it pained me somewhat to deliberately make my bedroom look trashy. Being thought of as a tramp however, was preferable to being thought of as a prima donna who was starving herself.

I remember how devious I had felt as I decorated my dingy eight-by-eight digs. There was no way I was going to actually buy food only to throw it out and keep the packet, so I improvised a little. Mother had left me with a box full of some of my "favourite" snacks in a last desperate attempt to feed me before she and my father had departed. I knew without looking what the contents would be: Cadbury's Boost, Marmite, Walkers Salt & Vinegar, and maybe some Lindt Lindor truffles. All the things that she knew I liked—*had* liked.

The hamper that she'd given me had been left untouched for over a month under my tiny, single, plastic-sheet-covered bed. I had gingerly pulled it out, then giggled at the absurdity of the way I was behaving. Anyone would have thought I were dealing with a box of spiders. *It's only food for Christ's sake!*

As I emptied the contents of a couple of packets of crisps into the bin, I felt exceedingly guilty. *Mum gave you this, she bought this for you to eat.* I stopped after two and pushed the box with the remaining crisp packets and chocolates back under the bed. I had taken the jar of Marmite and displayed it on the shelf above my bed; it reminded me of home.

Then, feeling rather like a criminal, which I have to admit gave the entire scenario an ever larger hint of ridiculousness, I crept up to the common room and raided the bin. Fingering through the rubbish, I looked for clean-ish pieces of wrapping that I could sneak back downstairs to my room with me. Sifting through rubbish was bad enough, but getting caught, hand-in-bin, rooting through the pizza-slimed, cider-infused, vomit-inducing common room rubbish had been the lowest point of that particular day.

I had realized that someone was standing behind me; someone must have slithered into the room without my noticing. I slowly looked over my shoulder with dread, a million excuses running through my head: *I lost my watch; I think I threw a ten pound note in here with my receipts; I heard a kitten mewing . . . it came from the bin . . . help me save it? I accidentally dropped my self-respect in here and I am trying to find it . . .*

Thankfully, it had only been Sid. Sid—a goth—whom everyone thought was weird. *Weirder than me?* Sid had just smiled at me that day, which had been kind of creepy as I had never seen Sid smile before, and I never saw it again.

All in all, it had been quite a task, the old room staging. But I had got there in the end. Then I waited. Waited for someone to come in and witness all the apparent eating that I had been doing. Nobody did, so I left my door ajar; more inviting. Still nobody came to see me. I left the door wide open—at least this way people would look in as they walked past and see the empty Walkers crisp packet that was on the floor about three foot from the doorway.

Despite not really understanding why eating was so stressful for me, I knew that I could not have people thinking the obvious about me. Nobody understood how and why I could be so thin and not have an eating disorder, least of all me. I did what I could to simulate that everything was fine; if I could convince other people there was nothing wrong, I might have a hope of convincing myself.

My A-level psychology course had taught me what causes eating disorders: vanity, trauma, horrid parents and/or a need for control; all influenced by Kate Moss along with all those other skinny supermodels of course. None of those factors described me or my life so far; I had always been confident, loved and relatively carefree, never wanted to look like a model, never been beaten by my parents, usually was not even vain enough to brush my hair in the morning and barely wore make-up. Why should I admit to having something like Anorexia when I knew that was not the truth? Why should I say that I was thin because I wanted to be thin when that was not the reason? I did not know what the reason was, and that had scared me almost as much as the thought of eating fat. I was worried that people would think I were crazy if I tried to explain that I *feared* eating. I could see no good coming from trying to talk to anyone about what was going on, so I had hidden it the best that I could.

University had been a nightmare. Not for the first time, I wished I had listened to my mother and not gone. I had known it when they had dropped me off and Mother, tears in her eyes, had asked me one more time if I was sure that I wanted to do this. I had known it when I watched Dad's Volvo drive away and felt something inside of me squirm and stir, something that had been waiting until it could safely emerge. That something had been skulking around inside of me for some time, deviously hiding its existence, but expertly meddling with my health and happiness. As I watched my parents depart that day, I understood properly what I had just consented to. It had been the strangest feeling, because despite knowing that whatever it was that had been rejoicing freedom to grow was not something that was going to be good for me, a part of me wanted that thing to thrive. It had been rather like the feeling of wanting another gin and tonic but knowing that having it will end in havoc, but wanting it all the same, except this feeling was bigger. This felt far more dangerous, and far less tractable.

I should have gone home. What would it have been like if I had not have stayed there? I mused. Never mind, I had stayed. I had survived, and there had been some good parts, some good friends. Not that I had been very open to friendships; for someone who had always been the popular kid, I had shied away from most social situations at university simply because I had been so ashamed of my thinness. Plus, social gatherings usually involve food, and food, the simple presence of it, by now sent me into a whirlwind of wittering whispers. *Eat! Don't eat! You're starving! You're stronger than that, you don't need food!*

One evening, about three weeks into term, a group of us had been sitting watching a film in the common room. There had been myriad snacks available: Maltesers, crisps, shortbread, Cadbury's chocolate fingers and Butterkist popcorn. Most of them were stationary on a table in the centre, but the popcorn was being passed around the room. Thankfully, the lights were out and nobody could really see if I were eating or not, so when the packet got to me I could rustle it about, making a big noise and pretending to eat, before passing it along to the person in the seat next to me. After the film was over, a math student whom I barely knew yet, Carrie, commented that she was surprised to see me eat chocolate:

"I never imagined that people like you ate chocolate."

I was taken aback. *People like me?* I hesitated in a moment of uncertainty, not quite sure how to respond.

"You know . . . the skinny model types," she clarified. "Is that what it is? Do you want to be a model?"

"No!" I had been unable to hide the scorn in my voice pertaining to her assumption. I felt the need to defend myself. "I am not trying to 'be' anything . . . I have been trying to put on weight!"

And that had been true, because I had wanted to put on weight, but I had been unable translate that want to my body, which was still losing it. I had not been successful in turning my intention of eating more into fork-to-mouth reality. My confusion had turned into anger; putting on weight should have been easy! Eating should not have been a problem! I had been so adamant that there was nothing wrong with me; that belief was all I had to cling to.

It had maddened me that it was considered perfectly okay for someone like Carrie to talk about my weight in public, but nobody ever said anything to Clark about his.

Clark was the largest boy in our digs. He was a sweet guy, but hideously overweight. Clark always wore corduroy pants with a green jumper and was very shy. Clark was studying computer science and I was very thankful to have him in the vicinity; he had already helped me work out how to login and set myself up as a user on the shared computer that we had in digs—something which I had been scratching my head about for the first week. I liked Clark a lot.

It annoyed me then, and still does now, that people did not assume that Clark *wanted* to be fat in the way that they assumed I *wanted* to be thin. It irked me that it was not okay or socially acceptable for anyone to ask Clark questions about his weight, but apparently it was fine to ask me about mine.

I imagined what the reaction in the room would have been if Carrie had said to Clark that evening: "Do people like you like being fat? Are you doing it on purpose so that you can look like the Fat Controller from Thomas the Tank Engine?"

That would have been considered beastly and rude. On the other hand, it was totally fair game for her to ask *me* why *I* wanted to be so thin. Everyone seemed to be under the assumption that I was doing it on purpose and out of a desire to be the next string-bean to saunter down a catwalk. The knowledge of this devastated me because it was not an accurate representation of the person that I was. I was a tomboy, a horse rider, a stable girl. (Ironically, as a teenager I had been "spotted" by a model agency while shopping at TopShop in London—and that was way *before* I lost weight. They put me on the books, but I hated, utterly abhorred, modeling because I found it boring, so it never really went anywhere.)

What upset me so much about comments as such from people like Carrie was that I was not the person who I had begun to look like. I didn't even like modelling for Christ's sake!

I became very self conscious; I knew that people were looking at me and thinking these things. I knew they were thinking that I was silly and vain. Half of them probably wondered what I was doing at university at all, or how I got there, because obviously stupidity and super-model wannabes go hand-in-hand as they strut through the shopping aisles.

Breakfast times I was usually alone, as most of my fellow students opted not to get out of bed before noon other than once a month when the fire alarms were being tested. I would always go. I found it incredibly hard to not show up at the canteen.

By the end of the first term I was turning up at breakfast and barely able to eat a bowl of Special-K cereal. I would sit there, on my own, and play with the flakes of puffed rice swimming in the milk in my bowl. I would eat one or two, but fighting the stress involved in doing so would surely have taken more energy than I could possibly have consumed. I would watch the rest of the flakes becoming bloated and fat with milk, before tipping the bowl in the bin. Eating took a lot out of me; every mouthful felt like a battle of wills. Often, I would end up just sitting back on my chair in the canteen, exhausted and defeated. Lunch would be fruit, which I had taken from the dining hall at breakfast time and saved.

Meat was a complete no-go area for me by then. I remember how thankful I had felt to the vegetarians, who made my passage into non-meat-eating so easy; not eating meat was now a totally acceptable, if not somewhat fashionable, dietary preference. One that I could hide behind if I need to.

During this time in my life, most people assumed that I was a vegetarian, and I was happy to meet this supposal. I did not eat meat, but despite my genuine compassion for animals, my reasons for abstinence were nothing to do with animal welfare. If somebody somewhere had invented a fat-free meat product, you could bet that I would have been all over it!

I had been very grateful for having a label to hide behind and a socially acceptable excuse not to partake in meat eating. Truth be told, until that summer I had been very partial to McDonald's.

At university, there had been an anti-McDonald's group, which I had joined. Their motivation had been animal cruelty. Mine: to rid myself of the guilt and horror of knowing that I had, multiple times over the span of my life, eaten cheeseburger and chips.

That had been somewhere in the middle of my first term. Struggling to find my social niche, I had hoped that this might be a group of like minded individuals. A couple of weeks after signing on for group email updates, I was alerted to a rally taking place on one of the Saturdays in the middle of term outside the McDonald's on Prince's Street. I had allowed myself to be cajoled into attending. It was November in Edinburgh and baltic. I could barely walk I had that many layers of clothes on. That was the first winter that I really began to feel the cold. I had always been a warm-running person until then.

I had not known what it was to feel cold before I lost weight. Sure, living in England I had experienced chilly weather, and spent many a day out on a horse drenched in rain and shivering. But that is an entirely different type of cold than the painful, eternal cold that one feels when one has no body fat. No, this was the type of cold that stays during the summer, only yielding marginally to a sunny day. This is the type of cold that becomes a way of being rather than a one-off result of failing to wear thermal underwear. The cold became me, and I became cold. The seasons and what the weather was doing were beside the point. I got cold in the winter of 1998, and I stayed cold for twelve years.

I had been cold during my wedding reception in June. I had felt cold after running the New York marathon in 2002. Hell, I could come out of a hot shower and still feel cold.

That stupid anti-McDonald's group. It had been frigid and frosty that day; we had stood on Prince's Street, a huddled, shivering mass of vigilante students, heckling lunchtime burger seekers.

I had been hovering, awkwardly, behind a dreadlocked boy with the most beautiful dazzling blue eyes. I still remember the conversation that I had overheard between him and the ginger-haired Scottish lad next to him.

"I'm so glad that I never actually had to eat in there mate, never had to taste that shite even as a kid!" Dreadlock boy had a Mancunian accent. Slightly unfitting.

"Me neither mate, me neither." The Scot replied through a frozen grimace.

"It's idiots that eat in that kind of joint, pure ignorant idiots!" Dreadlock raised his voice so that some passing school kids could hear him as they walked towards the glass restaurant doors. They sidled past us with sideways glances and whispered to one another before giggling and scooting on through the glass doors to join the line of people waiting to order burgers at the kiosk.

The Scottish guy tut-tutted at them, then continued the conversation he was having with Dreaded Manchester: "Yup, even as a wee lad I knew it wasn't good to go near

61

anything that came out of McCrap's."

I smirked at that. *McCrap's* sounded especially funny when said by a venomous Scot.

"Right mate . . . idiots!" Dread agreed.

"Right mate . . . idiots eating shite!" Scotty elaborated, raising his voice.

"Right mate . . . it's shite it is!" Dread confirmed.

"Right . . . shite." Scott officiated.

I left then; not only did I feel like a hypocritical imposter, I disliked their system of correlating the intelligence level of a person to the food that they ate. By their standards only idiots eat in McDonald's. If they were right, I must have been an idiot before.

Now I was a silly supermodel wannabe bimbo starving herself in a bid for catwalk stardom.

Not long after I stopped eating meat, I eliminated all dairy other than fat-free yoghurt and skimmed milk from my diet. I would take a supercilious pleasure in claiming that skimmed milk was actually the healthier option; I had read in some magazine that it is higher in calcium. However, secretly the only reason that I tolerated it was due to the reduction in fat. Eggs: I stopped eating them altogether; I was too scared of the yolks. I had read in one of the magazines left in the common room that the yolk contains all of the fat. I could have asked for a whites only omelette at the university canteen, but I did not trust the cook not to allow a bit of yolk in by accident, and then there was the frying element. Omelette meant frying in fat, yolk or no yolk. For a little while, if there were hard boiled eggs on the salad bar I would sometimes pick off the whites and eat those with my salad, but I stopped doing this after a bit of yolk fell in with the lettuce and I had to chuck the whole bleeding salad out for fear of eating it. Cheese a rather obvious forbidden food also.

There was always anxiety present around food, but I noticed that my disquietude escalated as the day progressed. By the afternoon I would have collected a growing unrest that, at some point, I would be overcome by hunger. It felt like the longer the day wore on the harder the battle between my mind and my body became. Most days, I knew that I would have to eat at some stage in the day; not knowing exactly when this might be or when I might cave to my hunger was torture. I found a solution to this, which was to eat one meal a day; when that meal was over, I was done with food for at least twenty-four hours and therefore less hounded by the stress of impending eating.

I remember the very first day I tried this one-meal-a-day technique was three quarters of the way through my second term. I had on my breakfast tray a banana, two apples, a low fat yoghurt and a small bowl of Special-K. The fruit I planned to take away with me and save if to eat for my dinner. I looked at the tray and I knew that would be it. It really pains me to write about this, as I can still see that tray of food, that measley offering, and I want to reach into the memory and slap myself in the face for being so stupid as to not see that I was sick, for not asking for help. I also want to give myself a huge hug and not let go until ten years have past.

But I can't do that. All I can do is remember how looking at my rations made me feel so peaceful and calm because I had just worked out a way that I would not have to worry about food and eating. By deciding on my daily ration in the morning, I would no longer have to go through the mealtime or food stress because there was not going to be any more mealtimes or food that day. It felt like freedom.

In a sense it was freedom. Freedom from the mental struggle that eating presented me with. Freedom from the angst of wondering when I would crack, when I would eat. Freedom from decision over what and when and where and how that food would come. The peaceful knowledge that there would be no more food to contend with that day stifled and quashed my anxiety a little, and I felt peppier as a result, more like myself again. Just for a while, I felt steadfast.

Chapter Ten

December 1998

When I returned home after my first term at university, my mother dissolved. The reality of my weight loss did not reveal itself to me until that moment. I had been avoiding looking at myself with eyes that were able to truly see the effect that the decreasing decimals on the scale had had on my physical form. My blindfold was whipped away from the second I walked through the front door. Obviously, this was emotionally distressing for my family, but it was also incredibly traumatic for me; after all, we put blindfolds on for a reason.

I had been so very excited about returning home for Christmas. I remembered how painfully exhausted I had felt after that first term of university. Tired, but not from the pressures of my studies—they are incidental. Tired, instead, from the relentless looping thoughts that swept like swallows though my mind. Tired, physically also, from the pressures of my eating and exercise regime, as I had also begun to make use of the university gym on campus. Tired of being cold.

In the final week of term I had felt as if I might shatter. I wanted so very badly to get home, as if in doing so all of this nightmare would stop. It would all stop, it had to stop, if I could just make it to the end of term. I kept telling myself that when I got home everything would be okay. The reality was that going home made my wretchedness suddenly very physical. It was not just in my head anymore, it was in my body, too.

Not only was my appearance a shocker, but my demeanor had also altered startlingly. Losing weight had sharpened my hipbones, my cheekbones, and the lash of my tongue. As my family were to learn that Christmas, being thin, being starving, and, most of all, being so confused about it all, brought out a sharp mean streak. I was changed, both physically and mentally, and if I'd been a bitch before I went to university, I'd perfected the act while I'd been away. The words that came out of my mouth were no longer mine, and they betrayed me.

When I walked into my parent's house, the look on my poor mother's face was enough to make me wish that I could walk straight back out again, or that I could wave a magic wand and put on thirty pounds. If I could have gained weight in a flash that moment, if there had been a magic pill of butter, fat and lard that I could have popped, I would have hammered it down in a gulp. I would have done anything in that moment, that moment of seeing her face fall, to undo what I had done. But I could not. I was to blame. It was me. I had done this to myself. I had exercised too much. I had not eaten enough. I had lost weight.

All I could do was promise her that I would gain it back; I promised and I promised and I meant every word; because gaining weight should have been easy.

Such a simple thing, it should have been such a simple thing to do. Should've.

The Christmas holiday passed and every day I found some excuse in my head telling me why the weight gain should start tomorrow. Telling me why the calories in the gravy and the roast potatoes could not be eaten. Telling me that in order to live I needed to avoid fat. Telling me that I was doing an excellent thing, and that I should continue to do so.

The one, the only, thing that my mother was asking from me seemed far far out of my reach. She was begging me to do something that seemed simple beyond belief and I promised that I would. I promised that I would put on weight. I vowed that I could do it and that I did not need any help doing it. Because it should have been easy, it should have been enjoyable even.

I may as well have been promising her the moon.

Chapter Eleven

When one discards nearly half of one's body weight in a matter of months, it scares people. I noticed the eye contact abatement among my friends at first; instead of looking me in the eyes when talking to me, they would gaze past me—over my shoulder or down at the floor—as they slightly shifted their body weight nervously from one foot to another. I can't say I blame them.

Social situations began to feel stilted and strange. Initially, I could not work out what was different; I was among people whom I knew well and in places I had frequently been before, but the scenes felt distorted. It was as if I were looking at a familiar photo but through a frosted glass frame rather than a clear one. Squinting and straining, I tried to translate what the picture in front of me was; why did it all feel so different now?

The difference that I was noticing felt familiar in itself; I knew I had felt it somewhere before. A little like an atmospheric déjà vu. Then it dawned on me one afternoon, after a particularly awkward cuppa with Jen and a couple of the other grooms from the stud, that I knew where I had felt this coldness before: London.

London: where you can walk for miles on a street chock-a-block full of folk and feel acutely alone.

My sisters still live in London, but I visit the city as little as possible; I hate the place. In the English countryside, or at least in Wiltshire where I lived, should one pass another person on a footpath over the hills, one would probably know them, and if not, one would greet them enthusiastically and wish them a good day. Because, in the countryside, people are people.

In the city, people are traffic; their eyes glaze over like car headlights and their rigid bodies zoom past without blinking or nodding a greeting. When walking about the busy streets in London, should I get in the way, I would often have my arm or shoulder bashed by someone else. Someone else, whose purpose, mission and direction in life was obviously much more important than mine. Or so they would seem to think. I might get a grunt of an apology on a good day, but most of the time I would get cursed at just for being part of the inconvenience that human congestion is. At least cars honk horns at one another, possibly making them more polite than the human traffic that swarms Kings Cross Station.

And that afternoon with Jen and the others had felt like that. I had been sitting, sipping tea and spying on those who were feasting on the generous offering of sandwiches and shortbread. "No, no," I had graciously declined when offered an egg mayonnaise sandwich, "I'm fine . . . I just ate."

Liar.

I had sat in a room full of people whom I thought I knew, but it had felt similar to sitting on the tube train in London; watching strangers look into their hands, at a book, at their phones, anywhere rather than at each other. Silent closed bodies gently swaying a synchronized samba back and forth as the train rocked and rattled over the tracks.

Energy can be inviting or repellant, and there is nothing more worthy of repelling than the sight of a person starving herself. Bodies locked like bolted doors. Well, most of them: not all; some people kept the door on the latch for me, indicating via a kind word or gesture that should I want a friend to talk to I had one. To those people I owe a debt of gratitude, because when one is hideous, a smile and a pair of sympathetic eyes are humbling.

In the months following that first-term Christmas break, my weight dropped another couple of pounds. I found that going out into the world was becoming a frightful task. I began to dread other people— especially those whom I did not know. That first contact when meeting a new person always reminded me of my external appearance. *This is not me! I am not thin, not vain, not weak!* I could see the alarm, the fear and the questions in their eyes.

Questions that I had no answers for.

Questions about my own body that I had no ability to respond reliably to because no matter how often I asked myself 'why can't I eat?', I simply had no idea.

I knew that people were thinking: assuming, that I starved myself on purpose, that it was my choice to be this way. I identified a curious disgust in strangers who peered at my beanpole legs and twiggy arms. I endorsed it; they were right: I was disgusting. I would pretend not to notice their horror as onlookers would pretend not to be horrified.

By the third term I had grown sick of trying so bloody hard to make new friends. I was the singleton sitting alone during study sessions at university. I was the girl that professed not to give a toss when nobody asked me to the freshers end-of-year ball. I remembered how I wistfully watched my housemates get ready for the ball that afternoon in our shared house of residence. I listened to the babbling gaggle of girls in the room next door to mine nattering and chattering as they picked out dresses and jewellery. The blow dryers dried and droned as they styled and straightened strands of hair. The giggles filled the corridors as someone spilt a glass of wine. I told myself that I did not care, because I was not a 'dressing-up' kind of girl. *It's a stupid dumb party and you should not want to go anyway.* Soft lonely tears tore streaks down my cheeks all the same.

As I think you can tell: being thin did not make me happy. It did not make me popular. The saddest lie that the media ever told was that skinny people have more fun. I had never been so wretched in my life. I also looked like shit, and I knew it.

I looked gaunt, tired, expiring. The bones sticking up around my hips would make me feel sick should I glimpse them. There were also these taut lines running from my hips down close to my nether region; my anatomy study years later, after university, taught me that these were the tendons around my hip flexor muscles. Whatever they were, they disgusted me, they scared me, they were not intended to be viewed, not meant to be seen; those tight lines were evidence that things were not as they should be. I tried not to think about it too much, because thinking about it never resulted in anything other than thinking, thinking, and more thinking; I covered my body at all times, haunted by my bones and skin, but, utterly unable to eat more.

How could anyone assume that I was choosing to be like this?

Plenty did.

Emaciated felt uncomfortable; literally, my seat bones would dig into even the softest of seats and sitting always gave me a sore backside. Often, I chose to stand rather than sit as a result. When I walked, my stick legs waned like undernourished saplings, rasping roughly against the inner edges of my rigid jeans. I felt fragile, and breakable.

The skin covering my prominent hips had developed callouses—from where the leather belt that I had to wear to keep my trousers above my wasting waistline kneaded into them—leaving me covered in ugly reddened patches.

Why would anyone choose this? I didn't; there was no choice involved in my thinness.

I would often overhear the girls in my digs whining and whinging about the fat on their hips and bottoms. I strangely coveted that. As much as I feared eating fat, and feared being fat, I wanted to have fat. The memory of how comfy my body had once felt would rouse a barren temper; it should have been me going to the ball, setting hairpins in place and puffing perfume.

It should have been me. It should have been me giggling and gaggling and gossiping with the girls.

It should have been me guzzling gin-and-tonic whilst getting ready. It wasn't; I was sitting alone and angry: sore and sorry.

I would try. Many times, in a fit of determination, I searched beneath my bed for my mother's hamper. I would open the box and stare at the chocolates and crisps inside, determined, absolutely adamant that I was going to eat.

Every time I opened the box filled with Marmite jars, Walker's salt and vinegar crisps, and Cadbury's chocolate, I came a cropper. I failed. When I tried to eat my hands would tremble; the cold sweat would cause my already frigid thoughts to freeze and fixate on a single word: No. The fear was so ferocious that my throat would close up; eating, even if I had got past the mental frost, would have been impossible due to the physical winter that had paralyzed my hands, my jaw and my tongue. When I gave up, when the fear that had replaced the rage that had replaced the loneliness was itself replaced by surrender, when I pushed that hamper back under the bed, it felt so good. Such a relief: so right.

I settled for thin, I settled for alone, I settled for sore; because, it was easier than eating.

I was running a lot—far too much—but this was not *optional* activity either. My head told me to run and my skin crawled until I did so. My jingle-jangle nerves clanged hard and loud when I was still; they would soften when I moved. When I ran, I almost experienced quiet. I did not relish running, I dreaded it, but it felt as relevant to my survival as breathing.

Of course, my condition had a terrible effect on my family:

My father, befuddled and at a loss, for the most part totally refused to acknowledge what was happening to me in front of him. He sat quietly when it came to mealtimes, always noticing but never mentioning my reluctance to fill my plate. I think that his silence was wise in light of the information that he had at the time and the situations that he had witnessed. I know that he often had to pacify his distraught wife, and I expect that rather than getting into a barney with me, he saved his energy for looking after her. I felt gratitude for him; my mother struggled to come to terms with my refusal to eat, so I was thankful for any support he could offer her.

My sisters had each handled me differently. Beth would ebb and flow between acceptance and anger, sometimes shouting at me to eat something and other times saying nothing at all. Candy, my younger sister, always held a silent avoidance rather similar to the way that Dad did. Both of them were obviously bewildered in the first year and clueless as to what to say to me. Scared; hoping that whatever was wrong with me would go away as mysteriously as it had come. It didn't; after a while, it was obvious that this was not a fleeting situation, so Beth became braver in her objections to my behaviours and increasingly verbal. Candy sunk further away from me.

Being avoided by my younger sister pleased me; Candy was the person that I felt most threatened by. Not threatened in the sense that she would be able to do or say anything to stop me running. Worse than that, I hated her for *being* what I had lost.

Candy, tall, athletic, and slim, looked just like I had been before I had become weak, pathetic, and thin. Seeing her reminded me of exactly what I was no longer, and that sparked jealousy. She had what I was and her physique presented me with how utterly low I had spiraled. She of course knew nothing behind my aversion to her presence. I never spoke to her about it. How does one admit to a sister that one considers her mere existence as a threat?

Well, one doesn't. One is nasty instead; or, at least, I was nasty. If I did speak to Candy I would be spiteful and mocking.

Then of course there was my mother; *Good grief.* I feel awful for what I put her through. The first year, at a loss for what to do, she would plead with me: begging me to eat more. After a couple of years of getting absolutely nowhere with that tactic, she learnt to bite her tongue and save her tears for after I was gone. I was thankful to her for this, because, I could not make it better. I could not do the one thing that I knew would make her happy.

One of the biggest psychological struggles that anorexia has left me with is guilt. The effect that my eating disorder had on my family is to this day something that I find incredibly difficult to forgive myself for. I'm still working on that.

Eating more, putting on weight and not constantly fretting about food was not only an aspiration, it was a frequent daydream. I used to fantasise about going home and eating a stonking great chicken sandwich in front of my mother. I would construct a monstrosity of thick white bread, butter, chicken breast, lettuce, tomato and a sprinkling of salt in my mind. I would build a sandwich that the Earl of Sandwich himself would be proud to eat! In my fancy, I would eat it all because I knew that my body needed it, and there would be no repercussion. Oh how I needed that sandwich!

I would think about this kind of thing every single night in bed. It seemed such a simple thing to do; just eat a sandwich and everything would be back to normal. Just eat a sandwich and heal some of the damage done to my family. Just eat a bloody sandwich and I'd start to put weight back on again, go out with friends again, be whistled at by boys again. Just eat a bleeding sandwich and ride that gluten pony back to a fuller figure and a succulent life.

I wanted so badly to be able to eat that fucking sandwich.

Family dinners, birthdays, weddings and holidays would cause my head to throb as I fought off the desire to scream, shout, throw things in anger and to run from the room. I contained it all. I would stand still and quiet; frozen like a sculpture out of fear that any expression would stoke the ugliness within me that was threatening to erupt. It is very hard to hold a conversation when you are fighting off a tantrum, so after a while, my wit, my laugh and my smile forgot themselves completely, leaving a numb, boring and chilly version of me that sulked into corners and festered in her own tedious, obsessive hellhole of a head.

Anger was my squatter: an emotion that had busted its way into the empty space left by humour and refused to budge out. Anger was one of the only feelings I could truly depend on to show up at a mealtime. I was brimming with so much anger that a single word from my mother would be all I needed to overflow, to release, to scream and cry and let out all the hate, confusion and frustration that I held within me every day.

And so it went on and on and on . . .

"Tabby, why do you have to be so rude and nasty to everyone?" Mother scolded me one afternoon when we were walking the dog though the village. An elderly neighbour, Mrs Holmes, had popped her head up from a rose bush in a garden that we were passing, and I, anxious to keep moving, had practically ignored her other than muttering an agitated acknowledgement as I stormed on past. Mother, on the other hand, had loitered to pass the time of day and had then had to scurry after me to catch up.

"Dear old Mrs Holmes was only asking you how you were, for goodness sake. The poor woman has known you since you were a baby, there is just no need to be so short and impatient with people!"

I had no defense: she was right. Usually, by the time I had noticed my ungenerous tone and impatience it was too late, the words or actions were already in the past, leaving me only with regret and guilt. I felt awful at the thought of having made Mrs Holmes think that I did not have the time to say hello to her, but I also I resented my mother for calling me on it; because quite frankly, my inability to be nice to others was simply another thing to put on my list of things about myself that I disliked.

Nowadays, Matt makes a joke about my irritability whenever I am hungry. It is usually very apparent when I need to eat as I get snappy and mean. If we argue—which, thankfully, does not happen often and is never very serious when it does—he will look at his watch and ask me how long it was since I last ate. To that, I usually crack a smile and agree with him: I get hangry.

Hangry is a word we use to describe the anger that accompanies hunger. I am very prone to hangry when I have not eaten recently. So imagine what I was like when I repeatedly starved my body. I was hangry all the time; I was in chronic hanger.

I bet you wonder why anyone bothered with me at all, seeing as I was such a bitch. I wonder that too. At the time, I was pretty clueless as to why I felt so uncontrollably nasty and mean. Nowadays, it is blatantly obvious to me as to why I was like this: A starving body is not a happy body. A malnourished body is not a relaxed body. A famished brain is not a rational brain.

"To be honest . . . I am rather . . . well, yes, rather . . . worried about your . . . your um . . . your weight." Doctor Smith, the resident University General Practitioner frowned intensely and shuffled his papers nervously.

It was mid-way through the first term in my second year and I needed a repeat prescription of the pill. I was on the pill, because—surprise, surprise—my periods had still not started.

"Are you . . . well, you know . . . are you, um . . . eating . . . you know, um . . . eating well?" He tried to keep his voice relaxed but I could hear the underlying accusation.

I felt myself bristle. All I wanted was for one single person in the world to understand that this was not my choice. I felt as if I were drowning and people were standing at the edge of the pool saying to one another, "Well, if she wants to swim she will."

71

Doctor Smith was just another blithering idiot who was wasting my time.

"Yes." I lied.

Of course I'm not eating well you bloody moron! Can't you see that by looking at me?

I cleared my throat for added authority, "I ate breakfast today even before I came here." I sounded so convincing and confident that I almost believed it myself. I looked at Old Smith for any sign of disbelief, wanting him to challenge me and simultaneously praying that he would not.

He coughed, then fiddled with his tie for what seemed like at least five minutes. Then he checked my notes, then he looked at me again. I sat stock still, glaring at him impatiently.

"I see . . ."

Really? What do you see? With glasses that thick I doubt that you see anything much at all.

All of a sudden, he seemed to brighten up a bit, as if he'd cottoned onto something. "Exercise . . . tell me . . . Tabitha . . . do you . . . exercise a lot?"

Yes. Every day. A minimum of four hours; often more.

"A bit." I muttered as I studied the backs of my hands with great interest.

I had never been a fan of the gym before I lost weight, but during the first term of my second year at university I had been like a pet hamster on one of those stupid running wheels. Not that I was going to admit that to Old Smith. He tried again:

"So . . . erm . . . what are things like at . . . well, you know . . . at, um . . . home?"

"I don't know, I'm living up here in Scotland."

Silence.

"Okay . . . I meant . . . um . . . when you are at home . . . you know . . . holidays and um . . . before you left . . . . . . before you came to . . . before you left to come to uni . . . university . . . what were things like . . . how are things . . . um . . . things with your parents?"

Jesus Christ! How the bloody hell does this chap get through a day?

I got it, bumbling aside, I could see his game. Hoping that I would fit nicely into his clinical textbook definition of anorexia nervosa with a juicy dose of childhood abuse to explain away my symptoms as a desperate yet understandable attempt to control my traumatic existence. Nice try.

I decided to play along with Smithy's supposition.

"Oh, when I go home?" I hedged, "Well, when I go home they beat me with a hosepipe and lock me in the cellar with no food or water for weeks on end."

Smith looked down at his notes.

I felt guilty for making fun of him then, he was just doing his best. My attitude was about as generous as my waistline. I apologised and left Doctor Smith's office with another prescription of the pill. At least I could keep my periods going.

Losing weight may have been the most obvious of my problems; my skinniness stood out like a turd in the snow. It was certainly my thinness that caused other people to worry, wonder and whisper about me. It wasn't, however, the physical aspects of my problems that dominated my meagre existence. The impact that my weight loss had on my life was practically incidental compared to the thoughts. The relentless, looping thoughts. The conflicting emotions surrounding food, exercise and eating and the constant barrage of self abuse was inexorable. My mind was deafening.

Chapter Twelve

Before 1998 I had loved eating food, but I had not been a particularly keen cook. Regardless of my preference for consumption over creation, my job in the pub morphed from pot-wash when I was twelve to kitchen-hand when I was fourteen to second-chef when I was sixteen. I liked the money cooking earnt me, but that was about it. I certainly never watched cook shows or looked at recipe books in my spare time.

Then I had begun to lose weight, and with this had emerged the obsession with food; not with eating it, but rather with watching it, looking at it, and thinking about it.

In the gym, I would spend my hours on the treadmill entertaining myself with *The Food Channel*. When I finally did sit down in the evening, I spent my leisure time leafing through Nigella Lawson and Jamie Oliver. Cookbook rifling was my guilty pastime, my dirty pleasure, my cheap thrill. Watching food on television or looking at it in cookbooks was like a drug; I got a buzz from it, but only when the threat of actually being faced with real food was low. I had no interest in pornography—no sex drive, remember—but give me Delia Smith and I'd be in heaven. My cookbooks were like friends to me. I knew every recipe on every page but never got bored of looking at those pictures of food. I could always soothe myself with cookbooks; it was my way of self-comforting.

I knew it was weird, so I hid my recipe-book collection; stashed under the bed like a teenage boy and his *Playboy* magazines.

Cookbooks is one thing; what about the rest of it?
Yes; there was more:
I watched for food. I listened for food. I *snooped* for food. I ferreted like a nark seeking whispers and trails telling of food consumption.

"Did you eat lunch yet?"
My antenna-like ears pricked, pulling my attention away from the research paper that I was trying to read; somebody nearby was talking about food.

I was standing in the foyer part of the University Library because I did not want to sit down. I did not want to sit down because my eating disorder prescribed that I never rest in daylight hours. Rules, rules and damned rules. I had no say, no voice, no options. I just followed the rules because, quite frankly, that was all that could be done.

"Yeah, I had a Pot Noodle before I came out," a second voice answered.
I looked up and found the source: two girls to my right were sitting at one of the study desks in the foyer. One was my age, medium build, sporty type with a beanie hat on. The other was a larger bottle-blonde with a ridiculous pair of fluffy purple high-heels on. I rolled my eyes; who the hell wears shoes like that in Scotland in winter?

74

Bottle-blonde giggled. "I know I shouldn't and that it's bad for me and all that . . . but I can't 'elp it . . . I just love 'em Pot Noodleses!" she twittered.

Pot Noodle is about four hundred calories.

Bottle-blonde and Sporty-beanie were just talking about their lunch, but I was transfixed.

No matter what I was doing, where I was or how hard I was concentrating, I could tune in on any nearby conversation involving food like a radio tunes into a music station; a violently loud pop-disco music station, commandeered by the most annoyingly enthusiastic disk jockey in Scotland. If someone was yabbering about food I was, quite literally, all ears.

I was also compelled to *watch* others eat.

Secretly, deviously: I would spy out of the corner of my eye to avoid detection. I would even place myself within view of people that were eating in a public place, fascinated with the process of each mouthful of food being consumed.

Everywhere, anytime, I would get distracted by hearing anyone talk about their diet; creeping closer to women in the changing rooms at the gym so that I could hear their conversations if they were talking about losing weight, food or fat. I would loiter by the locker room scales if I thought someone else was going to weigh themselves after me at the gym; pretending to fix my shoelace, I would kneel down close to the scales so that I could catch a glimpse, an insight to what they weighed. I would get distracted if I saw a shirt label sticking out, wanting to look closer, squinting my eyes to see what dress size they wore.

The most frustrating part was that I did not care; the real me did not give a toss what anyone else was eating or weighing or wearing. I was being overruled. I was being forced to care, forced to listen, forced to watch and forced to think. The part of me that did not care what anyone else was eating, or what some random woman in the gym weighed, would throw a tantrum like a bored child about the banal interruptions that caused me to stop and hone in on food conversations like a Scot to whisky.

Chapter Thirteen

In my second year at university, my usage of the gym was growing almost daily. Living in Scotland, it was rarely the case that the weather was good enough for me to run outside, so I visited the gym twice a day, spending a couple of hours in the cardio room each time.

Treadmills, stair-climbers, bikes, ellipticals: if it moved I would use it.

Taking my class notes into the gym, I would revise and swat there on those machines. Preferring solitude, initially, I never took part in the group fitness classes; I was not lacking in motivation to exercise and disliked the questioning stares from other gym members. *Gawking at the skinny freak on the treadmill.* The looks and stares caused me to start wearing my long sleeved tracksuit trousers and t-shirts when working out; I wanted to cover and hide my body.

One Saturday morning, as I had been pedalling away to nowhere on one of the upright stationary cycles, a cycle instructor approached me:

"Hi ... I'm Michelle," she introduced herself. I considered ignoring her completely and pretending that my headphones were so loud that I could not hear her. I did not want to be bothered. Reluctantly, I removed my earpieces and pressed pause on my Walkman.

"You seem to like cardio," she declared enthusiastically, "you should come to my indoor cycling class. It starts in half an hour."

Why the bloody hell would I need to come to your bloody cycling class? Can't you see I am already cycling? Moron.

I was savvy to the pressure that instructors probably had to fill their exercise classes. I had seen them try and recruit people from the gym floor before, but nobody had ever approached me yet. She was probably paid per attendee. Irritated about the interruption, I moved to lift my the earpiece back into my ear without even responding. Then:

"It's the hardest workout you can get . . ." she offered.

Done.

That was how I discovered indoor cycling. I followed Michelle up to the "spin room", a small square room on the top floor of the building which was crammed with twenty stationary bikes.

Spin bikes are similar to the type that one would ride outside, except that they are fixed to the ground and have a little dial that one can use to add resistance. When I first got on one, I discovered that with that resistance knob I could make myself work really hard. Heart-busting, sweat-beading, gasping-for-breath hard. There were only three other people in that class that day, but none of that mattered to me. The instructor, the music, the erratic breathing of the people around me all blended into the background as I kept turning that little dial up and pressing my legs faster.

I broke myself in that class. Incredibly, I came out dripping in sweat; I usually never sweated, even when I ran so fast that the treadmill wobbled and groaned like a freight train. It was glorious to feel liquid proof that I had eliminated so many calories. I could feel the confusion, the pressure and the frustration seeping out of my body.

Now I had a new tool, a fresh and superior way to exercise. The sense of freedom, the knowledge that whenever I wanted to I could come and get on one of these bikes and torch a ton of calories was liberating.

I could not get enough of those cycle classes. I went to them whenever they were on the schedule, even missing my tutorials should the time slots clash. Initially, there was certainly a sense of choice; I had been choosing to go to cycle classes. After a couple of months, this wore off; I became a hostage to that spin room. In the way that not eating during the day had quickly progressed from a resource that I used every now and then to an involuntary way of life, my daily spin class became part of me.

Until I began skipping them in order to take cycle classes at the gym, tutorials were the only part of my university schedule that I still actually attended. I had given up on sitting in on lectures entirely after the first year. I did not want to sit still for the length of time that the lecture would take and I preferred to read over the notes that I could pick up from the back of the lecture room whilst on the recumbent bike at the gym or the stairclimber. If I did go, my attention was rarely on the lecture. Someone would be rustling a crisp packet somewhere behind me. I would hear munching, smell food, making it impossible to concentrate.

I was hungry, but I could not eat, so sitting in an auditorium where other people were eating was utter torture. They were always eating the foods that I was not allowed. No, students do not sneak bags of carrot sticks and plain low-fat yoghurt into lectures. They sneak pickled onion flavoured Monster Munch, Terry's Chocolate Orange and Cadbury's Caramel. They sneak foods that reek of artificial flavouring and fantasy; they sneak chocolate that sounds like silky-smooth tooth-sucking satisfaction; they sneak snacks that come wrapped in happiness and fat.

Before giving up on lectures altogether, I tried a few different things to overcome getting distracted by people eating. I experimented with sitting right at the front of the room so that I would not be able to see anyone else, but generally I found that this would make things worse. Hearing someone surreptitiously unwrap food behind me and not being able to see it was like putting me in a straitjacket and tickling my feet with feathers.

My ability to recall anything food related was absurdly accurate; I might not be able to remember the topic of a lecture that I had been to the week before, but I could tell you what the guy sitting five rows in front of me had eaten during it. Cripes, I could even tell you *how* he had eaten. I would be able to recall if he had been a cruncher, a swallower, a sucker, or a scoffer.

Now, you might wonder how I did not actually starve myself to death in that time. I was not eating enough, and I was exercising a lot. So how is it that I am still here. Absurd as it sounds, it was the binge eating that possibly saved my life.

The first time it happened was towards the end of the first term—right before that awful return home for Christmas. I woke up at 2am, and as if possessed, went into the shared pantry and ate just about everything that was edible—I may even have eaten some things that would not quite make that classification in civilised society (these were student digs, after all).

After a couple of months of this binge-restrict cycle, I surrendered to the fact that I may not have been able to stop the binge; but I could control what it ate. I did all that I could to ensure that when that urge to eat overcame me there was only ever low-fat, low-calorie foods available: MullerLite strawberry-flavoured yoghurts that taste like stale potpourri; low-calorie cardboard-flavour cereal bars that scrape at the back of the throat; yoghurt-coated Special-K flakes of puffed corn that smell like loneliness.

I craved sweetness, so if I was going to eat at all, sweet stuff was what I would eat, as low in calories and fat as possible. Once I had taken that first mouthful of sweetened yoghurt it was as if the floodgates had opened and I would not stop eating until I could not physically fit any more in. Cramming fistfuls of empty, fake-sugar coated, insubstantial, fatless, tasteless, nutrient-void crap into my mouth, I ate without enjoyment. This was like the worst kind of out-of-body experience; I had no control, I did not give consent, and I was not actually tasting the food that I was consuming.

The next day I would feel like a dirty little tramp for eating all that food, so I would restrict again, and the cycle continued.

Chapter Fourteen

Toward the end of my first year at university, I had to visit the doctor again for another prescription of the pill. Old Smithy had finally retired, and a new lady, Doctor Willow, had taken his place. As much as I had considered Smithy to be a waste of space, I resented him having left me with this new and unknown quantity. I entered Doctor Willow's office with suspicion and distrust. After weighing me and sticking me with the measuring stick for height, she sat me down and started to quiz me about my weight.

"I expect that you know very well what I am going to say about your bodyweight Tabitha," she cut to the chase; a stern edge to her Scottish accent.

Doctor Willow seemed like a pretty savvy woman, she was relatively young—in her mid-thirties I guessed—with long chestnut hair and a straight-cut fringe at the front. Her address was forthright; I appreciated her manner despite myself.

I squirmed in my seat and considered bailing.

"I can also tell that you are not comfortable talking about this." She continued.

No shit. I tried to relax my shoulders. I said nothing, because, quite frankly, I had nothing to say.

"Well, I'm going to be straight with you." Doctor Willow leaned forward in her chair so that her eyes were level with mine; to my horror, she carefully placed her two hands over the white knuckle fist that my own were making on my lap.

"Your bodyweight is dangerously low . . . please, do not underestimate the danger of this to your long-term . . . and medium-term health." She removed her hands from my own and, keeping her eyes locked on mine, sat back in her chair.

"You need to put weight on and you probably need some professional help in order to do it. I am considering writing to the Dean, because I think that you need to be sent to an inpatient facility and should not be continuing at university without treatment."

My stomach hollowed out in fear.

When I was thirteen, a Welsh-Cob pony called Twizzle had kicked me directly in the stomach with both of his hind hoofs. I had been sent flying backwards into a wheelbarrow, and had landed conscious, but utterly winded. When I was finally able to breathe again, I had taken off my thick winter jacket and seen the rough imprint of his kick on my stomach. My Father had taken me to the hospital for a checkup as he was concerned that I might have internal bleeding. I was fine, but that was certainly the biggest shock to the stomach I had received. I still have a dent in my chest to this day.

This felt worse.

"I'm ok, . . . it's okay . . . I can put on weight on my own. I've just had a stressful term, that's all . . . I don't need any help!"

I was horrified to feel that prickly heat gathering behind my eyes, a tell-tale sign that I was going to cry. Tears were the last thing that I needed right now. I had to find the strength to convince this bloody woman that I did not need a bleeding shrink.

She said nothing for a moment, just sat. Then, she moved forward in an attempt to place her hand back over mine. I shifted back, snatching my hands back into my lap. I would not let her touch me again. I knew that if she had placed her hands over mine that I would cave to the water gathering under my eyelids. When one is close to tears, human touch, compassion, is usually all that is needed to turn the tap.

No way lady, you will not see me cry!

The action of jerking my hands out from her reach had the effect of allowing me to shift from a place of jittering self-pity to one of staunch self-defence. I was able to quash my rising tears and quieten the racket in my head. I pulled my shoulders back and broadened my chest. I could call her bluff; as far as I was aware, being thin was not against university policy and I had an inkling that she had no intention of writing to anyone.

She's manipulating you!

She's trying to scare you!

She's pretending to be kind with her touchy-feely bullshit!

She has no power over you!

Anger affected me like a drug in those days; like taking a large swig of whisky and feeling it flow through my body lighting me up bit by bit until my entire being felt warm and tingly. Except, anger was different from whisky in that it energized rather than sedated me. For me, the onset of anger feels rather like standing on the seashore and watching the sand. When the wave recedes, the sensation is one of oceanic sucking, being pulled in as the water hurries back into the sea.

That day, I got so angry so fast that my head swooned. I felt giddy with hate and my ears rang with the volcanic force of my internal shit-storm. This momentary disablement, caused by the onset of rage, was becoming somewhat common, I knew it. I also knew it would pass momentarily, and that when it did, I would be left clear, calm, cold, and one hell of a fucking bitch. Looking back at how my temper could surge in those days of my starvation scares me now. I don't know how I got through without physically hurting someone (I guess I was doing a good enough job at damaging myself to satisfy any need for violence).

Doctor Willow sat back in her chair and observed me for a second, a puzzled quaver on her brow. My abrupt change in posture had made it clear that I was no longer worried that she could impact my university degree. I was no longer upset by her, not phased, not bothered; *I don't give a flying fuck what you think* oozed out of me. She had every right to be confused, suddenly the room stank of attitude.

We sat in an uncomfortable stalemate. It occurred to me that I could just leave; I did not have to stay and listen to her. Yet I wanted to stay now; I was enjoying this too much. *Come on lady, say something ... threaten me some more ...* my temper begged and pawed at her. It wanted something to do now that it was awake.

The grandfather clock, who had been patiently observing my entire appointment from the corner of the room, saw his duty to step in and mediate the situation. He chimed five and the moment snapped. I remembered I wanted—needed—to attend a spin class at half-past five in the gym. A wave of guilt for having sat still, inactive, in this meddling woman's office for so long momentarily shunted my anger out of pole position.

I have to get to the gym!

I started to lift myself out of my chair. Seeing my notion to leave, Doctor Willow panicked and leant forward, extending her arm as if to try and touch my hand again. I snatched my hand back from her reach and targeted her offending fingers with a snarling glance.

"About your prescription . . . " Her voice was different, higher, as if it were being caught by something in her throat. She coughed, righted her position in her chair and continued: "You still need another prescription, correct?"

Dammit, she had my attention again.

Confident that I was going nowhere, she sat back again and continued: "You know . . . with your low weight . . . you are putting your life in danger. Your heart will not be able to support this low body weight for long . . . do you understand how serious this is?"

She might as well have been telling me about famine in Africa and asking me to do something about it. Yet another person who could not grasp that my physical state was not my choice. I wanted to cry in sheer frustration, and to my horror, self-pity.

No, no, no, not now! I needed anger back; I could not waste time feeling sorry for myself. Instead of having a use like anger did, pity only ever served to weaken me. Pity reminded me of how easy everything used to be. Pity was a memory of the way that I had used to look, the way that my body used to feel. Pity longed for flesh and to stop feeling cold. Pity knew that Doctor Willow, my mother, my friends were all right and that I needed help. Pity told me I was dying.

Pity scared the shit out of me.

Moisture simmered behind my eyes a second time. I was struggling to resist panic that my fear wanted me to feel. I needed something to hang on to or I was going to cry, and if I cried that was it; there was no way I could control the situation if tears came. I needed her to say something to anger me again. Thankfully, she did:

"I could refuse your prescription of the pill."

Bitch! What is it to you? Why are you trying to make my life harder than it already is?

"Fine, I will just go and find another doctor." I countered. "One who spends less time judging people on the basis of their physical appearance." I was angry enough to stay calm as I spoke. She looked slightly hurt by my words, so I continued:

"Tell me, do you berate overweight girls who come in here? Do you threaten to stop their prescriptions unless they work towards a size ten? Do you tell them that you will speak to the Dean unless they stop being fat?"

"I'm concerned for your heal . . ." she started.

I interrupted her, "My weight is none of your business, just like yours is none of mine."

She softened, dropped her eyes and swallowed. I continued:

"I do not appreciate being questioned, threatened and interrogated when I come into your office for a simple repeat prescription of the pill. I know that I look thinner than most other people, but that is only because the general population has got too fat over the past couple of decades. Being 'underweight' in relation to the general public does not mean that I am unhealthy or unwell and I would appreciate you keeping this appointment to the subject for which it was booked."

Like I've said before, I was my own worst enemy: anorexia has a knack of doing that to sufferers.

Doctor Willow sat in silence for a moment. She swallowed then reached towards the prescription pad on her desk.

Thank God! Hurry up and write the bloody thing so that I can get to the gym!

Then she paused.

Bloody Hell! What now?

"Well, how about I give you this prescription, on the promise that you come back in three weeks and allow me to weigh you? I would like to see at least a two pound weight gain in that time . . . sound fair?" She was trying to offer me a deal.

I shrugged, accepted her terms, agreed to make an appointment in which I would come and be weighed by her, collected my prescription and scurried out of her office in time to make my spin class at the gym.

I did not return to her office three weeks later, or ever again. Instead, I found myself another doctor. Doctor Willow had been persistent; she left me a couple of voicemails when a month had passed and she had not seen me. I deleted them without even listening. There was nothing that she had to say that I wanted to hear. None of her concerns or requests were helpful to me because I did not understand how I was supposed to process the information contained within them. The notion that I was underweight and that I should change that was about as much use as telling me that my green eyes were out of fashion and I should turn them blue, or that my size-nine feet were too big and that I should grow them smaller. Sure, I knew I was underweight, but I did not feel that there was any optional other way for me to be. By the end of my second year I was running for over three hours a day.

Well, I can tell you now that I wish I had been able to listen to Doctor Willow. I wish that she had been able to place me in an inpatient treatment center. It was the year 2000 that I saw her for that appointment. Should I have received some professional treatment that year, I might have saved ten more.

I didn't, so I continued to struggle with a torturously low body weight for another ten years.

Chapter Fifteen

In total, I was at Edinburgh University for four years. In this time I solidly maintained a robust schedule of eating very little and exercising a lot. My weight hovered ridiculously low and I looked like death on a stick.

I couldn't bear to hear people suggest that I had an eating disorder or anorexia. I would not even say those words.

All-in-all, I was a mental and physical catastrophe. I was confused, cold and existing in a cleft. The constant dissonance was breaking me despite my pretence of normalcy—which in its own right had become exhausting—after a while turning to disconnect. When doctors, friends, teachers or my parents told me that my life was at risk if I did not eat, it were as if they were talking about someone else, someone very far away from me.

You might wonder how my body stood up to all this abuse; that is something I often ponder also. For the most part, it did really bloody well at delivering a high level of physical endurance while being fed next to nothing of nutritional use. There was an incident in the middle of my last year, so four years in when I was twenty-three, that scared the shit out of me.

The trouble is that I don't really remember much of what happened, and because I never told anyone else about it, I have nobody to provide me with more insight. I do remember waking up one morning—hell-bent on running of course—and not being able to stand up. It felt like every time I got up I received a rush of blood to the head so hard that I wobbled and had to lie down again. I do not remember making the decision to go to the doctor, or getting to the university doctor's office, but I must have done.

I do not remember them transferring me to the bigger hospital on the outskirts of Edinburgh, but I remember being there and having an uncomfortable IV in my arm. Apparently I was so anaemic that I needed a drip, or something like that. The only person I remember is one particular nurse with curly brown hair; she was kind to me: I remember wishing that she would go away.

I think I was in hospital for three days, and the only part that I thoroughly recall was after they let me out and I had to try to get back into the centre of Edinburgh from where they had transferred me to. As I had left home in a state of goodness knows what, I had no money with me. The bus, which went from the hospital to town was two pounds and fifty pence for fare.

The buses ran every ten minutes and for the first half-hour, I loitered at the stop trying to summon up the courage to ask someone for the fare. I'd eye up people who I thought looked kindly, then bottle it at the last moment. By the time the fourth bus pulled in I had given up on trying to address one person, and just asked aloud:

"Please can anyone lend me the money for the fare, I don't have a penny on me and I need to get home."

Nobody even looked up.

Then, I burst into tears.

I got on the bus an hour later, when a driver, who noticed I had been there long enough for him to complete a whole round into the city and back, beckoned me aboard and waived the fee.

I'd left the hospital with a prescription for ferrous sulphate in copious amounts. I suffered with low iron levels for years and years after that. Even now, if I get run down, anaemia is right around the corner waiting.

Exercise had weaseled its way into my every waking moment. By the time that I left university I was not only running for a couple of hours a day, I had all these other rules too: I could not sit down during the day; I had to keep moving between the hours of seven in the morning and seven in the evening; I did all my study on an exercise bike; no food other than fruit in the daytime; and many more.

If life had been unpleasant before, it had taken a whole new level of discomfort now that I was not allowed to sit down. It might seem that the decisions that I was making to exercise were my own, but they did not feel like that. Should I sit down during the day I would experience fear and panic, so I stuck to the rules for an easier life. I did not enjoy doing what I did; I just had no other option.

I hated fat, and I resented that fat was present in so many foods; tarnishing them and making them unavailable to me. I used the low-fat recommendations from health professionals as a screen to hide my absurd behaviour behind: to excuse it.

At the end of four years studying Psychology in Edinburgh I returned home to live with my parents. I remember the day that I travelled back to the village from Edinburgh, feeling full of foreboding as I anticipated the upcoming arguments between my mother and I. I knew she would see having me under her roof again as an opportunity to feed me up. I knew that I would be unable to control my temper when she did.

Before I left Edinburgh for the last time, I called the leisure center in Andover, the town that was closest to my parents village. I set up an appointment to join the gym the very next day. I was thrilled to learn that had a full schedule of the indoor cycling classes that I had become dependent on. That was the only thought that gave me any sense of peace regarding the situation of living with Mum and Dad again.

My dismal forecast had been correct: at home the food battles began.

"I'd give anything to see you eat some real food." Mum would say as I messed around with miniature bowls of Special-K in the morning. I found such comments hurtful and unfair; from my own perspective the battle I had undertaken to eat anything at all in front of her was one worthy of a medal, instead I was receiving criticism.

If left to my own devices, low-fat yoghurt and Special-K would be all that I would eat for weeks, months or years on end. Due to the mental processing and turmoil that any new food entering my diet would cause me, I stuck to my safe foods, resisting and resenting anyone who might try and force me to eat anything different.

After a couple of weeks of being back in the village, I decided that I wanted to get back into riding. Not because I missed it, but because I wanted it as another form of exercise and an excuse to stay away from home. Home meant a full fridge and a concerned mother constantly clucking at me to eat: the more away-time, the better. To my surprise, horse riding was something that my parents seemed in favour of; they probably thought that the horses would do me good.

Getting back into riding was easy enough to do; despite having taken a four-year break, and in spite of my disparagingly low body weight, I could still ride well. My making it known to a few people that I was interested in getting back in the saddle was soon followed by an offer of some horses to train at a local hunt yard.

I pulled up at the stableyard gates that first day with butterflies in my stomach, which surprised me as I had not thought I would care one way or another. I felt excited and nervous about riding again—as if a little spark of something long forgotten was trying to ignite. I suddenly longed for riding to have returned back to the magical experience it had been when I was a child. I wanted to be that seven-year-old girl who would have done anything to be near a horse again. Maybe things had changed? Maybe I was getting closer to being the person that I once had been? Possibly this was that first step backwards!

But . . . no, that had not been the case. I had lost none of my skill, but when I got back up on a horse I felt nothing.

Blank.

I may as well have been sat on a bicycle. The only thing that I did know was that I was no longer interested in casually hacking about the countryside. Riding horses was nothing to me other than a means to earn some money and burn some calories whilst doing it. I would ride a couple of horses a day and get paid for my time. If I only rode in the indoor school, training them in dressage at a brisk trot I knew that I was burning almost as many calories per minute as if I had been out on a run.

I was horrid to myself in my own unhappy head; I was horrid to my parents and sisters; so it is probably unsurprising that I was horrid to the horses. I hated allowing the them any freedom; I rode with a tight rein, and should any horse I was aboard put his head up for as much as a second I would dig my heels into his side and bring him back under my strict control. I worked them hard and despite a couple of raised eyebrows from a couple of meddling old so-and-so's who I knew believed that I should not be up on horse at my frail body weight, people employed me to do all the disciplinary schooling work that they did not want to do themselves.

Riding served its purpose. I had an excuse to leave the house early each day. Often, I would tell my parents that I was spending the whole day at the stables when really I only planned to be there an hour before going to the gym.

I frequently trained a mare named Gaia—a beautiful dark bay with a blackened face and sweet brown muzzle. She was athletic and strong, young and frisky. I enjoyed the challenge of riding Gaia; she wanted her freedom and hated to be controlled. I would keep her head closely tucked to her chest as we trotted circles. I was always nagging her, correcting her form and her gait. She would pin back her ears and swish her tail in agitation, goading me into tightening my hold on her even further.

One afternoon I was schooling her in the enclosed indoor arena that stood to the back of the yard, behind the stables and in front of the pastures. I liked to ride indoors as it was so often raining and cold outside, plus, I could get the horses to concentrate better when they were not constantly being distracted by the sights and sounds around them. Most of the other riders preferred to school their horses in the outdoor arena that was adjacent to the paddocks, that way they could watch the sheep and other horses play about in the fields; their preference for this was another reason I opted to ride indoors. Alone, I was less likely to be inconvenienced by conversation.

Gaia had been typically defiant that session, arguing for her head and swishing her tail in frustration when I did not allow her to have it.

"Ya gotta let dat mare have 'er 'ed sometime!" A crumbly, aging male voice had startled me.

I had not been aware that anyone had been watching us. I looked up to see Bill, an old—really old—ex-jockey who Meredith, the hunt yard owner, paid to come up and muck stalls. He was standing in the doorway to the school watching me. Bill always wore this dirty old tweed jacket and grubby jeans tied up with baling twine instead of a belt. I seriously doubted that he had the first clue about riding horses, let alone training them.

"I'm sorry?" I questioned him. I was not sorry at all, but I was annoyed. I spoke without slowing Gaia's pace nor caring for Bill's explanation.

"Dat mare . . . Dat dere mare you got dere . . . too much control and not enough trust running down dem reins from yer hands to 'er mouth . . . dem 'orses . . . dem 'orses need a bit o' love and trust every now and den . . . you can danm'd be sure that if yer don't give 'er some freedom, she will take it when she 'as a chance!"

I scowled at him under my riding helmet and kicked Gaia on into an even sharper contact.

Crazy old fool.

Being able to get out of the house and go riding had diffused the home situation for me somewhat. I had more space, even with the likes of crazy old Bill to annoy me. But there were still far too many challenges presented every day when I returned home.

The fridge, or more to the point, its fullness, was one such challenge. Living at home meant that unlike at university where I would be able to control the foods that I bought, food was constantly being put in my space. Biscuits in the biscuit tin, cream in the fridge, peanut butter in the cupboard. My mother rarely shopped for low-fat products and would question me when I did.

"You're too skinny as it is . . . I thought you were trying to put on weight . . . why are you eating low-fat yoghurt?"

Good question.

Due to my embarrassment over my thin frame, I had taken to getting changed in the privacy of a cubicle when I went to the gym. One Wednesday afternoon, I bumped into one of my sister Beth's friends, a girl named Megan, in the locker rooms.

"Hey Tabby!" Megan was looking right at me, but her eyes were not on my face, they were on my arms. I cursed at myself for not having worn a long sleeved t-shirt.

"Hi Megan." I mumbled, diverting my eyes onto the floor rather than her face. I pushed past her into the cubicle that was now free.

As I got dressed, I prayed that she would not tell my younger sister that she has seen me in the gym.

She did.

Later that day, Beth was hammering on my bedroom door.

"What the hell are you doing going to the bloody gym?" She yelled as she cascaded into my room, her arms all a flurry, gesturing her complete and utter exasperation at me.

Panic flooded through me; I hoped Mum had not heard about this.

"Shhh, keep your bloody voice down and stop shouting at me!" I hissed.

"Why should I? Because you don't want anyone to know? Is that it?" Beth was still waving her arms in the air in a fashion that would have been quite comical in a different situation; she had always been quite the drama queen. For an absurd moment I wanted to laugh. I must have smiled because something infuriated her even more.

"Bloody hell Tabby what is wrong with you? You are supposed to be trying to put on some bloody weight! How do you think that going to the gym could in any way, ever, work out to help you do that? Huh? I mean most . . . normal . . . people will do anything to stay out of a gym! Nobody actually goes there because they want to! And here you are . . . someone who is as thin as a bush twig . . . and you can't get enough of the place! What the bloody hell are you thinking?"

I couldn't begrudge her that rant, or argue with her reasoning, because she was right. My mirth left me.

"Don't tell Mum." I felt dismal at the prospect of the row that would surely follow if Mother got wind of my gym membership.

"Why not?"

"Just don't Beth . . . please."

"I wont tell her, but you have to promise me that you will stop going!"

"Sure, yes . . . whatever."

"Promise?"

"Promise."

A little white lie?
Maybe, maybe not.

Due to night binges on the fatty foods in my parent's fridge, I did put on a margin of weight in the time I spent at home; just enough to be presentable if I covered my body in layers of clothes. To my surprise having that extra couple of pounds on me did not scare me when it was there. I hated the process of putting on weight but the outcome when it was realized felt good.

Looking healthier, I was able to get myself a full time job managing a local coffee shop; this suited me as it required me to rush around without a lunch break each day. It was also right next door to the gym. I could go before and after work, and in my hour lunch break. Most days there was a cycling class in the morning, at lunchtime and in the evening.

I envied overweight people. Seriously. I was jealous that they could walk into a gym and be congratulated whereas I was judged and forced to creep about in order to avoid sharp whispers and raised eyebrows. An overweight person could spend the whole day in the gym should they want to. I couldn't, and if I did the gym manager called me into her office to tell me that she was concerned for my health—that had already happened twice in the space of six months. I hated the judgement. I hated people assuming that I wanted to be thin.

Any time not spent in work, I was at the gym, running, or riding horses. I was desperate to move out from under my parent's house so that I could once again manage my own food and running schedule; it was exhausting having to be so secretive about my exercise and I could never really relax when I was at home. I was even more motivated to work and save money in order to be able to afford my own space. For a year that is all I did. I worked multiple jobs and spent nothing. My workaholic tendencies had meant that by the time I was twenty-four I had saved enough for the downpayment on my own flat and I swiftly moved out.

I finally got what I wanted: to be alone.

The side effect of being alone was being lonely. I was not in a human desert, and I had ample opportunities to go out and meet people; I just had no desire to take them. I associated other people with parties and the presence of food; for this reason, I was inclined to stay at home rather than go out. Life was just less stressful that way.

When I moved out of my parent's house and into my own flat, the freedom to run was liberating, and I ran more than ever before. The downside of this was I lost the weight that I had gained when living with my parents in a matter of weeks. This both comforted and distressed me.

My emaciation was apparent in everything about me. I felt it when I passed my hands over the skin on my face. I felt it in the dryness of my mouth and the arid quality of my eyes. I did not want to see myself nor did I want to be seen. My thinness existed as a quality present even in my speech. I hated the sound of my own lies: *Life is fine; I am good; I've already eaten,* when really I was shredding myself with my thoughts and starving myself with my actions. Life was not fine, I was not good, and you could bet that I had never "just eaten."

Chapter Sixteen

January 2007

I was twenty-five, and I was failing. My weight had dropped a little since I had moved out of my parent's house and any illusions that I had about me being able to look after myself were fading. Over Christmas I had lost a couple of pounds, an indication to me that it was over: I had lost. I was done. I had struggled at a low weight for eight years; I had run every day for over six of those years. I just wanted it to end.

Running, formerly something that presented to me as a means of survival, was beginning to show itself up as the traitor. I understood that I could not trust my instincts around exercise. I did not enjoy running one bit. In fact, I bloody hated it!

Running and I were coming undone.

But what to do? How to stop? The thought of change was difficult, and daunting; I doubted myself. Maybe I was wrong? Maybe if I took a day off running I would not be able to do it ever again? Maybe I was just letting lazy thoughts get the better of me?

Most of all, I was scared of being empty. Running was the only companion that I had. What would I do instead? How would I fill all that time?

I felt duped; I had been tricked into thinking that I had been going the right thing when I exercised, when all the while I had actually been aiding the very thing that was bringing me down. Running was not helping me eat more—the lie that I had so often told myself in order to justify those hours spent in the gym.

If you keep going another twenty minutes you will have earned a Snickers bar.

If you run again today, you will be hungry enough to eat dinner.

If you go to the gym you can have a toasted cheese sandwich for lunch.

Suckered every time. I'd go to the gym, but the food part never delivered as promised afterwards. The rules had changed before I'd even pulled off my trainers.

As depressing as all this was at the time, it was an important realisation for me to make. You many wonder why it took eight years for me to get there, and I'd tell you that with the strength of disease I was dealing with it is a miracle that I ever got to that understanding on my own at all. Anorexia grows stronger the longer that it is left untreated, and to this day I am not entirely sure why I was able to identify that exercise was a problem for me then where I had not been wise to it before.

I began to see patterns in my behaviours and thoughts that I had not been able to identify previously. I noticed on the weeks that I was able to convince myself to restrict my food intake less I was also inclined to run less. I noticed that on the days that I did not eat I actually found my compulsion to run was greater. *How could I have not seen this before?* I was more confused now than ever. I needed clarity but my brain felt foggy and dull. For the first time I was willing to consider that my behaviours were harmful to me, but I was so exhausted by them that I did not have the energy to fight for anything else.

So I kept running.

For a while the only difference was that I was doing so with rancour, but then, gradually, I felt unable to ignore the signs that change was needed. Signs I probably had seen or felt before, but my mind had hidden or squashed. Signs like my aching legs; the volume of their protests was deafening now. Signs like my clenched jaw as I jogged and the pain running down my arms.

I would watch other people run in the gym for twenty minutes then leave; something that once before I had attributed to weakness and now looked at as strength. I could not comprehend the willpower it would take me to leave the treadmill after only twenty minutes. I could only dream of such control. It both alarmed and excited me to realise that shortening my running time was in fact a dream for me now, whereas before it would have been a nightmare.

My thinness scratched at me furiously. There were things happening to my body that I had noticed before, but I had never really felt any concern over. Without fat in my diet my hair had become weak, unattractive and lank; for years I had noticed the shine dimming in the mirror and I had seen the fullness of my hairbrush whenever I combed it. I knew that my long blonde hair had been falling out at a greater rate since my second year of university, but I had not felt anything about this one way or another. As I pulled the strands out of the comb and deposited them in the bathroom bin I might as well have been peeling the skin off my toes. I felt detached, numb. So my hair was thinning? So what?

I had seen the soft downy hair that was growing thickly on my pencil-like arms, and the fear that I had felt had not been regarding the wellbeing of my body but rather that my mother, sisters or doctor might see it also and use it to argue that I had an eating disorder. I remembered from my psychology class that excess hair was a symptom of the weight loss that people with anorexia suffered from as a result of the body growing hair to try and keep warm. I felt anger towards my arms and legs for potentially betraying me. It was impossible that I could have anorexia at my age. *Wasn't it?*

Despite what I thought or knew, other people, people who were obviously not as educated as myself on the criteria for anorexia, seemed to want to assume this was my "problem". I scowled at the hair on my arms and pushed it to the back of my mind every time I caught a glimpse of it. Luckily, living in England, the weather meant that long sleeves are acceptable any time of year. I covered up, hiding that hair from others, and from myself.

Internal conflict was something that was a standard within me. There was no feeling that was not present with contradiction. Ravishing hunger lived next to satiety. The pleasure that I felt when I avoided eating went hand in hand with extreme guilt because I knew I was starving myself. The trophy of my protruding bones was presented to me alongside a darkness of sorrow and regret. When I looked in the mirror my eyes simultaneously saw victory and ruin. Each rib, hipbone and the way that the head of my fibula was prominent on the outside of my lower leg represented a prize in a game that I was going to win despite my own protests.

The unfairness of it would send me into silent tantrums. I had not asked for this. I never wanted to be this thin. *Where was my body? Where was my mind? Why had this happened to me?* All the things that I had dreamt of doing in my life were impossible now because I could not eat. I was too weak to ride a horse well. I was too emaciated to have a boyfriend. I was too preoccupied to have friends. I hated what my body represented to me: failure.

Each day my fear increased, because I knew that my body was losing the fight that it had been having with my mind for so long.

When I ran my fingers through my hair now I would feel a pang of anxiety as I felt the thinness of it. When I caught the odd glimpse of my hairy arms or my sharpened cheekbones I would feel more sadness and less glory than I had before. I was tired of feeling cold no matter what the weather. Most of all I was acutely aware of my solitude, and I could now attribute this to my thinness, as it was being thin that had taken away my confidence and desire to be present in the world. I knew that I had to do something.

So I got a kitten.

I hoped that having a cat might cheer me up. I called her Sprout.

Sprout was a rescue kitten, she had been starved and abused and she hated all humans including me. I took her home from the cat rescue in Southampton to my flat, let her out the box and she scarpered. Sprout was a very small kitten, but a fast one; I did not see her again for three weeks. I knew she was somewhere in my pokey two-bed flat because in the morning the food I had left out for her would have gone and a tiny cat turd would be found each day on my doormat. Right next to the clean litter tray.

Unfortunately, my plan of getting a cat did nothing to remedy the larger problem that I was facing. She made it clear that she neither needed or wanted my company. Who could blame her?

March 2007

Springtime came, and I was still running.

I distinctly remember a strange scenario one afternoon: I had ventured into a small corner store with the hope of buying a roll of sports bandage so that I could wrap my legs in it before going riding. I had been getting these horrid welts on my legs where the leather saddles rubbed and, in a bid to make myself more comfortable, I had taken to wrapping my shins in sports bandage. On my way to the yard that morning I had realised that I had forgotten my wraps, and had pulled over at this little store next to a petrol garage. I had not been in there before, and other than the cashier and one other shopper, it was deserted. The local radio station was playing ABBA tributes out of a crumbly wireless under the cashier's desk. I winced as I walked in; I hate ABBA.

The store reeked of mildew and sawdust. I doubted they would stock the bandaging that I needed, but to my surprise I found some over next to the Vaseline and cough medicines. I snatched a roll of Tubigrip off the shelf and headed to the checkout, sliding into place at the cashier's desk just a whisper ahead of the other shopper, who had also found what he needed and made his way over to pay. He grunted begrudgingly. I smiled victoriously.

As I passed a twenty pound note to the lady at the checkout, I was mesmerised by the Cadbury's Creme Eggs displayed on the counter. It must be nearly Easter time.

I tried to work out how long it had been since I ate one of those cream eggs; I remembered how much I used to love that soft and sickeningly sweet interior and the pleasure of finding it under the thick milk-chocolate shell. Over eight years for sure. I wondered about how much saturated fat was in a Cadbury's Creme Egg and felt some guilt for every single one of the things that I might have eaten in my life.

"You're tired." A voice broke into my thoughts; the cashier was talking to me.

"What?" I jumped clean out of my skin as I felt a stranger's hand touch mine.

The woman at the checkout had placed her right hand over my left. I started to pull away but she moved her left hand under my palm and captured my hand tightly between hers; the twenty-pound note remained crumpled awkwardly between my left fingers. She was looking right at me and seemed utterly oblivious to the impatient coughs coming from the gentleman behind me, who was still waiting to pay for his diet coke and Cornish pasty.

"You're tired of it aren't you? You're wanting to stop now." More of a statement than a question. She pressed my hands firm enough that I winced.

"Your energy for it is gone, you can listen now if you want to, you know that and it scares you doesn't it?"

What the hell!?

I whipped my hand out of hers, dropping my money on the counter in my haste, and shot out of the store. My heart was pounding in my chest and my ears were ringing with her words. I felt as if she had looked right into me, seen me. I put my hand against a lamppost to steady myself as Cornish-pasty man pushed his way out of the glass door entrance to the store that I had just come out of.

I was both disappointed and relieved that I had got out of there before she had said anything else to me, then, I remembered that I had dropped twenty quid on the counter and not waited to be given my change. I almost left it, but eighteen quid was more than I was willing to forget about. I took a deep breath and went back in. The store was empty other than me and the crazy cashier.

"You forgot your change." She had laid it neatly in a pile on the near end of the counter for me. I could have just swiped it up and left, but I loitered.

"You know you can stop?" She gazed into nothingness over my shoulder. I could not tell if she was actually talking to me or to herself, but I stood still and listened all the same. Then, she looked at me again, right in the eyes.

"It will end soon, one way or the other." She smiled, I felt goosebumps on my arms.

Enough of this rubbish talk, I snatched up my change and turned to leave without a word.

"Here!" She raised her voice to grab my attention back, I turned around to face her again as she gently rolled a Cadbury's Creme Egg along the counter towards me. I considered letting it drop to the floor, but stepped forward at the last moment and caught it.

"Cheers." I mumbled and left before any more weirdness could happen.

I still wonder about that crazy cashier. She looked like the kind of person that I should have just written off as batshit, and it irritated me that I had given her words any attention at all. But I had. She had known something about me, something that I did not want to be known.

Not long after that incident came another strange happening that played on my mind. I had been running on the treadmill in the gym while watching Food Network on the overhead television as was my usual routine. Now, I have to admit, that this type of thing is certainly not limited to eating disorder behaviour. I am not the only person who likes to watch cooking shows whilst exercising. I see it all the time in gyms, and it boggles my mind, as nowadays I can't think of anything more depressing than a cooking show and watching other people eat food when one is exercising. Back in those days, however, I could not get enough of them.

This was back in the day when we had to share televisions in the gym—unlike now where most cardio equipment has a built in private screen. To my great annoyance, some idiot in a Manchester United shirt changed the channel on the screen in front of me to football. I considered moving forward onto the line of treadmills in front of mine, as all of the televisions that served that row were still on Food Network (like I said, it's the most popular channel in the gym), but if I did that I would lose the calorie count on the dashboard of the treadmill that I was on. So I stayed put, and I plugged my headphones into the radio channel instead.

My ears were filled with such a loud buzz of static that I practically fell off the running machine. I righted myself and frantically pressed at buttons in an attempt to get connected to something, anything, other than the awful din of an untuned radio. I settled for the first station that brought me the contrastingly mellow sounds of human voices, and it was not until I had reconciled my running stride and taken a few breaths that I actually started to hear what the voices were saying.

It sounded like some boring science channel. I needed music. I lifted my hand back to the dash to change channels again. I paused; something caught my attention in the discussion I was hearing through my headphones.

"You see Fred, what actually happened was that rats that were put on a starvation diet started exercising more on the running wheels in their cages."

The discussion was about some kind of science laboratory study in which researchers had noticed that rats placed on a starvation diet had begun to exercise more than rats that were being fed the regular amount of calories that they needed. I don't know why I listened that day, but I did, and it dawned on me that I was that hungry laboratory rat! On the days that I ate less I would feel inclined to exercise more. I knew this; I had already observed it within myself!

Last year I looked that study up. It was published in 2003 by a fellow called Hebebrand and the paper was titled: *Hyperactivity in patients with anorexia nervosa and in semistarved rats: evidence for a pivotal role of hypoleptinemia.* I have no idea why a four year old nutrition study was being discussed on the radio that day, nor do I recall what station it was on, but if I could, I would write to that station and thank them, because the snippet that I heard that day instigated some exploratory work on my part, and marked the beginning of change. Well, almost.

It was hardly an easy or rapid turnaround. In fact, in the beginning all that happened was I had awakened to my own entrapment, and I was all the more wretched for it. I was still the one opting to go out running every evening, but when I ran past the amber lit window frames of people's houses and glanced in to see them nestled snugly in front of a film, I no longer pitied those who were not like me, nor did I think less of them for relaxing as they did. I envied them.

Chapter Seventeen

April 2007

One afternoon, Mother called me and asked if I wanted to join them on a family holiday to France. I said yes, and immediately regretted it. Honestly I do not know what I was thinking, because the entire trip was a disaster as far as I was concerned and did nothing to help family relations, either.

The day of the flight, walking into the airport, I might as well have been walking into a concentration camp. I looked around the departure lounge crammed with people. Folk sitting calmly reading books, drinking takeout coffee, and eating out of paper bags with *Dunkin Donuts* written on the side. Parents trying desperately to quieten noisy children.

People carrying on as normal while I silently panicked.

I knew that I was totally and utterly alone in my experience; nobody would be able to understand the fear that I felt at the prospect of being forced to *sit still* on a plane during the day. Not a fear of flying, not a fear of falling out of the sky, but a fear of stillness.

After our bags were checked in, while the rest of the family contemplated buying danish pastries and coffee, I went into the toilets and did jumping jacks in the tiny cubicle. I held my breath and was careful to be soft footed while doing them so that other travellers would not hear me. I did this until I heard the flight call for boarding.

On the plane I made frequent toilet trips so that I could run on the spot in the cubicle. The rest of the time I drummed my fingers and tapped my toes in anxious anticipation of that awful airplane food. When I smelt the air stewardesses making their rounds with the tin foil packaged trays of mush, I pretended to be sleeping.

Mother noticed that I did not eat. Of course, she always noticed.

When the food trolley was safely past, curiosity got the better of me and I peeked out from under my airline blanket at what Dad had been eating. It looked like some pulverised chicken and pasta in a white sauce. *Creamy sauces are full of fat, there must be thousands of calories in that!* I thought. *Disgusting!*

Despite the ordeal that it had been, when I got off the plane I had achieved something enormous: I had not run that day.

I had just done something that really scared me and I had survived. There was this moment of freedom in which I felt deliriously happy. In that moment, I saw a future in which I could take a day off running if I wanted to. As I walked through the airport I felt changed, a little clearer, slightly reset.

I fancied that by the end of the trip I might have eaten a croissant!

Chocolate croissant? Pain au Chocolat had been a firm favorite of mine as a child. I had this very weird and laboursome method of eating them, which entailed nibbling away at the layers of flaky pastry until there was only the chocolate in the middle left. Mother used to tell me off and instruct me to stop playing with my food.

What a fond memory that must have been for her now, I thought. I wondered if she dreamt of seeing me pick apart a Pain au Chocolat as much as I dreamt about being able to eat one.

My improved and optimistic mood had not lasted long after disembarking from the aeroplane. As we weaved our way in the family-size hire car through the busy French airport city onto the scrawny motorways and out towards the countryside I should have been filled with curiosity and excitement, but I was overcome with dread and foreboding regarding the week ahead. Surrounded by family and food, the holiday presented a nightmare full of uncertainty; I had no idea where we were staying, and wondered if I would be able to exercise.

Ugh, that holiday. Trapped in the middle of French countryside with my parents and cousins; it seemed that there was always some food related activity being planned. I suppose that for most people, that is what a holiday is all about: eating. Like I said before, I cannot fathom what I had been thinking when I agreed to go. There was food everywhere.

Cheeses of each and every description were showcased by street vendors at each town and village that we visited: soft and creamy Brie; tangy and buttery Camembert; strong, salty and stinky Gorgonzola; mild and milky Mozzarella; rich and decadent Roquefort. All displayed on rickety old tables shaded by even ricketier canopies and sun-brellas. Deli meats hung on every street corner: Salami, Boudin Blanc, Andouillette, Saucisson, Rosette de Lyon and a thousand or more variations; these were the worst for me to look at, as I could see the white speckles and fatty marbles in the meat. Plates sat threateningly on the rims of the tables, offering patés and mousses smeared over white fluffy rounds of bread for tourists and potential customers to try.

My parents oohed and arrrrhed, tested and tried. Delighting in the delicacies, they bickered gently over which Brie was the smoothest and whether it would be better suited with a baguette, a brioche or a boule.

All I could see were mountains of saturated animal fat.

Fat: *on* the dinner table, *in* the fridge, *at* the markets that we went to each day. Merchants brandished their fat offerings. The tourists, like lemmings, lined up for it.

While others relaxed and decompressed, I held a constant silent state of panic for the entire ten days that we were there. The unpredictability of the situation stressed me the most. At any time, someone could suggest an ice-cream stop. Any corner turned could present us wandering tourists with more merchants offering foods.

I had to do something to help me manage the constant adrenaline that I felt. Running was all I knew, and I needed it more than ever, but I was presented with the problems of when and how I was going to achieve that. There is no room for privacy on a family holiday in a shared villa—no sanctuary for secret workouts. Well, apart from the night.

When everyone was awake in the day that villa was like a fort and I was trapped within it. But at night, when everyone else was sleeping, I could get out. I would quietly pull on my trainers and tiptoe my way to the front door.

The floorboards on the outside deck were problematic; they would creak loudly when stepped on, meaning I had to clamber my way around the side of the deck, clinging on the handrail before jumping down to the soft undergrowth below. Then finally I could run.

If it were not so desperate and sad, it would be funny, but the things that I used to do and the binds that I would get myself into just so that I could run. Take for example, the time when I got to the university gym and had forgotten my trainers, so ran barefoot on the treadmill until the manager came and told me I was violating health and safety. Or the time that I snuck into a toilet in a cafe to do a hundred jumping jacks and my mobile phone flew out of my pocket and into the loo. Or the time that I tried wearing a disguise so that I could go to the gym for the second time in one day without the gym manager noticing and pulling me into her office to tell me that unless I put on weight and worked out once per day or less my membership would be revoked.

Maybe when I have finished writing this book I will start writing comedy sketches about people who workout too much.

There I was, in France, an unfamiliar country, in the dead of night, stumbling up unfamiliar roads. I ran fast, because I have always been a little afraid of the dark and the strange sounds and shadows spooked me. At four in the morning I would return to the villa, sneak in the same way I had snuck out and curl up in my bed.

I remember one night, about midway through the planned stay, pulling my knobby knees into my chest and sobbing at the feel of them. *Where had my legs gone? What were these alien icicles that had taken their place? Why was I doing this to my body?*

That holiday, I watched my family gorge on cheeses and crusty French bread. I got away with eating mostly just fruit and salads, but I could feel my mother's eyes on me at mealtimes. I knew that she wanted to say something to me, I knew that she wanted to ask me if I could please eat some "real food" like cheese or salami. But the public setting meant that she was biting her tongue to avoid a row.

That holiday I had wanted nothing to do with the rich foods that seemed to be the focal point of our French visit. I wrinkled my nose at the sight of croissants in the morning with pasture butter and peach jam. I was supercilious in my attitude to the custard pastries that my father delighted in. All I could see in what he and the rest of my family ate was fat, and it was okay for them, but not for me.

I once listened to the story of a pastor who lost his faith, and realised that he no longer believed in God. It was a Radio Four broadcast re-run that was on the radio as I drove home from work one night. The story described how the hardest part of this religious man's severance from the church was realising that his whole life had been geared around it. His marriage, his home, his friends and family. He talked about how for years he continued going through the motions of being a pastor, but without his heart in it he felt burdened, fatigued and depressed. I understood then that I was feeling something similar, everything I had been for the last eight years seemed nonsensical. The only difference between that pastor and me when I was twenty-five was that I had much more to contend with than the lifestyle and identity changes that he spoke about. I also had this monster in my head telling me, convincing me, that I needed to do what I was doing in order to survive.

But, oh, did I want to stop!

Every run that I went on my legs felt heavier. Before now, I had been tired. Before now, I had been bored. Before now, I had been resentful. But before now, it had always made sense somehow. I had had some greater understanding about what I was doing, as if I knew where I was going. Now I felt lost, but trapped in the habitual processes that had developed so strongly. This period of my life was the hardest yet; my habits, my compulsions, were goading me.

Breaking a habit or changing behaviours is one thing, but my problem was not only my habits and behaviours. I could deal with breaking habits, I had done it plenty of times before, I had given chocolate up for lent, broken the habit of sucking my thumb as a child and when I was ten I had worked really hard to break the habit of tensing my arms when jumping fences on my pony. What I was facing now was far more than just habitual behaviour. I think that is something that a lot of people do not understand about anorexia, it is not simply a web of habitual behaviour, it is not simply addiction—although both of these things can be aspects of the problem—it is a complex mental disease. For this reason, overcoming it is more than a full time job, and managing it, even after recovery, is paramount.

101

Chapter Eighteen

The first day that I thought about suicide was remarkable. I had never considered it to be an option before, and suddenly there it was. The idea politely presented itself to me one afternoon; offering itself up as a tool that I could use if I wanted to. The part of this that was remarkable was that this understanding brought no fear with it, only peace.

Escape.

Hold that thought. Let's pause there for a second, because things are getting rather gloomy and I think that it is worth pointing out that I did not commit suicide; if I had I would not be writing about it. The point is, there was a time in my life when killing myself felt like a good option.

The feeling that suicide presented a welcome freedom makes me think about a statistic I have written about more times than I can remember: *Eating disorders have the highest mortality rate of any psychological disorder.* I understand why this is, because I have lived through wanting to die in preference to the daily battle of eating food.

One of the reasons that anorexia is so dangerous is that it is very misunderstood. Sufferers therefore are bounced from therapist to therapist, give up and suffer alone, then ultimately decide that enough is enough and want to end it all. This is infuriatingly common, and I use the word *infuriating* because every suicide resulting from an eating disorder could have been avoided with correct and adequate treatment.

So far in this story, I have presented three versions of me. There is the one that is stuck right in the heat of hell; that's the me at college and the me that runs for hours on the treadmill every day. This girl has no idea that she is as sick as she is. She cannot see her problem. All she knows is that fat is the enemy and exercise is the path to glory. She is dying, and is at a point of exhaustion where she is contemplating speeding up the process, which quite frankly, is understandable.

Next we have the just-married, seemingly-normal-just-rather-skinny version of me sitting at her parent's kitchen table reminiscing about the most hellish years. She is doing better, but she is still unable to admit that she has an eating disorder and for this reason, is not out of the woods yet. This is the halfway house girl, she is almost happy, but not quite. It is not a random assignment that I write about her. That night, when I sat on the kitchen floor after having binge-eaten a tier of wedding cake, was a huge turning point in my personal story. That was the night I realised that I was utterly fucked. What led me to this conclusion was the fact that it was my wedding night, and I had not enjoyed it in the slightest because I had spent the entire evening, and possibly the entire previous eight years, fretting about food. That was June 2010.

For some reason, it took an event as big as a wedding, my own wedding, and the understanding that even a happening as grand and life-changing as my own wedding had not changed anything at all, to make me understand that I needed to change, that I could not wait any longer, because if I did, I would wait-out my entire life.

Ultimately, the experience of getting married, and recognising that I had done so and all I had really thought about was the amount of calories within my wedding cake, really shocked me. Some might say it shocked me to the point of action.

And now, now we have the current version of me. I am here, now, typing. This version of me has just sent Matt a text asking him if we can get pulled pork barbecue takeout for dinner. She has no idea how many calories are in that, and doesn't give two hoots. Yes, this third version of me, the one writing this, is well and truly happy.

The reason that getting to the point of recovery took so long was because I truly believed that I did not have an eating disorder. I had been told that anorexia was about wanting to be thin, about not having any self confidence and being star struck by skinny models on the telly, and that was not me.

Now, this is a big problem. As a sufferer, I had been told so many untruths about eating disorders that I did not think it possible for me to have one; therefore, I did not seek out or receive any treatment for anorexia. I am not the only sufferer who has faced this conflict, but I am one of the luckier ones because I survived. In the next couple of paragraphs, I will briefly outline a few of the reasons why this is a problem, and why misinformation puts lives at great risk.

One of the things I had been told about anorexia was that sufferers do not eat at all. I ate. Sure, my eating was dependent on my running. Sure, I only ate low-calorie foods. Sure, I binged uncontrollably at night. And sure, my eating habits were ridiculously erratic; nonetheless, it was undeniable that I did eat, and because I ate, I thought I could not have anorexia. That, by the way, is myth number one but the fact is:

Eating disorders do not follow a straightforward set of mapped symptoms.

Another reason that I did not think that I had an eating disorder was because what I was going through was not about wanting to be thin. Nor was it about wanting to look good. I had been told, that people developed anorexia only if they had a desire to be thinner than they already were. That is myth number two, and for the record I hated being thin. Thin never looked good on me. Thin was ugly.

Not *all* people who suffer from eating disorders are, or want to be, thin.

Myth number two was continuously reinforced by other people, usually people who were in a position of professional contact with me. Any doctor who had tried to talk to me about my weight had started by asking me questions, like: "Do you like your body?", "Do you think that you are overweight?", which to my mind was testament to their belief that I was starving myself on purpose because I wanted to be thin like some idiot supermodel. If I had a problem it was not the problem that they thought I had.

(I pick on supermodels a lot, and that is just because I have a warped sense of humour. I do not have anything against supermodels, rather the societal ideal that they represent. For the record, I know of many people who are supermodels and are not stupid. Also for the record, I was a model for a little while—albeit a very bad one because I turned up for shoots covered in mud and stinking of horses—and my agency pulled me off the books at eighteen when I lost too much weight. They did everything in their power to encourage me to gain weight and stuck to their guns about not using me when I looked unhealthy. Model agencies are not the problem and most of them prioritise the health of their models. Agencies are, after all, only responding to demand, and demand is for skinny girls because skinny girls sell clothes. The problem is not supermodels or agencies or even those manufacturers who demand size zero girls for shoots; the problem is with consumers.)

Before the age of seventeen, I'd never experienced trauma; not unless you count the time that I went into the ice-cream shop on Winchester High Street and was told that they had sold clean out of their secret recipe, homemade double-chocolate fudge ice cream. Fact number three:

Eating disorders do not *all* emerge as a result of trauma, as the sufferer attempts to take control.

Control. What a joke. So many people have and still do try and psycho-babble me about how my eating disorder was a symptom of me trying to regain control of my life. I had control right up until I developed anorexia thank you very much. Then it all well and truly went to shit.

Fact number three leads into myth number four:

Eating disorders are not *caused* by parents.

This one I cannot stress strongly enough. I feel so sorry for any poor parent who has to watch their child starve themselves. It is adding insult to injury for anyone to then accuse them of causing the problem. Eating disorders have a biological base folks; parents can't *make* them happen. Sure, a parent—or anyone else for that matter— can provoke an eating disorder in a child who is already genetically predisposed to developing one, but that would be a result of an action that resulted in said child going on a calorie restrictive diet, not by being a controlling/neglectful/indifferent parent.

Now, when I was twenty-five, I did make a large step in that I worked out that I had a problem with exercise. It happened one day after I had been for a particularly long run. I returned home, stood leaning against my kitchen counter, exhausted, and thought:

I have an exercise addiction.

That thought, that single hanging isolated thought and my own calm acceptance of it was really bizarre. I watched that thought run across my mind like a star shooting across the sky in slow motion; as if it were a thought in another person's mind not my own. When it passed though and left me with nothing but a whisper of a trail, I wanted more of it, so I set it off again:

I have an exercise addiction.

I had never heard of an *exercise addiction* before, so I was pretty sure that I was making it up. *Did such a thing even exist? Can a person get addicted to exercise?*

As I replayed the words in my head I understood that in simply allowing myself to acknowledge that I had a problem, that my behaviours and my running were not normal, I had just given myself permission to stop running.

I can stop running?

That was too much. My legs buckled and and I slid down the kitchen counter onto the floor. Heaving sobs and a mass of tears. I cried in mourning for the eight years that I had lost to running. I cried for every step that I had forced my struggling body to take. I cried for the time it had stolen and the damage it had done. But most of all I cried out of relief, as I knew that tonight marked the start of change.

I also knew that my exercise addiction was a symptom of something larger than I could fully comprehend in that moment. But I had no idea what, and was in no fit state to go searching out deeper truths that day. You see, despite being well up for not running anymore, I was terrified. Exercise defined me. Running defined me; to consider stopping felt like I was giving up on the very thing that was *me*.

Well, run or live; what's it to be?

That night I decided that I would rather die than live through another day in the prison that I had built up around myself. That night I softened to the possibility that I had a way out.

I cold-turkeyed the running. That firmly decided I would not run the next day, and I welcomed the battle; because, in understanding that death looked like peace for me, I had nothing to lose.

Whilst this is my story and I must tell it as it happened, I have to express that this was not the easiest or the ideal path for a person suffering from an eating disorder of any type to take. Had I known then that one could have Anorexia and still eat, or that I could have anorexia and not like being thin, or had I known that activity-based Anorexia was something that the DSM were considering adding to the diagnostic criteria, and that my problem was a mental disorder, and that there were people that understood this, people who could help me understand this, and had I been in a nourished enough mental state to understand all of these things, not only would I have not got so low and desperate to see suicide as a possible way out, but I would never have tried to overcome my disease alone. Had I known any of these things I might have opted for professional treatment.

As it was, I did not consciously know that I had a disease. Anorexia will hide itself from those who suffer from it, and it is very hard to fight a demon that has no face. At that time, I was fighting in the only way that was available to me. In labelling one undesirable behaviour as *exercise addiction,* I had found a way to section off a portion of my monster to deal with; a more manageable chunk.

The ideal way to tackle a monster as big as anorexia is to rally some troops to help you. Treatment centres, nutritionists, psychologists, medical interventions, friends, and family are all comrades that one should utilise when one embarks on the road to recovery. Because I did not understand that I had anorexia, because my malnourished brain was struggling to think clearly, and because I was deeply ashamed and confused about whatever it was that was wrong with me, I felt there was no choice for me other than finding my own way out, or giving up. While I would not wish that feeling of desperation, loneliness and fear on anyone, for me getting to a point where I was low enough to surrender my life to the fight was the turning point that saved my life, and something somewhere within me knew it because I slept well that night for the first time in months.

I woke up in the morning and immediately remembered that I could not go for a run that day. I lay motionless for about three minutes in a complete state of what-the-fuckness. I was scared to move a limb in case I woke up the demon within me that would force me to go running. I lay stock still, barely breathing. I wished that I could go back to sleep, to not have to do this in full consciousness.

Silence, waiting, hoping that it would not come, hoping that I could lie here and not feel it. Praying that my resolve would hold and that I would have the strength to get through this day. *One minute at a time* I whispered to myself. *You can do it, just take it one minute at a time.*

Then it came.

The urge, the desire, the want to get up and run like I had done every day for eight years. Taunting, manipulating, convincing thoughts:

Just one more run will not hurt.

You are giving in. You are failing. You are lazy.

If you do not run today you will never be able to be as strong and as powerful as you were yesterday. You have to run. Without running you are nothing.

106

The thoughts pretended to be on my side, they disguised themselves as my voice. They beckoned, they pointed and they pulled.

Just one minute at a time, I told myself. Hold fast.

I lay still and was subsequently trampled over by anger, pain, confusion, frustration, denial, acceptance, grief, sorrow, fear, victory, pride, and at some point: happiness. All the emotions seemed to want to come at once in a mishmash.

Then peace. Just for a second, as I fought off the desire to run, I tasted peace. I saw what my life had the potential of being. And that tiny slither excited a hunger and a power that I knew in that moment would result in my victory. Peace was there for me. Not right now; I had a lot of work to do to get it, but it was there somewhere ahead.

I called my boss at the café and told her I was sick; I would not be in that day.

Not running was the first battle that I declared, and unbeknown to me, the first step in my recovery from my eating disorder. My cold turkey approach worked for me that first day. That is not to say that it was easy, because it was not. There would be times when I would feel as if I were suffocating in my own skin and my body would physically start to panic. My breathing would elevate, my heart rate would speed up and I would feel dizzy from the pressure of the screaming thoughts in my head. The first day was the worst, I was acting on faith and had no idea if I could actually do it or not.

I had been unprepared for the waves, so I almost got knocked down by them a couple of times that first day. "The waves" were what I labelled the pattern of calm and storm. I would gradually feel calmer, and my emotions would subside to the point that I would wonder if I had imagined the whole thing, maybe there was no such thing as an exercise disorder at all.

Maybe I was absolutely fine.

Maybe this has all been a bad dream.

I would feel myself relax physically; my shoulders would fall away from my ears and the line of my jaw would cease to ache. Then, boom! The wave would smash into me. I would want to run, the monster inside of me was back, tantruming because I was not doing as it wanted.

As soon as I identified the wave pattern I was able to manage it. I could pre-empt the waves and prepare for them. On camping holidays to France my sisters and I would play in the surf, running towards the waves and jumping up so that the salty water would not get into our eyes and mouth. I was jumping waves again now; but this was much less fun.

After that first day my confidence grew somewhat; I could remind myself that I had done this once already and I could do it again.

On day two this terrifying thing happened: my legs swelled up.

My knees and my ankles filled with fluid and they felt so weak I could barely stand on them. I could only think that this must have been a delayed concussion as a result of running for so many years never allowing a rest day for my body to heal. It was painful, but still not as bad as the mental anguish I was in. I considered going to the doctor, but the thought of it depressed me so much I stayed put. I could not fathom gathering the energy to answer questions only to be told to go home and rest and eat.

I ate very little those first few days, but I allowed myself to concentrate on one thing at a time, and my body, given an opportunity to rest, began to recover. When I did eat, it was fruits and vegetables and mostly at night.

Day three: My legs were still a little puffy but I went back into work. It was very hard not to park up at the gym first thing in the morning as was my usual pattern and spend a couple of hours on the treadmill before my shift started. That morning seemed like an ocean of time where I should have been running. I almost caved.

You did two days, that's enough.

One run in the gym will not hurt, you have proven what you needed to prove, you can run again now. It will make you feel so much better.

The thoughts, so convincing, nearly had me in the gym on day four. I had fully intended to exercise as I left the house that morning. It was a premeditated, conscious act of rebellion. What exactly I was rebelling against I have no idea. My own best interests?

I put my workout kit in the car. I parked up outside the gym, put the car in neutral, pulled up the handbrake and turned off the ignition. Then I stopped; my eyes fixated on my hand as it hovered on the ignition key. My wrist was *so* thin. It were as if I had seen it properly for the first time in years. It was so very shockingly thin.

I saw my pale, translucent skin. I saw the prominent veins running down my arm. I saw the jarringly defined groove between my ulna and my radius. I felt an overwhelming surge of pity for my frail wrist, for my body. My poor wrist had done nothing to deserve this. My loyal, hardworking hands—that for years had held the reins of horses, pens, books, my Walkman as I ran—were pallid and wan.

I knew that I had to be better than this. I had to be stronger. I picked up my mobile phone—a flip-screen version called a Razor—and dialed the number of the gym reception. I didn't even trust myself to get out of the car.

The receptionist answered, "Leisure Centre."

I recognized her voice. Her name was Tracy and she usually worked in the mornings. I could see her in my mind's eye leaning back on her chair, her bottle-blonde hair pulled back in a tight ponytail, studying her nails and chewing gum as she spoke to me.

"Hi, I would like to cancel my membership please." I was harried, rushed. I needed her to get on and do this for me before the next wave came. Before I changed my mind.

" 'ang on a moment (sound of bubblegum popping) . . . the membership representative is busy with someone else, can I put you on 'old?"

"No!" I was on the verge of tears and did not want to stay on the line. "No, I cannot hold, my name is Tabitha Alderson and my membership number is 84526. Please leave a note and have my membership cancelled!"

"Well . . . look alright, if you just . . ."

I hung up.

Now that I was not allowing myself to exercise, I had this wealth of extra time on my hands and at first this felt overwhelming; I felt as if I were being strangled by space and choice. Choice was hard, as if I allowed myself to think in terms of what I would *like* to do with my time, my preference would have been to run. I was choosing to walk against the tide of hammering thoughts in my head and it was an onerous task. Without running to shield me my fear of fat was taking even more space up in my mind.

I had to keep myself occupied. I would have to fill that space with something. I decided to absorb myself in studying again, but this time I would go formally into a career field in the only area that I really felt I had any interest in: exercise and fitness.

I know what you are thinking: bad idea. You'd be right of course. This was a very, very bad idea.

I knew that studying and working in a gym would be potentially a very challenging space for someone who was trying to overcome what I believed at the time to be an exercise addiction (I would like to interject here that I now know that eating disorders, and all the various behaviours that accompany them, are not addictions. At the time, however, I had to call my exercise compulsion something, I had to label it, and addiction was the word that seemed to make the most sense to me then).

When I revealed my new choice of career path to them, my parents reacted in the way that I expected: an awkward silence and a couple of long deep sighs. I knew they were thinking that this was simply another expression of my obsession with exercise. I suspected that they were right, but I was desperate to put my energy somewhere and exercise was the only thing I had an interest in studying. Well, that and cooking.

I enrolled on a training course that would teach me how to be a personal trainer. Most of my learning was to be done from home with coursebooks. I was also required to secure an internship position at a local gym in order to gain a certain amount of apprentice hours. A small portion of the course had been classroom based, and the nutrition section was part of this. In order to complete these segments, I had to travel up to London for three days, sit in a classroom and sit still. Stillness: a pleasure for some; a snake-pit for me.

The personal training course was expensive, so to get myself some additional income I went back to a job that I had had as a teenager: assisting the chef in the kitchen of a local pub called The Barley. Working in the evenings had been a good move because it had given me something to do in the time I would have previously spent in the gym.

Returning to work with food caused almost as many raised eyebrows as the personal trainer qualification did, but my sister Beth was the only member of the family who outright said what she thought:

"You?" Beth squawked. "Work in a kitchen as a chef! Are you completely crazy? You don't even eat anything Tabby, how will you know what the food tastes like?"

"I do . . . " I began to defend myself, but she wasn't done.

"Well . . . at least they won't have to worry about you eating all the produce! But seriously, do you realise how bloody weird that looks? You, in a kitchen, surrounded by food, and skinny as hell?" She smirked. "Why the bloody hell would you want to work there?"

"Well, I . . . " I tried again, but she still was not done.

"And by the way, the personal trainer thing . . . well, I know that nobody else wants to say anything to you because they are scared you will bite their head of, but I think it's completely nuts. Working in a gym is the last thing that you need to do. That's like an alcoholic working in a bloody bar!"

And so she continued for at least another ten minutes.

Of course I argued, and I stated my case, and I was persuasive enough to stop her ranting and encourage her to see my point of view. I convinced Beth that day that what I was doing was a good idea, but in truth, I was struggling to convince myself.

The hardest behaviour to break had been the one which required me not to eat during the day. Another titbit of information that I had retained from my Psychology course was that a person's eating patterns are designed to be relentlessly strong because humans need to eat to survive. Any habit that is related to food is formed in the basal ganglia—which lie close to the brain stem—and by design of nature, these habits are very difficult to break. This is a wonderful blueprint which keeps most people alive and delighting in food, but in my corrupted and overthrown brain, the strength of my habitual behaviour around food was crushingly hard to take.

It's about time that I explain about the "voices" in my head. Those voices and thoughts would whittle and worry like nagging old hags at the back of my mind all the time. When they felt threatened, for example by the presence of food, they would leap to the forefront of my consciousness and scream.

In the years since recovery, I have worked with a number of people who suffer from anorexia; we all have these voices. We might call them something different, some sufferers refer to the voice as "Ed" and others have their own names like I did, but it is there.

Now, try and tell me that this is not a mental disorder?

Anyway, the point is, that when one has voices in one's head demanding that food not be eaten, eating is a rather troublesome affair. When I attempted to eat during the day, the hags in my head went apeshit. Embarking on even the smallest piece of fruit was a rollercoaster of emotion, distrust and blind faith. Eating was so traumatic that I had to be totally alone in order to even attempt it. Tears and shaking were something I was not prepared to let another living soul witness.

At that time, I was still working at the café during the day. In order to be alone for my food battle, I would take my apple up to my manager's office and eat in there. Something that should have been so easy, so simple and so enjoyable was everything but. Now I know what you are thinking, "An apple! She's scared of an apple? But there is no fat in an apple!" And you would be right. There might be no fat in an apple, but what pissed the voices off was my disobedience. My choice to eat during the day was a direct act of defiance against what they were telling me.

Now, another problem with these voices is that they do not present themselves as bad; especially not at first. It is not as if they take on a voice or tone different from all the other thoughts in one's head, or as if they just suddenly present one day and declare: Hello! I am your eating disorder and I am here to ruin your life!

No, they disguise themselves as normal thoughts. They sound just like the ones that tell you to remember to brush your teeth in the morning or that you really need to mow the lawn this weekend. The voices camouflage themselves and hide amongst the mundane and helpful daily task thoughts. Like weeds, they grow up in between the healthy flowers of idea, lovingly strangling, until one day, all that is left is ragwort.

The irony was that, come nighttime, I could eat and eat and would never want to stop eating. I was two completely different people living in one exhausted shell of a body. I ate at night, because at night, one voice told me to eat, and tricked me into believing then that if I ate at night I was in control of the situation, when really, it was like feeding Gremlins.

You must have watched that film? The one where the cute little creatures turn into nasty monsters if they eat at night. Yup, that was my eating disorder. When I binged at night I was feeding it, making it stronger and weakening the Mogwai. Needless to say, my decision to eat during the day did not go down well with these voices.

My first on location training was a three-day weekend, and the preliminary segment of my personal training course that was to be taken in London. I was going to be three days straight in a classroom and there was going to be a lunch break each day. Had I embarked on this course any earlier I would have not considered the lunch break at all—instead I would have gone for a run. But, this approaching weekend presented itself to me in my mind as a possibility of change. To change something that for a while had been wanting to be tackled. I decided to pack myself a lunch.

Intention is one thing, and that alone was a big step for me. But intention does not always result in actuality. When the midday break came on Day One I opened my packed

111

lunch salad and stared at it. I felt the eyes of my colleagues on me, I was convinced that everyone in the room was looking at me. I looked up, sure I would be met with ten pairs of eyes, but instead, people were chatting happily as they tucked into their own sandwiches. Nobody was watching me at all. I looked back down at my salad, again, I felt hot eyes scrutinising me from the other people in the room.

It's your imagination, nobody is looking at you. Just eat.

Then, the opposition:

Don't do it.

To eat now will be failure.

To eat now will mean that you lost!

I felt the pressure to eat mount behind me like a dark shadow. The adrenaline, the heat, that familiar lump in my throat. I wanted to move. I *needed* to move. I pushed back my chair and excused myself for the loo.

I wanted to run; I managed to negotiate a walk instead. Out into the fresh air and away from my lunchbox I felt my stress lessen. I walked a while before returning indoors. Taking my salad with me this time, I went back outside and sat alone on a graffiti-adjourned bench that stank of piss on a small patch of grass close to the building. There, alone, I anxiously began to eat.

I did not really taste my salad that day, but that is not what mattered to me. There was probably barely a hundred calories in the entirety of the undressed lettuce leaves, cucumbers and tomatoes that I ate that lunchtime, and that mattered very little to me either. What mattered was that I had won, I had broken the cycle, I had eaten something other than an apple during the day.

The nutrition course that was part of the personal trainer package I had purchased was pretty run of the mill in terms of the recommendations given for optimal eating: low-fat, high-carbohydrates and moderate proteins. It was all based on that widely circulated food pyramid with carbohydrates and grains on the bottom and fats along with sweets at the top —you know the one.

This delighted me. Fat was considered a danger; the food pyramid said to limit fats, and that came from science. Science is never wrong, is it.

Part of the process for those of us on the nutrition course was to keep a food diary. We would then have to analyze it, and break it down into the macronutrients fat, protein and carbohydrates before writing a short essay. This was a great tool for me to use to actually return to eating during the day and I set myself the goals of a steady breakfast-snack-lunch-snack-dinner-snack schedule. Nobody on my course knew that on that particular weekend I ate lunch for the *first time* in a number of years. It was the perfect opportunity being among strangers and in a neutral space where there was less of the emotional baggage attached to mealtimes as there would have been at home or with my family.

When I returned home to my little flat after the initial weekend of my nutrition course I set myself the task of those three meals and three snacks. Every bite was a battle, and not one I was always able to win. I stuck to variations on a fatless salad or low-calorie yogurt because, quite frankly, that was plenty difficult enough. When I wrote up my food diary I looked at it and thought it looked like the food log for a person with an eating disorder.

I did not believe that I had an eating disorder, because I ate food at night, but I was well aware that anyone reading my food diary would think so. I considered adding some of the items from my night binge, so that it would balance out, but that would have looked equally as ridiculous. Salad followed by a mountain of chocolate?

Hell, I didn't know what to do, so I lied. I made it up. I added a fictitious couple of pieces of whole wheat bread and a chicken breast in the lunch section. I fabricated that I had eaten a salmon steak with noodles and vegetables for dinner. I knew that would be what my tutor would want to see as he was forever harping on about the importance of carbohydrates and protein. I was cheating, but regardless, I tried not to let that detract from my victory. I was pleased with myself. I had eaten! In daylight!

The nutrition course also gave me some rules to follow, like not eating too many eggs due the the amount of cholesterol in them, not eating processed or baked goods and eating plenty of fruit and vegetables. I like that, I liked the rules, especially the ones around fat! Low-fat everything! That was a nutrition rule that made my eating disorder very happy.

At the same time, my chef job meant that I could further indulge in my food obsession, and best of all, it was valid! I had a reason to look at cookbooks all day and night. This is where things get really weird, as despite being terrified of eating fat, I absolutely loved to make foods for other people to eat. It was like the best of both worlds! The Whispers told me that other people eating fat made me stronger! If I saw another person eating food, better still if it were something which I had created for them, I felt good. Simple as that! I felt good when I saw others eating.

Now, the enjoyment I gathered from watching others eat is interesting, because I am not an overly compassionate person. In fact, nowadays, watching another person eating something yummy is rather tourtuous! I am rather an "all the more for me" type of person. As a child, I would sneak into my sisters' bedrooms after Easter and eat their Easter Eggs so that my own stash would last longer. As an adult, a recovered adult, I scowl and growl at anyone who is silly enough to suggest dessert sharing, and I cannot go out for Tapas because I get all possessive about the small plates and try to stab the other diners with my fork. In short, when it comes to food, the only pleasure I derive from watching other people eat is that which comes after I have pushed them aside and stolen whatever it was they were eating!

Yet, when I could not eat, when I did not want to eat, watching others eat felt great!

I would bake and create foods laden with all manner of fat and calories. Working in a kitchen was thrilling! I would be handling butter, cream, fats and oils all day, but I would not go as far as to lick my fingers. It was exciting; like playing with fire. I was hyperactive, anti-sociable, and obsessively dedicated to making good food. I also never ate on shift; all in all I was the perfect employee.

In my cooking, I was able to make foods using all the ingredients that I wanted to eat but was unable to. Meat, cheese, sausages and all the fattiest tastiest wonders that I had once loved so much went into my dishes. In the restaurant trade fat sells food, because it tastes good, and my dishes were full of it. Steak and stout pie, double chocolate cheesecake, lasagna and banoffee pie were some of my favourite dishes to make and often my best sellers. I have no idea what my food tasted like, because I never tried any of it. If I did have to taste a sauce to season it, I would hastily spit it out again.

Some chefs got fat, always eating the tempting foods that they were creating. Not me; I was stronger than that.

Chapter Nineteen

In the restaurant trade, fat sells.

In the fitness industry, low-fat sells.

By night, I was a chef filling customer's bellies with food. By day, I was a personal trainer promising customers weight loss.

I completed my nutrition course and started to work as an apprentice personal trainer. The only difference between an apprentice personal trainer and a personal trainer is that an apprentice does not get paid. I was supposed to apprentice for six months, but I negotiated myself a paid job within two. I was popular as a trainer, and much as I would have liked to say that my popularity was testament to my shining personality, in reality it was because I was so thin. I guess people thought that some of my thinness would rub off onto them if they hired me, or that I had a secret formula for weight loss.

Subsequently, I earned good money working in the gym. When asked, I would also supply dietary advice; because, after all, I was now a qualified nutritionist. Remembering how I used to counsel other people about nutrition in a time when I was suffering from an eating disorder appalls me. I could not see that the advice I gave to others was driven by my own problems with food.

Do me a favour: never take nutritional advice from a person with an eating disorder.

Unfortunately, it is not uncommon that people suffering from eating disorders work as professionals in the diet and fitness industry. In fact, when I was in the thick of it, helping other people lose weight was something I felt passionately about. I truly believed that I was doing a good thing when I told clients to cut the fat out of their diets and instructed them to drink only diet beverages. Now, because I know that I was misguided, and because there is nothing more dangerous than a deluded enthusiast, I can see that it was downright reckless for me to be allowed to act as a health guru.

I was thin, and other women—those who envied my thin frame—sought out and listened to my counsel. Whenever this happened, it depleted any notions that I had that my low body weight was unhealthy. How could it be bad if everyone else wanted it? The compliments I received from others did a lot to reinforce my disordered behaviours. Eating disorders are not directly caused by the thin-seeking society that surrounds them, but they can feed off it.

Part of the personal training course had covered marketing. Our tutors had sat us down and taught us the art of conning potential clients into wanting a personal trainer. There is a distinct formula that most trainers use: First of all, each day, I would scour the gym floor for fatties. New members were often a good bet, as most people join a gym in the first place wanting to lose some weight. The sales team would point me in the direction of any newbies, whom I would approach and, generously, offer a free demo personal training session. During this session, I would wow them with my skill and expertise. I would also promise them their dream body for the bargain price of thirty quid a session (twenty-five if they bought ten).

Most other trainers had to work bloody hard to attract clients. Not me. Some days, I felt as if I were a cheat, because for me it was ridiculously easy. Clients would seek me out! They would be given a free training session with another trainer, and then see me and ask if they could sign up with me instead! At first I was both relieved and thrilled about this, but there was also a creeping sensation that people were not coming to me for the right reasons. Were people approaching me as a trainer because of how very thin I was? Was it ok that this was a selling point for me? It did not feel so. But regardless, what could I do?

I must have sounded like a broken record:

"Eat less fat."

"Eat plenty of fruit and vegetables."

"Fill up on low-calorie, low-glycemic index carbohydrates."

"Drink more water."

" . . . eat even less fat."

One of my very first paying clients was a girl called Rachel. She was just a couple of years older than me, single, and the first thing that I thought when I saw her was how attractive she was. She looked perfect. I was confused as to why she believed that she needed to lose more weight, because she looked fine just the way that she was.

Rachel was nice; she worked in human resources for a local firm. One of the first questions that I asked her was what her primary motivation to be in the gym was.

"I want to lose some weight," she answered, straight and simple.

"Oh" I said, outwardly feigning surprise whilst inwardly yawning. Everyone was in the gym to lose weight. "Well, you actually look a pretty healthy weight for your height." This was the truth, she looked great.

"No." She insisted, "I'm fat."

Wow. I was shocked to hear her say that. She was *far* from fat. I was quiet for a while, as I did not really know how to answer this. A paying client gets what a paying client wants, and if she wanted weight loss, surely I should help her with that regardless of what my personal opinion was? I wondered if there was a section in my *Personal Trainer's Guide to Success Manual* that dealt with the ethics of helping people lose weight even if they did not need to (I had checked when I got home that night: there was not).

I figured I could work with her and try and get her to understand that she did not need to lose weight; maybe if we toned her up a bit more she would feel better about herself.

"Well, what makes you say you are fat?" I queried. "I don't think that you are!"

"I've been wanting to lose some weight for a while . . . ever since I broke up with my boyfriend last November . . . I know he thought I was fat because his new girlfriend, the one that he dumped me for, is a size six or something . . . skinny bitch . . . anyway, I would just feel better if I was skinnier . . . I want a thigh gap . . . you know?"

I did not know.

A thigh gap?

I had absolutely no idea what a "thigh gap" was. I had to ask one of the other trainers, and when he explained the concept to me, all I could think was: *why?*

I had one myself—a thigh gap—but it was not intentional. I had never considered it attractive or something to work towards in life. Yet here it was, a whole *thing* that women put on their top ten lists of life achievements. In recovery, it was my mission to lose my thigh gap, and I still shudder when I hear those words now. Really, the concept of the thigh gap neatly encompasses the ridiculousness of society's obsession with thin: dangerously unhealthy, ironically unattractive and utterly nonsensical.

Rachel was the first of a series of women that came to train with me because they wanted to lose weight. It was surreal; when I had set out to become a personal trainer, I had envisaged that most of my clients would be obese, and that I would be doing the world an incredible service by helping fat people get thin. I had not imagined that the majority of the people coming to me and asking me for weight loss would be already perfect and healthy-looking young ladies.

Training these women did not feel good, or virtuous. It felt kind of dirty. Like I knew that they wanted something that was not right for them. Like I knew they were attracted to something about me that was not healthy for them, or me. Despite my inability to put on weight, I would have hated for anyone to think that I looked the way that I looked on purpose, or that it was desirable; or that it made me happy. I had been happy before I had lost weight, not after.

One afternoon Rachel came to the gym for her session with me in one hell of a mood.

"Bad day at the office?" I hesitantly enquired.

"I'll bloody say so!" She scowled. "My boss, Tony, you know . . . the one that I told you about . . . the cute one? Well, word is that he started dating Amy . . . this girl that works in the marketing department . . . you know, I think I told you? The *thin* one . . . skinny bitch.

Well anyway, Tony, the idiot, is going out with her!"

Something else which had come as a surprise to me when I started working as a trainer was that most of my clients treated me like an agony aunt. People told me all kinds of things! One lady told me about having an affair with her husband's best friend, then pointed him out to me in the gym before paying me to train her husband. That was awkward. Another girl confided in me that she fancied her boss and that she was planning on seducing him at the next work party. "He's married, but his wife is a bitch so it's fine . . ."

Rachel's admissions were quaint in comparison.

"I just want to look like that!" she blurted out and pointed at a magazine that someone had left on the bench in the trainer's office. On the front cover was a model in a bikini. "Get your beach body. Lose the belly fat!", was the cringingly unoriginal headline.

"That? Rachel, *that* is photoshop! Nobody looks like *that*! Even the model does not look like *that*."

She pouted at me.

I laughed, "Come on Rachel! That model has arms so skinny that it looks like she's had part of her bicep surgically removed!"

She smirked back at me, "I guess you are right, but I still want to drop a couple of sizes, everything will be better if I lose a bit more weight!"

I doubted that very much.

Thankfully not all my clients were like Rachel. I did have a few that truly needed to lose some pounds. Hilary for example.

Hilary was in her late forties and lived in one of the small villages close to where the gym was. She was a mother of three children, the youngest of which was seventeen. Hilary claimed that she had never been able to regain her pre-baby figure. Technically, she was in the "overweight" range. Hilary liked to garden, and sometimes she walked the dogs with her husband, but other than that she seemed to spend her time housekeeping and baking. She told me that she was at her happiest when at home with her Aga, creating delicious things for her family and neighbours to eat. Fruit loaves, home baked sourdough bread, Bakewell tarts and chocolate brownies were a few of the things that apparently Hilary was considered queen bee for in her village.

Hilary reminded me of village life—before I went to university, and before I began to hate the foods that I had once loved. Our village had a number of "Hilary" types: ladies who loved to bake using local resources such as eggs from Mrs Holmes chickens next door, or butter and cream from the local dairy. Pies, cakes and crumbles galore; walk into any one of these women's homes and there would certainly be something fresh out of the oven to delight in. The Hilarys of the world love nothing more than sharing their culinary masterpieces.

My own mother was a Hilary: a feeder. Always wanting to offer everyone food. To feed is to love for many women.

I really liked Hilary. She had never been in a gym in her life before the day that she walked in and enquired about personal training. The only reason that she was there at all was because her doctor had told her that her cholesterol was too high, and that she needed to lose some weight and eat less fat in order to be healthy.

It was rather a shame really, because Hilary's body suited her personality. She carried her weight really well; in fact, she looked just right. I felt awful breaking the news to her that the first thing to go from her diet would have to be all the pies and cakes she was so fond of— and so very skilled at—making. In some respects, losing weight would be relatively easy for her, because her diet was so high in fat and she was pretty inactive. I felt optimistic that she could slim down in a matter of weeks on a low-fat diet coupled nicely with some moderate daily exercise.

Two weeks later, Hilary came into the gym looking harried and stressed. I was thrilled, because she had indeed lost a couple of pounds, but she seemed a tad fed up.

"You okay this week?" I asked her after she had been silent for the first fifteen minutes of our session. She was usually very talkative.

"I'm fine I guess, I just feel a little flat this week . . . unlike me I know . . . I'm not usually one to lose my chipper." She feigned a smile, but she certainly seemed to have lost some spark. It seemed that a low-fat diet made Hilary depressed, and she was not the only one.

My clients, on the whole, were miserable with their diets. They would lose control and binge on fatty foods at the weekends, only to return sheepishly to the gym on Monday looking to me to help them exercise off their shame. I was so staunch an advocate for the low-fat diet, that I would do anything in order to help my clients achieve success with it. I wrote them weekly diet plans and instructed them to keep food diaries. Science, the government, and my schooling told me that I was right, that fat was public enemy number one, and that in helping other people learn to cut fat out of their diets, I was helping them be healthier.

And so it continued.

But what about me? Did I manage to stick to my no-running resolve even when working in a gym?

I would love to be able to say that my recovery for my "exercise addiction" took a smooth and organised linear path. Maybe it would have done had I had professional help. But the truth is that it did not. It had its very own cycle of recovery and relapse.

One of the only truly consistent aspects of my life was that I would at night binge on food. I would go through phases of being able to eat a salad at lunchtime if all the conditions were right and I was alone, then I would get thrown out of sync if my routine was interrupted, and any disruption would result in a return to not eating, putting me back to square one.

Exercise crept up on me, if I allowed myself to go a walk one day, and then have feelings of guilt and anxiety unless I went the next day too. A walk one day might turn into a jog the next; a jog one day might turn into a run the next. My haphazard work schedule of working in the café during the day, and in the kitchen some nights, made trying to settle into an eating routine difficult. My stress levels and my temper remained high.

One evening, when I arrived to work in the kitchen after a particularly irritating day of dealing with café customers, my boss offered me a full time position as second chef. I took it and handed in my notice at the café. I worked lunchtimes and evenings at the pub, allowing me to train clients and ride horses in the late afternoons. Every morning I allowed myself to go for a forty-five minute walk, as a compromise to not running. For a couple of weeks at least, this structure and daily routine worked out pretty well.

As a personal trainer, exposure to various types of fad diets was part of my job. I remember one time, about three weeks into our training together, Rachel asked me what I thought of the Atkins diet. I could not hide my wide-eyed disgust.

"Oh. My. God! It's disgusting! All they eat is fat! Seriously Rachel, I have heard some bullshit in my time, but Atkins is something else! It really takes the biscuit . . . not that Atkins himself would eat a biscuit because biscuits are too high in carbs . . . but you know what I mean, it's ridiculous!"

She pouted at me, "Well my friend Amy is on it, and she lost some weight. I just want to *do* something, you know, not for ever, but for a couple of weeks. I just need to lose a few pounds." She motioned towards her perfectly flat stomach.

"Can't you set me a weight-loss diet? I know that you do that for other people."

I felt uncomfortable.

Now, remember, I did not know then, as I do now, that when a person is genetically predisposed to an eating disorder, the act of reducing calories or dieting can act as an environmental cue and trigger the disease. I did not know then that when I had dieted in order to lose enough weight to ride Kit-Kat, that the illness my genes harboured had begun to stir. I did not know that all the myths I had been told about the type of person who has Anorexia Nervosa were untrue, and that the disease can affect any person, male, female, black, white, tan, young, old, and even stoic horsewomen. Most of all, I did not know that eating disorders could affect people who did not want them to, as the general consensus at that time was that they were chosen by sufferers.

Not knowing any of these things, it made no sense that I felt so very apprehensive about the situation with Rachel; but I did. I felt deeply uneasy about placing her on a calorie restricting eating plan.

I could refuse, but I thought that if I did she would probably just go and do the

120

Atkins diet on her own. I wondered what I could say to make this girl understand that there was nothing wrong with her body, and that being thinner would not solve any of the problems in her life. Even then, as ignorant as I was to eating disorders and their triggers, I did know that thinness does not equal happiness.

The problem was, that no matter what I said, all the magazines that Rachel read showed her pictures of skinny people having fun and looking fabulous. They were of course, supposed to be selling clothes, but they functioned to sell thinness. Everything Rachel looked at gave her the message that to be thin was to be popular and happy.

"Let's think about that." Was all I could say. I changed the subject, "I think we should work on your upper body strength this week."

Let's think about that indeed. Nowadays, I frequently give talks in schools about eating disorders, and I write about them in abundance too. One of the biggest misconceptions that I come across is that the media—which undoubtedly contributes to negative body image problems—actually causes eating disorders. I want to address this here, as despite my abhorrence for the portrayal of the 'perfect woman' by the media, I cannot agree that this *causes* eating disorders. This is fact number five:

Eating disorders are not *caused* by the media.

Now, what seeing these images of emaciated and ridiculously beautiful women can cause is a negative sense of self, which can in turn lead to dieting behaviour, which can—in a person who is genetically predisposed to having one—lead to the enabling (triggering) of an eating disorder.

What I am trying to make clear, is that a person can only develop an eating disorder if they possess the biological make-up for it. Negative body image is often present in individuals who suffer from eating disorders, but not all—as demonstrated nicely by my own case. I never thought that I was too fat, and I never dieted for any other reason than because I wanted to be lighter in order to ride that bloody horse. The concept that eating disorders are only suffered by individuals who do not "love themselves" is utter tosh, and it leads to fact number six:

Eating disorders are not *caused* by low self-esteem.

When a person has the genetic setup for an eating disorder, he or she can develop that disorder at any time, or potentially not at all. As weight loss and calorie reduction (this can be intentional or not) are things which trigger the illness, people usually get triggered in their teenage years, when they are more likely to be lured into thinking that they need to diet and are more inclined to care what other people are thinking or doing. This can, however, happen at any time in life, and it can also be triggered by all sorts of stress. The reason, as you can (hopefully) now see, that people equate negative body image and the media with eating disorders, is that those things act as a trigger in the majority of cases; they are a common environmental cue, but nonetheless, they are not the actual cause of eating disorders.

What does cause eating disorders!? I hear you cry!

In my opinion: genes.

All that aside, body image and the media is a hellishly important issue. It is imperative that society stop giving people the idea that they are fat and ugly. If less people think that they are too fat, less people will be led down the dieting route. If less people embark on diets, less of those who are genetically predisposed to eating disorders will go on to develop them. See how it is all interwoven, but how the cause and effect elements can become confusing?

A negative body image can be awfully detrimental to a person's health and happiness and this alone is reason enough to support the groups that advocate for truth in advertising, and a ban on photoshop.

Now we have that cleared up, let us get back to the story!

Where were we: oh yes, I was twenty-five and working three jobs.

One morning at the horse yard, I was training Gaia when something spooked her. I was in the covered indoor school, riding "on the flat" (which was what we refer to the process of schooling horses for disciplines that do not involve jumping over fences). I loved to ride on the flat in the school as it meant trotting an endless twenty meter circle with my horse on the bit. It's pretty hard work, causing both horse and rider to generate a sweat, which is why it was my preferred way of riding.

Gaia was going well for me that day despite her natural inclination to want to chuck her head in the air and have her own way, she was listening to me. At least, she was behaving right up until Boris the yard cat jumped down off one of the rafters and spooked her. She jumped in the air and threw her heels up in a buck. Annoyed with her disobedience I pulled her back into my firm contact.

The second buck that followed took me by surprise and saw me scrabbling to stay in the saddle. I dropped my right hand rein and grappled to get a grip on Gaia's mane in an attempt to stay on. A second's opportunity, a slack rein, and she was gone! She pulled the remaining left rein right out of my hand and exploded underneath me into a flat out gallop. We flew through the school gate and out the open stable-yard, where Gaia almost fell on the slippery cobblestones. She found her feet and continued across the yard and into an adjacent field before I even had a chance to do anything more than clutch at her mane and avoid the fall that seemed inevitable.

Faster and faster she ran. Seeing the fence on the far end of the pasture looming closer and closer every second, I had no option but to grasp at one flying rein and haul with all my might in the hope that I could turn her. I haphazardly managed to get both hands on the rein dangling over her left shoulder; I lent back and hauled.

She turned—too sharply—and almost had me off over her left shoulder as she swerved to the right and reeled on her heels. Before I knew it we were headed back in the direction that we had come, and just as fast!

Shocked that I was still aboard, but understanding that this would not last long unless I could slow her down, I managed to get a grip on the rein again. Leaning back, I hauled, I pulled and I prayed. We finally came to one of the most undignified stops I have ever made on a horse.

Phew. Heart racing, sweat dripping down my back, I sighed complete relief. I could not believe that I had stayed on and was thankful that there had been nobody else in the yard to witness my embarrassing loss of control. I patted Gaia on the neck.

"It's alright lassy, no harm done!" I murmured.

I pressed her into a controlled walk back towards the barn with her head firmly back down in a contact.

"Aye you see!" I jumped out of my skin as Gaia startled at the sound of a human voice.

It was Bill, with his wheelbarrow, emerging from behind the muck pile at the back of the barn. I groaned with embarrassment as I realised that he must have watched the whole sorry episode.

"I told you that mare would take her freedom." He chuckled to himself as he waddled with his empty barrow back towards the stables.

"'em horses, 'em 'orses got to be allowed to be 'orses, you got to give them a bit of freedom otherwise they will take it from you when you least expect it!"

My head swelled in anger towards Bill, mostly because I knew he was right: Because I rode so tightly, the horses were ticking time bombs.

Rather like my food consumption.

During the day, I ate tightly: vegetables and fruit. At night: boom-o-binge!

This dichotomy left me feeling torn between being two different people; neither of which were very likable versions of me. They were two polar opposites of attitude and behaviour towards food. During the day, eating brought fear and struggle; at night, a demon forced food down my throat to the point of sickness.

Chapter Twenty

One morning, it must have been sometime in April 2007, something wholly disturbing occurred: after a month or so of being really good at the three meals a day lark, I didn't eat breakfast. I had got out of bed in the morning and simply felt too weak to embark on the breakfast battle with myself. Instead, I pulled on my jodhpurs, got in the car and drove to the horse yard. This was the first time I had not eaten one of my structured meals in a number of weeks and it felt so unbelievably good just because my head was quiet for once.

I'd taken a break from the fight and allowed myself a morning's respite. Surely this would not hurt just once in a while, *right*? I felt happy. When I got to the yard I even cracked a smile at Bill and bid him a good morning. I tacked up Gaia and started our training session.

I probably remained happy for half of our ride, but then came the guilt. How awful I was for starving my body. I felt overcome with regret. Why had I done that? I should have eaten. Back came the discord. Back came my scowl.

At the end of our session, I dismounted Gaia and set off in my tight-shouldered walk to return her to her stall. I had to walk past Bill again, and as I approached him I regretted my warm greeting toward him earlier. I hoped that it would not encourage him to try and talk to, smile at or even look at me now; because I wanted no attention.

Unfortunately, Bill, standing there in his dirty old tweed jacket and grubby jeans, was beaming at me as I strode past.

"Aye, not learnt that lesson yet 'ave ya lassy," he chuckled at me.

I had no idea what the hell he was talking about and any other day I might have walked past him without acknowledging him or his absurd comments. But I was brimming with anger already and I needed an outlet. Bill would do nicely.

"Bill, what the hell are you going on about now?" I turned and looked him square in the face. My fury had no visible effect on his smile. In fact, if anything I saw it broaden and touch the space behind his eyes.

"'em 'orses. 'em 'orses need a bit of love and trust every now and then, because you can be sure that if yer don't give 'er some freedom, she will take it when she 'as the chance . . . just like she did t'other day when she ran with yer lass. Just like that she will!"

"Jeezus Bill! What the hell do you know about schooling horses?!" I demanded "Nothing! You have no idea what you are talking about!" I pulled Gaia behind me as I stomped back to her stall.

I was still angry at Bill as I drove to The Barley. How dare he question my techniques with his idle prattering nonsense. My bad mood affected everyone else that day. The two waiting staff got yelled at by me for missing orders, serving unpolished cutlery and being too slow at coming in to retrieve the food once it was ready. I cursed at the pot wash girl, a petite twelve-year-old called Lucy, who insisted on showing up to work with red nail varnish. I made her go and scrub it off in the staff toilet.

The head chef, Gary, was a small, Scottish, gremlin of a man, and not particularly pleasant to work with. Not that I ever enjoyed working with anyone, but Gary was particularly obnoxious. He would wipe his nose on his chef's whites—a habit that would make me feel ill to observe—and had an annoying way of breathing loudly, which made it impossible to try and forget that he was there. Gary had once told me that women made excellent second chefs if they were not too "girly", but should not be employed as head chefs because their changing hormones led them to make inconsistent flavour choices. Tosser.

"Yer a good lass now, don't get me wrong . . . but lasses just don't make 'ed chefs."

"Really Gary? Why is that? Is it because we all insist on tying red ribbons on the racks of lamb? Or is it because we make the gravy taste of perfume? Maybe it is because we spend so long dressing the salads, you know, worrying about what style of olive oil is in fashion?"

"No . . . no, it's science actually, it's to do with the hormones. The hormones change a lot in lasses and because of the hormones they can't taste stuff right." He answered stoutly, puffing up his chest like he knew what he was talking about. I imagined that was something he had read in *The Sun.*

That day, even Gary commented on my snarkiness.

"In a mood today aren't ya? That time of month is it?"

Idiot, I don't even have periods, not unless I'm on the pill.

"Not married are you Gary?" I said, and smiled at him sweetly.

"Neither are you!" He shot back.

Touché.

That day, after shift, when everyone else had gone, I stayed behind to finish mopping the floors. Usually this was Lucy's job, but I told her to go home early; maybe that was my way of apologising for being so beastly to her. Or, maybe it was because I wanted the extra activity involved with toiling the mop around the kitchen. Who knows.

The only thing that I really knew for sure that day was that I felt like crap. I considered skipping another meal. I knew I would feel better if I just went without lunch. Then came the guilt: *You are supposed to be eating. You will lose more weight if you skip another meal.* I began to make myself my usual salad.

I opened the fridge to pull out the lettuce and came face-to-face with a sticky toffee pudding. I had seen, and ignored, that pudding a hundred times already that day as I had opened and closed the fridge, but this time was different.

This time, I grabbed a spoon. I scooped up some of the squelchy golden syrup that the sodden sponge cake was swimming in. *Just a taste. I just want to taste it.*

As soon as the sugary-sweet sauce hit my tongue I knew a binge was coming. I had never binged during the day before and I was unprepared. I had no energy to give resistance as the spoon continued to dig sections out of the gooey sponge.

Squatting down there in front of the fridge, I shovelled pudding and syrup into my mouth; barely tasting because I was eating so fast. Every now and then I would be forced to stop and gasp for breath before eating more.

I ate what would equate to six portions of sticky toffee pudding within a couple of minutes. When I was finished, desperate and confused, I sat on the floor in the kitchen and wept.

That was the first daytime binge. My demons were merging.

Things got worse after the sticky toffee pudding episode; food teased me with a growing insistence. My demons were starting to show up within each other's space. My nighttime binge-eating voice—whom I subsequently named Succubus—had begun to try and wheedle in on my daytime activities; when I was cooking at the pub during the day she taunted me, trying to goad me into eating. Feeling threatened by the the binger's attempt to rule the daylight as well as the dark, my food-restricting daytime voice—whom I am going to call Sister Catherine after Catherine of Siena—tried to assert her frigid self by insisting that I skip meals.

I've given these voices names now, because at this stage in the story I want you to see how I was being torn in two directions. On the one hand, the night-time binge voice, Succubus, who had previously only come alive in the evenings, was beginning to try and take over during the day. She wanted me to binge eat all the time now. The other, Sister Catherine, wanted me to restrict.

Catherine, incidentally, brings us on to fact number seven:

Eating disorders are not just a modern day problem.

Actually, quite untrue. History tells us that Catherine of Siena had a condition called anorexia mirabilis, which I believe to be the early form of anorexia nervosa: the conditions are the same, the name just changed over the years. Now, in Catherine's time (1347-1380) fasting denoted female holiness or humility and underscored purity, so people who fasted themselves to death were considered saintly. Catherine—who in my opinion undoubtedly suffered from an eating disorder—strongly believed that she was walking the path of God when she denied herself food.

I commiserate with her, as anorexia can be very convincing. Had I lived in the

1300s, I certainly would have believed the same: that my eating disorder was in fact a superior way of being. Anorexia does that; the disease makes the sufferer feel as if the illness is actually *correct*. This is why—as anyone who has ever known a person suffering from anorexia will tell you— it is so difficult to get them to eat.

Anyway, the point is, that around this time almost ten years now from the time when my eating disorder emerged at seventeen, it was changing again. The voices that had until then stayed separate—Sister Catherine and Succubus—began to both shout at me at once.

Like the time I tired to eat bread …

My parents had a glorious tin bread bin. It was a very old-fashioned country-kitchen type, with blue lettering and rim liner. Mother loved good bread, so there was always a variety of loaves in stock: sliced for sandwiches and toast; or crusty homestyle rounds for dipping into soups and stews. The bread tin was like a talisman for me; every time I went and visited my parents it shook, beckoned and rattled at my resolve. I had this great ambition: to be able to eat a slice of bread during the day. Normal style.

Normal style, meant not sidling up to the breadbin and teasing off the lid as if it were a Jack-in-the-box. Normal style, meant not picking up a slice of bread and sniffing at it like a neanderthal. Normal style, meant not gingerly tearing off a square inch of crust and nervously putting it to my lips, then hastily throwing it down to the spaniel, who, knowing only too well what was coming, would plaster herself to my heels whenever I was in the kitchen.

Normal style, meant simply eating a slice of bloody bread. I thought it was impossible, but I had this dream of doing it anyway. I had even planned it all out; in my head it was a simple operation, an achievable goal. In reality it was mission impossible; an operation that required meticulous planning, dedication, precision, perfect timing, and a lot of luck.

I would have to do it at my parents' house, because buying myself a loaf would not work. Having a whole loaf of bread in my flat would be a red flag to Succubus; she would undoubtedly make me eat the whole bloody thing. I knew that I had to be alone to do it, and that was the timing piece. Finding a peaceful moment in my parents' house was hard, even during the middle of the day when Mum and Dad were out working, because my two sisters were still often in and out despite no longer living there.

Then, one day I got lucky. I pitched up at my parents' house and there was nobody home but the dog.

Now's the chance! Today is the day!

Seriously? You are going to try this now? You're not prepared enough. You will fail.

It's too much, too soon. Give yourself more time.

Wimp! Sissy! If you can't do it now you will never do it.

After minutes of mental bickering between Succubus and Sister Catherine, I hovered close to the bread tin. Sister Cathrine pleaded with me to resist, to walk away; Succubus sniggered excitedly. I lifted the lid a couple of inches to peek at what was inside. Ears pinned, I listened in case anyone else should come into the kitchen and see me nervously peering into the crumb lined tin. Silently I placed the lid on the side of the counter and with shaking hands.

Put it back, you will regret this! If you eat bread you will undo all the good work that you have done. You will forfeit all these years of withstraint. You will be weak.

I unwrapped a loaf, wincing at the sound of the paper bread sleeve. I knew I should hurry in case someone should return home as I would have hated for anyone to have seen me; to witness this strange behaviour. I told myself this was nothing, that I was just looking, just feeling, that is all that I wanted to do.

I gingerly tore off a piece of the crust and cautiously placed it on my tongue. Suddenly the bickering ceased. Quiet. Perhaps I could take a single chew?

WHAT THE HELL ARE YOU DOING!

I ran over to the bin and spat the bread out.

It should have been the simplest task in the world: to eat a slice of bread. I may as well have been asking myself to put my hand in a tank of piranhas.

Unless it was salad or fruit, I was unable to eat a food that was not packaged. packaged foods came with the neat and convenient little table on the reverse that provided me with the exact calories and fat content. Homemade foods were a great source of stress and to be avoided at all costs. Mother was constantly trying to feed me something homemade, so living in my own flat had been a great way of escape.

At night I ate sweets because Succubus craved sweets. Now, this is interesting, as sugar can help increase the absorption of tryptophan, which is involved in serotonin production. I also understand that serotonin influences one's feelings of happiness and I have often wondered if I were craving sweets so that I could be happier. If I were craving sweets to help me make serotonin, I wonder why I did not crave tryptophan dense foods like turkey and pork? Looking back, I think that I craved sugar so much simply because sugar is very addictive, and Succubus wanted the highest calorie foods she could find because she believed that she was starving to death. I would eat far past the point of enjoyment, so it was not even as if I ate sweets because doing so was something that made me happy. No, those binges were horrid, frenzied, panicked acts of desperate bolting down food.

The more stressed that I felt, the less I could eat during the day; the less I ate during the day, the more I would eat at night. I tried to educate myself on the effects of stress, hoping that this might be the key to overcoming my night feasts. One afternoon I went to the library and did some research on stress and eating. I learnt that when one gets exhausted due to stress or lack of sleep—both of which were things that I had an abundance of—the function of one's adrenal glands can get disrupted.

I also came to understand that when the body is in search of other sources of energy it will look to sugar to provide it with the most immediate source. This adrenal fatigue seemed the most likely reason that I would lose control over sweets. But that evening after being in the library, like any other, I binged. It seemed that educating myself on the why of my issue was not influential in curbing it.

But I had to keep trying.

The next week I went back to the library and read up on sugar addictions. I learnt that when I eat something sweet, my brain releases opioids which give a feeling of pretty intense pleasure. The brain recognises the correlation between sugar and pleasure and then craves it. It would seem that fake sugar has the same effect on the brain as real sugar when tested on laboratory rats, and could also be highly addictive.

Ugh, I read that and thought of all the artificially sweetened low-fat yoghurts and cereal bars that I ate—plus the diet drinks. I understood then that I was priming my brain for a sugar addiction. Once I had taken that first mouthful of sweetened yoghurt it was as if the floodgates had opened; I would not stop eating sweet stuff until I could not physically fit any more in. I was beginning to understand that sugar in the quantities that I was eating it was a bad idea, but what was my alternative?

Fat?

Chapter Twenty One

Working at The Barley and resisting the food I served was getting harder. The smells that once had little effect on me during the day were now making my stomach restless. Hunger mingled with frustration within me, making me even more foul tempered. I was particularly drawn to the puddings: Banoffee Pie; Sticky Toffee Pudding; Apple Crumble with custard; Spotted Dick with cream; Rocky Road Marshmallow Cake; and Death by Chocolate would shamelessly flirt with me. I was careful not to allow myself to be alone in the kitchen. I knew I could not be trusted.

I had no close friends at that time. My flat sounded hollow when I moved about within it. Unmistakably empty. The only thing that I had as an escape from the silence was work, so I had thrown myself into my various jobs. I had acquaintances: clients at the gym;

other personal trainers; other kitchen staff; other riders at the stables . . . erm . . . can I count Bill?

Acquaintances are not the same as friends. On the odd occasion that I had a day or night off, there was nobody for me to "hang out" with. Nobody whom I wanted to be with; or who wanted to be with me. I couldn't relax and eat in public, which made socialising awkward and embarrassing because, let's face it, most social situations revolve around food. I was restless, so I could not sit still to do "normal" things like watch a film or go for tea. It is hard to have a conversation when one cannot stop still.

For a number of years I had problems sleeping, and I am sure that this added to my tetchiness. If I managed to fall asleep, I would be awoken every couple of hours by the din of my own teeth being ground against one another. Bruxism meant that not only was my sleep interrupted, but my jaw hurt a lot. Sleeping—or rather, lying awake trying to sleep— was an altogether rather depressing, wholly frustrating experience; I was better off working at night and keeping myself busy.

It is worth noting that I slept terribly the entire time that I was underweight. When I recovered to a restored weight my sleeping patterns returned to what they had been before I was seventeen. I now sleep like a baby. I have observed over the years, that people who do not eat enough food—or, more to the point, enough of the right *type* of food—during the day struggle to sleep well, and often wake up in the middle of the night to eat. I am of the opinion that when the body is underweight or hungry, it doesn't want to sleep. Maybe this is a survival thing? The hunter-gatherer part of the brain is getting messages that food is needed and therefore sleep is an inappropriate behaviour? Well, that's my theory anyway.

I highlight *type* of food there because I think that it is important to understand that calories are not all equal. There were times when I was eating enough calories, but still avoiding fat. I did not start to sleep well until I began to eat a balanced diet and therefore was consuming adequate calories from fat.

One Saturday, Gary did not show up to work. Simple as that, and I heard hide nor hair of him ever again. I was unaware of the full story that led to him leaving, but it seemed that the landlord owed him wages, and he had had enough: a pretty standard scenario. Chefs come and go, and they go quicker than they come. It's a fast paced high stress job, and most chefs are cooking on four hours or less sleep per night and pure adrenaline.

The landlord, a beastly man called Boris, contacted a chef resource agency, and the next day, Thierry showed up.

Thierry was tall, with light brown hair and bright blue eyes. He displayed none of the antisocial traits that most chefs, including myself, tend towards. Most of us are so focused on food that people are but a trite inconvenience. Not this guy; he was quite the opposite actually. Looking me directly in the eyes as he greeted me, Thierry offered out his hand for me to take and shake. My reflex was to look away from his gaze, but no sooner

130

had I diverted my eyes did I turn them back to his. I shook his hand briefly and turned back to dicing onions.

Within half an hour of sharing a kitchen with Thierry, I felt as if some of his confidence and joviality had transferred to me. It was impossible to stop the corners of my mouth turning up into a smile as he delivered his daft jokes in his lullaby French accent.

Thierry was thirty-two-years old, good looking, and an incredible chef. Best of all, he had a wicked sense of humour. We got along well working with one another right from the start. He was incredibly careful when he cooked and would arrange the meal components on the plates with precision; making the wait staff stand back until he had inspected every dish. Then, with a brisk nod of his head, he would allow his masterpieces to travel from the kitchen to the dining room where they would be swiftly destroyed by our ravished diners. In his food, Thierry showcased perfection and diligence. Lucy, the pot wash, had obviously fallen in love at first sight; she stood at her sink chewing on her hair and gawking. Who could blame her?

I could.

I had no time for silly girls who go all gooey around a good looking guy. Just to prove that I was not as featherbrained as Lucy, I acted a lot colder towards Thierry than I had any business being. I hated to think of his inflated ego, and did not want him to assume that I was struck as Lucy was.

Nonetheless, I had just met someone whom I liked, so my cold-shoulder resolve did not last long; before the end of that first shift we were hurling banter at each other across the room.

Incidentally, the term "cold-shoulder" came about from the days when one would entertain visitors with a banquet. Unwelcome guests would be given yesterday's meats, which would have been cold leftovers from the previous day's roast; often, a shoulder of lamb or the like. When one gives the cold-shoulder, one is displaying indifference at another person's presence. That has nothing to do with this story of course, but I thought it somewhat relevant as at The Barley, shoulder of lamb was one of our best selling meals.

For me, a person who usually dreaded having to spend time with other people, it was disorientating to actually look forward to being greeted with Thierry's wide toothy grin when I walked into the kitchen. Work was suddenly a whole lot more fun. Sometimes, our playful charade would be heard as far out as the bar, and Boris would come in and tell us to "shut the hell up". Other times, when the pub was busy, such as a Sunday lunchtime, we could go hours without speaking; dancing around one another wordlessly in the cramped and tiny kitchen, always knowing just where the other was. We worked as the perfect team, passing knives, chopping boards, hot pans and plates; seamlessly meeting the onslaught of orders. Thierry's food was a hit with the customers, I secretly adored him, and everyone seemed happy.

The French chef was able to help me access a part of my personality that for over eight years I had totally lost. He never looked at me with the concern or distance that other people did. It was as if he were blind to my exterior and when he looked at me he looked straight into *me; without judgement, assumption or projection. When I was with him, I too was able to access that person that I had once been, the one that laughed, played pranks and was popular. It were as if I hit the reset button when I was around him.

I enjoyed being the person whom I became when I was with Thierry, but there was something even more remarkable about his influence on me: he could get me to eat.

It first happened after a chaotic Saturday evening shift at The Barley, a couple of weeks after Thierry had started working there:

"Are we going out into the bar for a drink, Tabs?" he asked as he threw down the red gingham dishcloth he had been using to help Lucy dry and put away the last of the evenings crockery.

I wanted to. Of course I wanted to, but my head exploded with the usual conflicting thoughts surrounding the caloric value of alcohol. This internal bickering exhausted me within milliseconds. It was just too hard. I had to say no, if only for an easy life.

"Well, I might . . . I should get home. I have to feed Sprout."

Thierry looked confused, "You have to feed Sprout?"

"My cat."

"Yes, I know that Sprout is your cat . . . who could forget that you named the cat after a small green vegetable that smells of fart . . . I am confused as to why Sprout cannot get fed in thirty minutes time from now? After we have celebrated the victory of me surviving yet another shift with an idiot second chef such as yourself."

He garnished the insult with a theatrical twirl.

I smiled, Thierry seemed to understand that compliments made me nervous, but insults had a relaxing effect on me. He knew he was winning and continued:

"What? You want to go fester in your flat on your own?"

I said nothing just shrugged.

"You are coming out for a beer with me, right now!"

So that was somewhat decided for me. Any other person I would have scolded for bossing me about. Not Thierry. I just conceded and did what he told me. Unfortunately—or fortunately, depending on which way one chooses to look at it—the biggest test for me that evening was yet to come.

"We need something to eat first." He muttered, as he opened the fridge door and hoisted out a whopping great industrial sized tray of homemade apple crumble.

In fact, I had made that particular pudding myself, and I had been told it was delicious. I had never tasted it of course. I had made it with butter. Lots of butter. Sticks of butter, which I had rubbed into white flour and sugar to form the crisp crumble top. The apples I had peeled and cored, sliced and spiced before sautéing in even more butter. I had lined the metal baking tray with butter before I had poured my apple base and crumbly top into it. Then, just before I had carefully positioned my crumble in the oven, for the final touch, I grated some butter, and sprinkled it with brown sugar onto the very top.

I watched, wide eyed, as Thierry pulled a couple of serving bowls down from the shelf to his right. I stood, in a daze, as he used the big metal serving spoon to portion out dollops of the butter-laden, calorie-hell of an apple crumble into the fancy edged bowls. I was still staring as he placed them in the microwave to heat.

The spell broke, and I understood with a jolt that he was making *us* food, and that would mean *me* being expected to eat, with *him* in public. I was terrified. Sister Catherine and Succubus kicked off.

Leave now! Before it is too late. Make an excuse and just go.

No stay! You can do this. This will help you get better!

Leave! Make up an excuse and and leave. Think of all the butter in that pudding!

I stood, my brain a babble. Transfixed, watching the process. Thierry removed the bowls from the microwave after the ping. He placed the steaming hot puddings on the stainless steel counter between us and paused for a second.

"Aha!"

What he did next horrified and thrilled me: he dove into the fridge and emerged with a bowl of whipped cream in his hand. *Holy Shit! Cream! Not cream too! Not cream on top of all those calories and all that butter!*

Of course, we served cream or custard with every dessert. No pudding ever left the kitchen naked. I dolloped cream, custard, toffee sauce or ice-cream on top of every pudding I prepared for a customer. That was different. That was for someone else; this was for me.

I felt my whole body lurch in fear as he dolloped a generous slop of whipped white fat into each bowl. I watched it elegantly melt into the pile of hot crumble beneath it. I was rooted to the spot somewhere between a complete relieved surrender and utter despair. In the seconds that it took Thierry to gather a couple of spoons and place one in each bowl, I went through panic, anxiety and anger. By the time he had placed a julienned apple slice on the side of each bowl, I had cycled through towards a calmer, numbed acceptance of what was going to happen next.

Finished, he slid a bowl over the stainless steel counter towards me. I stood, unblinking.

He looked up at me, then down at my bowl, and nodded at it as he took a spoonful out of his own.

I stared at him. Stuck. My head was eerily silent; Succubus and Sister Catherine must have both fainted. Maybe they had murdered one another?

He frowned at me. "Eat dammit!"

And I did. Shaking hands—which I hoped Thierry did not notice—lifted the first spoonful of apples, oats, sugar, butter and cream toward my mouth.

Thierry stopped stuffing his own face for a second and watched me. I hesitated. He nodded, ever so slightly, motioning for me to continue. *Eat*, his stare told me.

Open. Close. Chew. Swallow.

"There you go!" Thierry smiled and gave me a wink, then turned his concentration back to his own bowl.

That moment in my life was indescribable. I am trying, believe me I am trying, because I am writing a book and the very nature of this work demands accurate description. It's just that there was no single emotion, and I was so struck by the absurdity of it all that I think I had a moment's out of body experience.

I was excited; I had just done something that I had never thought I would be able to do again. I had overcome something that terrified me. I had broken down all sorts of barriers. I was ecstatic about that, but I was conflicted as to what that meant. I had just lost my identity. I was left unsure about who I was, where I was and where I was going. The possibility of anything being possible was overwhelming. I had been holding myself in the safety of the behaviours that I knew because that was all that I knew, it defined me.

In that bite I had shot the bottom out of everything that I believed myself to be.

I had taken a step forward, a leap backward to the person who I used to be, and was clumsily stumbling my way over unfamiliar and yet known ground. In short: I was lost as a cow in space.

At least I was going somewhere, and with Thierry I continued to do so. It was as if he was holding me in this new space of the person that I used to be, not allowing me to think or look back. I do not believe that he had any idea that he was playing this role for me, and this is just what made it possible. Thierry never treated me as if I had any kind of problem around food, and because of this I could relax better. It was never easy, but Thierry was like a cheering squad that gave me that extra boost I needed to help me perform crazy, terrifying and unbelievable feats: such as eating.

I ate that whole bowl of crumble. Bite after bite brought a spike of adrenaline, but the strength of the shot lessened with each spoonful and by the time I was done I felt my nervous system beginning to calm.

"You could eat another one of those couldn't you?" he smiled at me. My stomach lurched as another shot of fear hit; I was at my edge. I could not eat another thing. I needed to process the life changing event that had just happened to me first.

"Well, better not, we wouldn't want you to get fat, eh?" Thierry joked as he playfully picked up his dishcloth and threw it at my head. "Come on, let's get out of here!"

Perhaps he knew that making me eat more would be pushing too far, or perhaps he was just in a rush to get a beer.

Chapter Twenty Two

Around the same time that Thierry started at the pub, I remember arriving for a Monday morning training session at the gym to find a young woman and her newborn baby waiting in the reception. She was apparently there to pick up her husband, who was working out.

"Is there anywhere we can go?" she asked quietly. It took me a couple of seconds to join the dots in order to understand what she was asking me: the baby needed feeding.

"Oh, right. Gosh . . .erm, yes, you can use the office."

Nobody really used the office, which was really nothing more than a glorified cupboard, but I showed her how she could lock the door behind herself anyway. I was very intrigued by the whole breastfeeding scenario. I wanted to know how many calories were in breast milk, and how many calories that woman had to eat a day extra in order to do it. I also wanted to know what the milk was composed of. What was the ratio of fats to protein to carbohydrate? I had all sorts of questions that were not really appropriate for me to ask, so I did some research that afternoon.

In my personal training course we had sped over the post-natal training part in about half an hour, but the one thing that had stood out to me as completely absurd was the lecturer telling us that breastmilk is very high in fat. As far as I could remember nobody had mentioned the dietary requirements of a breastfeeding women being different than that of anybody else. I knew that there must have been some good reason why breast milk was so fatty, because why would nature give babies something as damaging as fat otherwise?

We had been told by our lecturer that, as children, our bodies use all of the different types of fat: saturated, monounsaturated, and polyunsaturated, to build. He also emphasized that fat is a key component of breast milk—which is why it is so abundant—so that the child can receive a good amount of the fat soluble vitamins: A, D, E and K.

Was that true? Did new mothers have to eat more fat? Surely that was not right.

My pressing curiosity led me to conclude that I really needed to ask a mother about this: someone who had first hand experience. I picked up the phone and dialled my mum.

"Darling!" Mother answered excitedly, "how are you Sweetie?" Then without waiting for a reply, "I can't believe the phone is working . . . can you hear me?"

I sighed impatiently. Mum had just been bought her first mobile phone. My dad had given it to her for her birthday. I was actually quite impressed that she had remembered to take it out with her, and that she had worked out how to answer it.

"Mum, you don't need to shout. I can hear you fine . . . listen, quick question . . . what did you eat when you were pregnant with me?"

"What? Why on earth do you want to know that Darling?

"Oh, I'm just doing some research into pregnancy for my nutrition course Mum, that's all." I lied, because in all honesty I had absolutely no good reason to want to know what my mother's diet had been like when she was breastfeeding. I was just curious, and that was weird.

"Well, let me see . . . we used to eat a lot of cheese, still do. You used to love cheese Tabby, do you remember?"

I shuddered. Yes, I remembered.

"Oh, and real butter! We ate a lot of butter back then, there was none of this horrid margarine stuff that your father insists on buying. Did I tell you that I had to tell him off last week? I caught him spreading about an inch of that bloody St Ivel Gold stuff on his toast one morning. I told him . . . I said . . . 'Michael, you are going to give yourself a heart attack,' then I made him scrape some of it off."

"That's good Mum, you should not let Dad eat all that fat. He'll have high cholesterol . . . what else?"

"What else? Well he was having tea and that strawberry jam that he loves . . . "

"No Mum, not what else did Dad eat, I mean what else were you eating when I was a newborn baby?"

"Hmm lemme think . . . We had just moved out of London and into the village, it was a real change of pace for both of us. There was no fast food like there had been in London. I have always loved to home cook and bake Tabby, you know that. I always used proper butter, we loved to eat cheese, still do, I've never been a big fan of ready made meals or pizza . . ." She trailed off.

My parents, who had both spent their childhood and early adult lives in London, decided to pack up and move to the countryside when they learnt that they were pregnant with me. They did this in the belief that it was a healthier environment to bring children up in. Although they were probably thinking in terms of fresh air and less cars, they inadvertently avoided the trans-fat generation that was beginning to emerge in cities and towns. What happened around that time was the amount of baked goods, snacks and fast foods that were available to be consumed had increased. If my mother had continued to live in the city, it was highly likely that her diet would have been filled with pizzas, Pot Noodles, Chicken Drummers, blended oil, mayonnaise, corn oil, Viennetta ice cream, Angel Delight and margarine. Despite being sickened at the very thought of saturated fats, I was happy that my mother was eating real butter and lard, rather than margarine, because at least these are fats that my brain could grow from.

About a year after I was born, St. Ivel Gold—a particularly prolifically marketed margarine spread—arrived on the shelves of Tesco and other supermarkets in the United Kingdom. Gold touted itself as a "butter" that could be spread straight from the fridge. To many, this seemed too good to be true, as butter kept cold and fresh in the fridge tends to be a nightmare to spread on bread; I'll go as far as saying that clumpy butter which rips off

137

the top layer of bread when ones tries to spread it is one of the biggest first world problems to affect the modern human being. So good on Gold for tackling this substantial issue head on.

Gold apparently answered the prayers of consumers everywhere. My Mother had never liked it, but my Father loved to slop the golden gloop thickly onto his morning toast with an inch or so of jam to follow. St. Ivel Gold was recommended by health experts as the seraphic alternative to butter because it was lower in fat, so my father took that as an excuse to use even more of it!

Prior to margarine's marketing debut, my parents had always eaten butter, and even when marg was considered to be all the rage, mother preferred the taste of butter still; this is mostly what she gave to us in our sandwiches, leaving the margarine for my father to eat on his morning toast.

And eat it he did. When it came to putting anything on toast, be it butter or St. Ivel Gold, my father did not mess around. In my early twenties, his fat consumption—and even the memories that I had surrounding it—haunted me. I remembered often the time, one morning, when I came downstairs for breakfast to find my father eating a slice of toast with what looked to be an inch of cheese on top. I must have been fourteen, so this was before I ceased to eat such things, and what he was munching on looked delicious; when he got up to pour himself a cup of tea I flew in and stole a large bite.

Turns out that It wasn't *cheese* my father had been eating on his toast: it had been butter. Butter spread an inch thick.

"DAD!" I'd squawked after rinsing my mouth out with tea. "Mum will go bonkers if she knows that you are eating that much butter on your toast, I thought it was cheese for God's sake!"

"Shush," my father warned me, worried that my fuss would alert my mother to his butter-piling antics. He knew I was right: if she caught him eating an inch of butter on toast he would be in trouble. Mother was concerned about my father's heart and blood pressure, and everybody knew that butter and fat were responsible for heart disease, *right?*

The coast being clear, he sat down at the table, pulled up his morning paper and using it as a fashion of a barricade, hid his tea, his toast, the butter dish, and himself behind it.

I cannot help but smile at the memory even now. Over twenty years have passed since then, and my Father seems no worse for his butter-eating ways. Neither did I come to think of it, because as a baby I had been a huge fan of butter.

One more childhood story? Can you stand it? Last one, I promise:

This is a story that I absolutely adore now, but it haunted me to the point of bad dreams when I was suffering from anorexia. What was even worse for me then, was that my parents have an old polaroid photo of the incident.

The picture is of me, age one, sitting on the kitchen floor next to the refrigerator.

My mother has told me the story many times, about the day she noticed that she had neither seen nor heard me for a couple of minutes. Investigating the house, she found me in the kitchen where I had pulled open the fridge door and was sat on the floor eating butter straight out of the tub. Butter, glorious, golden butter smeared over my face, my hands, and of course my neat little Oshkosh dungarees. Incidentally, the St Ivel Gold low-fat margarine which had sat next to it in the fridge remained untouched.

I must have eaten half a bar of butter that day. Like I said, when I was suffering from anorexia, the memory of this was almost too much to take. Looking at the photo sparked off all sorts of guilty thoughts:

How many calories is that?

One hundred grams of butter equals seven hundred and seventeen calories.

You probably ate closer to one hundred and fifty grams that day by the way, so more like a thousand calories plus!

That is so disgusting!

How could I have eaten that?

Well I had, because despite the hate of fat that governed my life in my twenties, I had loved butter as a baby. Loved it to that point that, once I was mobile—a crawler—my parents had their work cut out to keep my fingers out of the butter dish. As a child, I never thought twice about the calorific value of the food that I was eating. I never judged fat as bad, I just loved it.

When one is a baby, one's small body is limited in the amount of fat that it can store itself. Because of being so physically tiny, babies need their mother to keep eating fat in her diet so that they can receive the benefits though her milk. Rather like blood-sucking ticks if you think about it.

Even after delving this far into the world of breastfeeding, I still had unanswered questions. I was interested to understand why and how breast milk was enough to feed a newborn baby. *How could one single, natural product be enough? Enough to build bones and tissue and brain cells*?

I decided that I would have to get a book out of the library on this. So I did.

Apparently, immediately after giving birth, a mother feeds her baby something called colostrum; the word *colostrum* is from the 1570s and refers to the *"first milk of an animal"*. Colostrum is commonly referred to as foremilk, and is a thin and yellowy looking fluid that is rich in protein and antibodies. Yukky as that may sound, this stuff provides a baby with a passive immunity as its own immune system is not fully developed yet. That is a pretty nifty design idea from good old Mother Nature don't you think?

In time, the milk the mother produces changes to become mature milk, otherwise known as hindmilk. This is a gradual transition into a thicker and creamier variation of colostrum. What is happening here is that the fat content of the milk is changing to suit the baby's needs as he or she is growing.

This struck me as rather incredible at the time that I read it, and it still does now. Breasts are like the most effective and efficient fast-food service in the world! A drive-thru that already knows what one wants and has it all ready, optimally geared towards what one's body needs that day. Not that I ever went to drive-thrus in those days, but I still considered that if I were to want fast-food, it would be pretty impressive if the cashiers were as smart as boobs.

The next thing that I read was a 1985 paper published in the *American Journal of Diseases in Children*, concluding that, in comparison to milk from other mammals such as horses, cows and elephants, human breast milk is relatively low in protein. Apparently, this is because human babies are designed to grow and mature much more slowly than the offspring of other mammals. The researchers offered that humans need to grow slowly so that our massive brains can develop gradually. We also need to stay small enough for our mothers to be able to hold us in their arms for a good couple of years, that way we learn from them how to communicate with other humans.

As I read this, I reflected on the horses that I had seen being born at the stables. Horses and other animals don't need to cuddle as much as humans, nor do they need to save as much energy as we do so that their brains can develop. If they did, I guessed that I would have been sitting next to a horse in my lectures at university, and that would be absurd.

Horses are smart, but not as smart as people. When I was twelve, I began working as a stable girl at a horse stud in Wiltshire, England. I remember that first spring when I had the pleasure of watching newborn foals play in the buttercup scattered pastures. Those babies were born big and able; their knobbly knees would hold them upright within an hour of hitting the turf. A nudge from the mare's muzzle would encourage her foal to his feet, his soft coat still glistening and his ears still wet. Horses and other prey animals need to move practically as soon as they are born so that they do not become someone else's dinner. If they don't move soon after breaking out of the afterbirth, chances are high that they will get eaten. Prey animals do not have the luxury that we humans have of just being able to take our time and lie cradled in our mother's arms for a year while our brains are busy getting themselves setup for superior intelligence. Human babies are allowed a lazy start; horses have to run first and think later.

Despite the relatively low protein makeup of human milk, it is high in an amino acid called taurine. The word *taurine* comes from the same origin as *taurus*, which refers to the bull, and this is because taurocholic acid was first discovered in ox bile somewhere in the middle of the eighteenth century. According to a scientist called Hernández-Benítez, taurine positively increases the number of neural stem cells that a baby has, so it is important in the development of the human brain. Taurine is also essential to vision, it is the most abundant amino acid in the retina, and other parts of the eye structure; it is one of those special amino acids that our bodies cannot make up out of other sources so we need to ingest it.

I have to admit, I find all of this information fascinating; I found it captivating then, and I still do now. The difference between then and now is, that my motivation for wanting to understand these types of things has changed a great deal. Then, was interested about how and why breast milk contained so much fat, because my belief was that fat was always a bad thing. Nowadays, I simply enjoy learning and re-learning about the genius of the human body and its design; there is nothing more to it than pure awe.

Calories from fat are responsible for over half of the total calories in breast milk, plus, babies need cholesterol too. They actually need cholesterol! Can you imagine that!? Cholesterol, as hated, slandered and ostracized as it is, is actually important!

Apparently, cholesterol is essential to life; especially to new life. This presents a problem for babies who have mothers who believe that cholesterol is a bad thing and are overly vigilant on the low-cholesterol diet for their children. If a baby does not have enough exposure to cholesterol when it is building systems, it stands to reason that, when that child reaches adulthood, there will be processing problems. Then, what would I know?

I do know that if I had fallen pregnant when I had an eating disorder, there was no way I would have eaten fat or cholesterol. In fact, I bet I would have used that little bun in the oven as an excuse to eat even more orthorexically. Luckily for my unborn children, when I had anorexia, all I could think about was anorexia, so men, sex and sprogs were not on the putting green. Eating disorders are selfish like that; they do not like to share their host's attention.

Getting back to mothers and breasts; there was more:

I read that a new mother should not try and lose her baby weight too soon. This confounded me as a personal trainer! Why had we not been told this on our training course? In fact, we had been led to believe the opposite, and told that new mothers were prime pickings. "Women who have just given birth are golddust," our lead trainer told us, "if you cannot convince a new mum to train with you, you are not worth your salt as a trainer!"

According to the paper that I was then reading titled *Polyunsaturated fatty acids in human milk: an essential role in infant development*, on the contrary, new mothers should be coupled with an exercise program that slowly, patiently, returned them to their pre-baby size; preferably *after* they had finished breastfeeding. The reason for this was because the baby needs a certain amount of fat from the milk it receives, and therefore, Mummy needs to eat some, and she also needs to have some on her body. In particular, the levels of omega-three and omega-six polyunsaturated fatty acids that are delivered to baby via breast milk are very dependent on the amount of fat that the mother eats.

I remember feeling as if I had been led somewhat astray by the course I had taken.

I considered that personal training was something of a sales scam. The trainers had been so focused on teaching us how to build a client base that we had never covered such things as when it is not relevant for a person to want to lose weight. It seemed that there was a lot more to fat than I had imagined, and that it did have a role in life; this, above all, was a prickly pill.

Chapter Twenty Three

After a successful Sunday lunch shift in the second week that Thierry had been working with me at The Barley, he swung out the back door with a wave of his hand and his wide Cheshire Cat grin. I wondered as always did, where he went to after work. I knew that he still had a gig somewhere in a nearby town because I had quizzed him about it a couple of days before. He had shrugged and told me that he also worked in a pub called The Ship.

I was fascinated by Thierry. I just wanted him to be my friend. I would daydream about us simply hanging out together and doing normal stuff like watching a film on a Sunday afternoon. I thought it strange that I would feel this way about a person that I had only known a week, but it was not surprising that I would desire this platonic type of relationship with a guy, rather than looking for a girl to be friends with. Truth is that I always got on better with guys than girls. Girls can be silly when it comes to serious things like parallel parking, yet serious about silly things like brushed hair and perfume. Boys are easier to get along with because they are more straightforward in their communication and don't worry as much about their fingernails.

The weirdest, and most welcome difference in my life that week after I met Thierry was something that I had never dreamed could possibly happen to me: for the first time in almost ten years, I was thinking about something, or someone, other than food!

I was also doing things differently, such as cutting my morning walk a bit shorter so I would be at work early in the hope that I would catch Thierry as he was having his pre-shift fag outside the back door of the kitchen. *Fag* is a British slang term for cigarette; it is also a derogatory name for a homosexual man; a phrase used to describe a young public school boy; and a term to describe a bothersome task. For reference, whenever I use the word *fag* I am referring to cigarettes. Thierry was a smoker, and each morning before work he would stand outside in the fresh air and take advantage of nicotine, not young boys.

Every chef that I had ever worked with smoked. At The Barley, I was the only person who didn't take a fag break every half hour. Back then, it was still legal to smoke inside the pub, so everybody did it and the bar stank as a result. I hated the stale smell of cigarette smoke, and resented the way it hung on my clothes and in my scraggly blonde hair, so I avoided the bar if possible. Not that the kitchen left me smelling much better; I stank like a deep fat fryer.

I would leave The Barley feeling grubby inside and out. My hands were either covered in food or the chemical soap that sat next to the sink. Clumsy and impatient, I was forever nicking my fingers with the paring knives, or the cheese grater. There were burns on my hands and up my arms from holding hot plates or getting things in and out of the oven in a hurry. I would wash my body after work in the evening only to get up and walk back into the grease pit the next day. My flat reeked of stale fried food as my discarded chef whites sat in the washing basket. The one thing that helped me feel fresh was my walk in the morning. Outside—usually in the rain—I could breathe. I might have been cold and damp, but at least I was not being suffocated with grease.

In the couple of weeks since Thierry had started at the pub, I had began to hurry my morning walk because I wanted to get to the kitchen earlier; I wanted to see him.

Why did I want to see him? Why did I value his friendship so? I did not understand it, but I knew that Thierry, despite his excessive smoking, swearing and lude jokes, was good for my health.

That Sunday evening, I arrived to work early and was disappointed not to see the tell-tale trail of smoke wafting above the kitchen roof as I pulled into the car park. Usually, Thierry arrived before me and stood by the back door smoking. It was unlike him to be later than me to work.

Looking around the car park, I noted that his muddy black Saab was nowhere to be seen. Deflated and annoyed I went on in and started the preparations for shift: chopping carrots; parboiling potatoes ready for roasting; washing lettuce ready for the salads that accompanied the sandwiches and cheese ploughmans; and warming gravy for the meat pies and sausages.

Half hour late then turned into an hour. When the kitchen opened for service and Thierry was still absent, I knew I would not see him in The Barley again. I felt as if I had been kicked in the stomach.

Boris bumped me up to the slot of head chef that day. I should have been thrilled, even little Lucy came up and gave me a hug of congratulations, but I wasn't. I was sad and angry at Thierry for coming into my life and leaving me, for giving me a taste of what it was to have a friend, a taste of what it was to be me, and then going. I wanted to leave it at that, lesson learnt and carry on, but I could not.

The next day I found the phone number of The Ship; the other pub where I thought Thierry had said that he worked. I called it. When the squeaky-voiced Liverpudlian front-of-house girl answered, I asked if a French chef called Thierry worked there. My heart was beating hard as I waited for her reply. I felt like some crazy stalker.

She told me he did, that he was working in the kitchen at that very moment, but that they were so busy she could not disturb him. I left my number and told her to have him call me back. I waited. I cleaned my flat. I went for a walk. I checked that my phone had reception. I cleaned my flat a little more. He did not call back that day, but the phone rang just as I was headed out on my morning walk the day after. I was pulling on my shoes at the time and I tripped into the kitchen with a trainer half on in my hurry to grapple for my mobile phone.

"Hello Darling!"

It was my mother.

"Mum," I could not hide the disappointment in my voice. "What is it? I was just on my way out." Or the irritation.

"Morning Darling!" My mother seemed oblivious to my curt tone, or perhaps she was just desensitised to it. "I was wondering if you wanted me to bring you some of this wonderfully delicious homemade beef stew that I made yesterday, it would do you some good Darling."

I let out an exaggerated sigh. Why did she insist on trying to bring me the disgusting fat-ridden slop that she and Dad adored so much? Why could she not just accept that I was never going to eat that type of food?

"You used to love my stews, remember?" It was as if she had read my mind. Her tone was searching and aspirant; I felt sad for her. She was always so hopeful that I would eat like I did when I was a teenager again one day. I felt a lot of love for her in that moment; Mum never gave up on me.

"You know Mum . . ." I spoke gently this time, "there is beef stew at The Barley, and chicken stew, and fish pie, and shepherd's pie . . . if I wanted to eat beef stew, I could eat it every day at work."

"But you don't eat it at work though do you sweetie, and you are still so thin. I just thought that perhaps having something homemade for you might be nice and tempting for your appetite Honey . . ." She trailed off.

I would have laughed had that not have seemed like a mean thing to do to her. Appetite? The last thing that I needed was my *appetite* being tempted. My appetite was not the problem, feeling hungry was not the problem. Eating was the problem. How could I make her understand that asking me to eat, especially to eat such fatty food, was like asking me to drink cyanide?

I couldn't; there was no explanation.

"Mum I have to go . . . I'll be late to work." I hung up the phone.

After a couple of days, I stopped hoping Thierry would call me. Then on a Tuesday afternoon I picked up my shrilling phone thinking it was my mother. This was back in the olden days, before caller identification was an option on mobile phones. Anyway, my mother was the only person who ever phoned me.

"Hello?" I winced at the irritated tone of voice as I answered.

"Tabs, you moody old cow, lighten up would you dammit!" It was Thierry.

"You working tonight?" He asked. I wasn't.

Later that evening, Thierry turned up at my flat with, to my horror, a Tesco's Bakery box containing a dozen donuts. Atrocious eating habits are a pretty common theme among chefs.

Imagine my conflict: I am thrilled to see Thierry, but the opportunity cost of having him over is deep-fried sugar-coated hell. Had it been my mother on the doorstep offering a box of donuts I could have easily told her no, but this was much much harder. I could feel rhythmic shots of adrenaline coaxing my body towards panic.

Keep it together, you don't have to eat them, you have to stay calm and focused.

Impatient at being kept on the doorstep while I gawped like a blithering idiot, Thierry pushed past me and made his way into my small kitchen.

"Nice place Tabs!" He mused, then turned to me, "Donut?"

I had tried to protest. I had opened my mouth with the intention of telling him that I had already eaten and that I was not hungry, or that I already had my dinner salad planned, or that I was allergic to donuts and eating one would certainly cause me to spontaneously combust . . .

"But . . ."

"Tabs, shut the hell up and eat you skinny fool."

I ate. Just like that. I ate a whole donut in the company of another person. To this day, I do not really know how I had been able to do that. It were as if something had reached a point of surrender. Eating the thing was not exactly pleasurable, but the adrenaline disappeared to be replaced with a numbness that brought a sense of calm.

I ate one donut; Thierry ate five. When I was done, he had hounded me about eating another one. I declined firmly; one had been enough. I was both proud of and disgusted with myself. I also felt rather faint and unstable; I sometimes experience lucidity after a large amount of adrenaline has been pushed through my system, so was used to that lightheaded blurriness, but it made me wonder if I had actually eaten that donut at all, or if I had dreamt it.

As we sat in my living room watching Fawlty Towers videos, my system began to recover and I knew it had happened. I had eaten a donut during the day, which meant I had eaten something bad for me during Sister Catherine's rule.

Why had I done that? How had I done that?

I felt a creeping guilt towards my Mother. She would have given anything to see me eat something that she had brought round. What made it worse was that I knew anything she would have brought over would have been home made with good quality ingredients and a lot of love. Yet here I was with Thierry eating utter crap from the Tesco's bakery.

We fell asleep in front of the telly, then around midnight, I woke up to find Thierry's foot in my ear. He was snoring loudly. On the table in front of me, glaring and gloating, was the box of donuts. It had been a box of twelve, and I had eaten one, then Thierry had eaten five, so, six gone meant there were six left. I couldn't take my eyes off them.

A grunt from Thierry's direction snapped me out of my daze, he was waking up.

"What time is it?" He asked groggily.

"Midnight."

"I'm outta here . . . work in the morning."

I watched his car pull away, then returned to the living room where the dreaded box of remaining donuts was holding court. I picked it up, intending to take it straight outside to the big trash bin that the block of flats shared; I wanted it out of my house.

Just one more bite?

Succubus was awake. Of course she was, it was night: her time.

I picked a donut out of the box with my thumb and index finger, carefully and cautiously, as If I were handling something particularly dangerous. I held it at arm's length for a while and talked myself in and out of tasting it.

Just one bite, you owe it to yourself, you deserve it.

Fat, laden with fat, you should never have eaten that one before, throw the box away.

Succubus won the fight easily. I took a bite.

One bite turned into two. I ate one donut, and then another, and then a third. As I took a bite out of the forth, I stood up and made my way—donut in mouth—out to the bin in the car park. I had to throw these out before I ate the last two. I had to. I pulled the fourth donut out of my mouth as I tipped the box with the remaining two still in it into the bin. I tried to throw the half-eaten fourth donut in where the box containing the remaining was now mingling with empty cartons of milk and boxes of egg shells.

Just one more bite, don't throw it away, one more bite.

I ate what remained of donut number four.

Next I was reaching into the trash bin, holding my nose against the stench of rotting vegetables and leftover meals, leaning over the edge so that I could get my hand around that nasty donut box. I pulled it out from where it was mingling with half-eaten apples and blackened banana skins. Having successfully seized now slightly soggy box, I opened it up and crammed the final two donuts into my mouth. When the donuts were gone, I desperately ran my fingers around the inner edges of the empty carton in search for any stray crumbs and sugar that I might have missed. I sucked at my hands and fingernails until there was no trace of donut or sugar left; until I was sure that I had eaten it all.

Then I cried.

A couple of days later, Thierry pulled up at my house at eight in the morning and informed me that we were going out for coffee. I protested lightly, knowing that it would do no good, then went with him feeling guilty because I was not on my usual morning walk. I noticed that it was not as hard as it might have been previously to opt out of my usual routine, maybe Sister Catherine was becoming more accustomed to being disobeyed?

We wound up down the road in a small local café that was very close to my flat, but that—to Thierry's surprise and rather obvious distaste—I had never been in. Of course I had never been in it; I did not like to consume anything in public, why on earth would I ever go to a bloody café other than to work?

There was nobody else in there as we sat ourselves down at a small round table next to the window, so the waitress came up to take out order almost immediately. I had not yet had a chance to see the coffee menu. I felt jumpy and on edge. *Why am I doing this? What is the point? Why is Thierry able to make me do things that I do not like to do?*

"What can I get you two?" The waitress looked bored, she was chewing gum, but her breath still smelt of cigarettes.

Get me? All I wanted to be got right then was outside, on my walk like I should have been. The thought of sitting down and drinking coffee instead was pushing me towards panic. I needed to tell Thierry that I could not do this, that I had to go or something, I needed to make up an excuse to get out of there.

"Two café au lait please Darling" Thierry ordered with a smile and an exaggerated French accent.

"Wat?" Our waitress looked less than impressed.

"Café au lait? Latté? Coffee with frothy milk?"

"Right, two la'ees"

I snapped back to reality when I understood that one of those was for me.

Latté, that means milk! Full cream milk.

"I will just have mine black please." I corrected him.

"Tabs . . . shut up," Thierry said to me, then he turned to the waitress, "She will have a latté, with a couple of sugars, and use the whole milk, not that low fat crap please."

When the Barista brought the latté over to our table. She also placed a plastic bag over my head and tied some string around my neck. Well, at least that is what it felt like. But Thierry just kept on talking to me as if nothing was wrong. Blabbering on about the new car he wanted to get; about the idiot that owned The Ship where he cooked; about this fantastic steak pie he had made. His lullaby voice was like an air hole for me, it stopped me suffocating. Sip after sip, I conquered that latté.

The French chef has no idea how he affected my recovery. Thierry walked into my life just when I needed him the most. Had it been a couple of months earlier, I would never have been in a space ready to accept him. In him I found some ethereal form of authority that I could listen to. When I was with him, my habitual behaviour was put in contention. He was my catalyst.

Despite having Thierry's unwarranted help in those first stages of my recovery, it was not all smooth sailing and good news. Sister Catherine still berated me for eating the fatty foods that he insisted that I eat, and she would sink her sharp little claws into me when I was alone. When I returned to my flat that day and got ready for work, I felt regret for drinking that latté instead of going on my walk.

How could I had been so stupid and so easily tempted?

I felt disgusting, like my skin was crawling at the thought of the fatty milk inside of my body. I would have given anything to get it out of me. I could imagine the fat molecules being absorbed into my bloodstream. I had to battle incredibly hard not to pull on my trainers and go out for a run. Running had been my shield against the barrage of thoughts that would come at me, so after that latté I craved it more than ever.

Crouching on the ground, I put my head between my knees. I just wanted it to stop, I could not think clearly with all the noise that was in my head. Thought after thought hit me like shots out the barrel of a gun, each one that touched left a splash of emotion: hate, fear, disgust, shame, guilt.

I was defenceless against the onslaught of abuse delivered by my own thoughts; how can one negotiate with a force that one cannot see? How could I protect myself from thoughts in my own head?

This abuse became a regular hangover from spending time with Thierry. We would go out, he would order us lattés, or beer, or hot chocolate, sometimes with a side order: a croissant, some coffee cake, flapjacks, or a slice of cheesecake. I would eat, then, when I was alone, the abuse, generated in my own head, would slap the shit out of me.

One Friday afternoon Thierry had come over with a couple of pieces of strawberry cheesecake that he had made himself. He rarely created desserts, as he preferred to concentrate on the savoury components of meals, so he was particularly proud of himself, and insisted that I eat this enormous slice of pudding.

I had, and it had been delicious; a delightfully light, melt-in-the-mouth creamy texture with a hint of strawberry sweetness. The base, made of a mixture of McVities HobNobs and Digestives was just right: crunchy, crumbly and buttery. It would hold its place when bitten into, but then disintegrate into a sand-like softness on the tongue. Thierry's cheesecake was quite perfect.

"Hmm, yes, it's good."

"Come on Tabs, admit it, it's better than good! That is a *fabulous* cheesecake!"

"Maybe.*" I winked at him.

When the cheesecake had been eaten, we had spent some time sitting on my miserable excuse of a balcony in the spitting rain. Looking out over the bleak industrial estate opposite my flat, as we chatted about the goings on in our kitchens. Thierry liked to hear the latest gossip from The Barley and wanted an up-to-date account of which waitress was dating who, and what Boris's latest idiocracy had been.

Usually our talks would turn to food, and discussing recipes. That afternoon, we had been having a heated discussion on the various ways to make mashed potato. Thierry preferred to blend a couple of eggs into his along with butter, salt and pepper. He also liked to serve mash that had been whipped to a consistency that could be piped onto the top of a beef and ale stew, rather than the thicker, chunkier style that I liked to dollop onto the side of the plate. I never used eggs in my mash, but instead added butter and cream and seasoned with salt and pepper. Mash was just another example of how I would use ingredients that I would never contemplate eating myself in my cooking for others. Apparently, this had not escaped Thierry's attention.

"It always surprises me the amount of butter and cream that you put into the food that you make when you are so scared of eating anything with fat in it yourself."

There it was. That was the first time that Thierry had spoken to any observance that he might have made regarding the way that I ate. I was mortified. In that instance, Thierry had joined the rest of the people in my life who reminded me that I was weird, that I was too thin, and that I was different.

I also felt angry. Had I not eaten everything that he had ever asked me to? Had I not just sat and eaten a whole bloody slice of cheesecake in front of him? How dare he question me when I *had* been eating fat in his presence. I felt that prickly angry heat percolate behind my ears. Thierry must have noticed my shift in posture because he playfully smacked me on the hip and told me to lighten up.

"I just mean I can tell that you don't actually like to eat the food that you make, that's all." He backpedaled.

"Yes I do!" I sharply defended myself despite knowing that my retort was a lie.

"I just tend not to eat in the kitchen at work too much because I think it's unprofessional," I felt smug about that answer; being able to throw in some moral high ground.

"Come off it Tabs. Look around your kitchen. Look in your fridge. There is nothing to be seen other than Special-K cereal and skimmed milk!" He exclaimed waving his hands in the air.

I looked down at my fingers and picked at the rough edge of one of my nails. Thierry was not oblivious to my strange eating habits and I had been so naive to think that he might be. I felt embarrassed and exposed, but mostly, I felt sad; as if I had just lost something.

"Look, I'm not trying to get at you," he softened his voice and playfully prodded me in the ribs. I squirmed and could not help but crack a smile. "But, you need some fat in your life girl, and not only when I am here to make you eat it."

I looked up at him, somewhat awkwardly. This was the first time that Thierry and I had ever had any sort of serious or personal conversation. I realized that I knew very little about him other than he had come over to live in England from France about five years ago. I did not know why, nor did I know anything of his family or his life before we had met just a couple of months earlier. It dawned on me how short a space of time I had known this guy, and how large the impact that he had had on me was. I wished that we had never strayed off the safe ground of talking about work and cooking. Now we were talking about food and eating, and within that was so much more than I was willing to give. A boundary had been stepped over.

With companionship comes vulnerability, and that was something I was still not ready for.

"Whatever Thierry" I brushed him off with an intentionally detectable cold current in my voice. I removed my gaze from his face and and returned my focus to the industrial park. The conversation was over; any door that had been nudged open had slammed shut and firmly bolted itself.

We sat in silence for a second. After a while, I felt guilty for snapping at him, and I racked my brains to find something, anything, to change the subject with.

"You know," I hedged, "that really was a bloody smashing piece of cheesecake."

"It was too sweet actually . . . that's why I wasted a piece on you . . . not good enough for paying customers," he winked at me.

"Yeah, you're right . . . it tasted like shit." I agreed. I earnt myself a sharp dig in the ribs for that retort, but I had also successfully masked the uncomfortableness of the preceding conversation; sore ribs were more than worth the effort.

Chapter Twenty Four

After Thierry left that afternoon I was a mess of emotion. Desperate to divert my attention away from the call of my running shoes, I took myself over to the local library and started looking back into scientific studies that had been done addressing the role of dietary fat. That day, the name Ancel Keys came into my research for the first time. Ironically, what that bloke did for the world of fat rendered him a hero in my eyes then. Nowadays, I see Mr. Keys as more of a well-meaning but misguided contributor to one of the largest scientific mistakes that the world of diet and nutrition ever made.

Nevertheless, back then, I was thrilled to have found such a champion to read about; here was a chap who seemed to feel like I did about fat and see it for the dietary villain that it was. The main difference between the American scientist and I was that Ancel Keys had what was thought to be a scientifically-backed reason to avoid fat, whereas I, until that day, had a hate and fear of it based on no good reason at all.

I learnt about the *Seven Countries Study*, which had began in 1952 and was established with the intention to explore the epidemiology, or presence of, coronary heart disease. In fact, Mr Keys had been a player in the field of researching heart disease since the 1940's, when, as a University of Minnesota researcher, he had postulated that the surge in heart attacks in middle aged American men was through their own fault: a lifestyle choice problem. I can still remember the rush of adrenaline that I felt when I first read the conclusion that Mr. Keys had come to.

The *Seven Countries Study* was the first ever multicultural comparison of heart attack risk in populations of men coming from differing backgrounds and therefore differing attitudes to health and fitness. You can probably imagine how reading about how Ancel Keys came to his conclusion that fat was to blame for heart disease put a real spanner in my so-called recovery from my yet-to-be-admitted-to eating disorder. It was not really as if I needed anything more to work against me; my own mind was doing a good enough job at keeping me in the cognitive hell that Anorexia is. But nutrition study, and reading about the benefits of a low-fat diet, certainly played a large role in stalling my progress and confusing me even more.

Cholesterol was also in Ancel's firing line right from the beginning, strung up right next to fat ready to be proven worthy of damnation. In the *Seven Countries Study*, Ancel and company assessed the levels of cholesterol and fat in the diets of two separate groups of men: the workers, and the wealthy. It appeared that the wealthy people ate higher fat diets, and this is where Ancel got his first hypothesis. He theorised that serum cholesterol was related to fat intake—saturated fatty acids in particular. When the team of scientists compared that data across countries, they concluded that countries with a low prevalence of coronary heart disease were characterised by low blood cholesterol values.

What happened next is that Ancel Keys presented this hypothesis about fat and heart health to the World Health Organisation. It seemed evident that the wealthy of the world were dying of heart disease at a greater rate than the lower classes, and that this must be because wealthy could afford to eat a diet higher in fat. Ancel's hypothesis made perfect sense to me, but then of course it would. I would have readily jumped on board any bandwagon that set out to put fat in a lynch. In fact, they could have put me in charge of kicking the stool out.

By 1961, the American Heart Association adopted the recommendations made by my new hero Ancel Keys. Saturated fats were beginning to get the bad guy label and polyunsaturated fats were seen as *good* or *better*. That same year, a four page report came out that concluded:

"The best scientific evidence of the time strongly suggests that Americans would reduce their risk of coronary heart disease by reducing the fat in their diets and replacing saturated fats with polyunsaturated fats . . ."

Hallelujah! I thought then.

Crap, I don't have a chance! I think now.

The information that the *Seven Countries Study* gave me was like ammunition. I felt justified and validated. I had been right all along and there was nothing wrong with me. Reading studies that reinforced my position gave me a buzz, and researching became somewhat of a pleasure activity as well as another sidelining obsession. I became absorbed in reading about the long-standing problem that fat had been in the human diet. It stroked my ego to know that I had guessed right all along: fat really was the demon I had believed it to be. I had unraveled the mystery, and I had done it all by myself.

My work at the gym was steadily picking up and I was busier than ever, which made it easier to have an excuse not to see Thierry. I was gradually taking less shifts at The Barley and more at the gym; at least my career seemed to be headed in the direction that I wanted. I handed in my month's notice at the pub in late May. I was going to be a full time personal trainer.

One morning, after Thierry and I had eaten a rich and gooey chocolate fudge cake the night before, I got up and went to a cycling class at the gym.

I justified going because I had eaten enough the day before to warrant it. I told myself that it was just a harmless exercise class and a one off. Even then, I think that I knew that walking into a cardio class meant a lot more than that. It meant I was losing.

My body felt trashed after that class, but my mind was basking in it; I felt warm, happy and loved. Regardless of the promises that I had made myself about that class being a one off, the next morning I got up and went to a cycle class again. I was sure that I could control it this time; I promised myself that I would be able to exercise in moderation.

Soon enough, I was taking spin classes every day, and I felt guilty about it. Needing an excuse for my presence in biking classes, I enrolled in a certification course to teach indoor cycling. Now I had a valid reason to be in those classes as I was furthering my education as an instructor. Getting qualified had meant that I was on a stationary bike and being paid to teach the very activity that had for a long time been one of my addictive behaviours. Brilliant.

Over the weeks that followed, Thierry frequently called me up and asked if I wanted to hang out. More often than not, "hanging out" would involve eating a type of food that lay acres beyond my comfort zone. I had gone from being in a terminal low to a rollercoaster of food related emotion. I was either up high, eating something terrifying with Thierry, or sitting on the cold floor of the burrow that followed on my own. I ricocheted from one extreme to another, in a different form of binge and purge cycle. When I was alone I would eat salads or low-fat foods and feel miserable. When I was with Thierry it was a whirlwind of fun and fat. I was a mess.

After a couple of weeks of this fluctuation, I decided that Thierry was a bad influence on me, and that I should probably stop hanging around with him.

Why am I planning to push away the one person that I want to spend time with?

Thierry was the only person that could help me access the version of myself that I liked. I would have to choose one or the other: the fat-eating, fun-loving, happy me, or the fat-fearing, solitary, irritable bitch. My heart was leaning in one direction but my head was strongly rooted deep in the other: fat does a person no good.

I considered my career; I felt like a hypocrite telling my clients not to eat fatty foods and then doing it myself when I was with Thierry. I had to be smarter when choosing friends.

Despite a substantial amount of thought telling me that I was doing the right thing, a part of me knew that I was slipping backward, and that I had pushed away the only person that would have been able to pull me out of this spiral I was in. I had been thrown a rope, but the reality was I had not been ready to take it.

Despite my uptake of exercise classes, I had been able to put on a bit of weight. I wish that I could tell you this gain had been due to eating good healthy meals in the day; it was not. No, the reason that I had put on a couple of pounds was because my night binges were getting progressively bigger. I would wake up each morning and feel so disgusting and dirty. *Dirty fat calories on my body.* I was not opposed to the gain in weight, but thinking about the foods it had come from made me feel sinful, used and unclean.

On the plus side, regardless of how I had achieved it: I had gained weight; I was looking better, and I knew it.

Chapter Twenty Five

"All you ever eat is salad!" I looked up from my plate. Annie, the landlady of the pub, was scowling at me. Not the reaction that I had been anticipating.

It was the seventh of June, 2007, and this was the very first day that I had come and brought my lunch from the kitchen to eat it in the bar. *In the bar*, where there were *other people* sitting and finishing off their afternoon pints. This marked a huge achievement. I was practicing eating in public, and I was proud of myself; or at least I had been until that moment.

I could not expect Annie to understand that I had almost turned back three times at the door of the kitchen. I could not expect her to know how I had felt sick, and nervous, and sweaty, as on my fourth attempt, I finally walked out into the public space clutching my lunch. I could not expect her to appreciate that today I had *almost* been brave enough to put some dressing on the lettuce that I was about to eat, and that I had made the decision to put some sun-dried tomatoes in amongst the leaves even though I knew full well that sun-dried tomatoes are drenched in oil. I could never expect her to have an inkling of the fear that I felt as I had watched the globules of fat rise to the top of the dressing bottle after I had shaken it; for this reason I had not got as far as pouring it on my salad. I would never find the words to explain to her the battle that I had with myself when I made the decision that this time I was not going to take the three sun-dried tomatoes that I had carefully selected over to the sink in order to scrub the oil from them. I would never be able to convey to her the disappointment I had felt when, after arranging those three, oily, sun-dried tomatoes in my salad, I had panicked at the last moment and picked them all out. She would never be able to comprehend why, even after removing all traces of sun-dried tomato from my salad, I had thrown the entire thing in the bin and started again due to suspicion that the fat they were preserved in might have contaminated the remaining green leaves.

(Sigh)

How would Annie be able to understand that my big victory today was eating in public? How would she know that me, sitting in the bar, eating a salad, in the middle of that day, was actually the most daring feat accomplished by a human since Philippe Petit's twin towers stunt 1974?

No, I could not blame Annie at all. She had no idea, but I still felt my stomach knot up with her accusatory tone all the same.

"It's no wonder you are so thin. You need to get some fat in you! Eat a proper meal is what you need!" She continued to scold me as she busied herself wiping down the bar. A couple of the beer drinkers looked up to see what she was nagging about. I wished I were thin enough to slide between the floorboards and disappear.

I said nothing. There was nothing to say other than *Go Fuck Yourself Annie* and I doubted that would have gone down too well.

I would never be able to get someone like Annie, who was plump, rotund, and snacked on pork scratchings, to understand me. I doubted that I would ever be able to get anyone to understand me. Hell, even I did not understand me!

Still, I wanted to tell her just how bad fat is for the human body. I wanted to show her my books that said that the low-fat diet lifestyle I was living was scientifically proven to be correct. But no; I would not waste my breath on her. Instead, I used her scorn to fuel my motivation to continue my studies into fat. That very afternoon saw me back in the library.

By 1961 Ancel Keys had made it to the front cover of *Time* magazine. He told *Time* that the ideal heart healthy diet should consist of almost seventy percent carbohydrate and only a marginal fifteen percent fat. This same figure was the one I had been given in my nutrition training in 2006 and what I had been using with my clients ever since.

By 1970 the *Seven Countries Study* had reached new heights, and as a result of its recommendations the American Heart Association committee formally recommended that all Americans—including infants, children, adolescents, lactating pregnant women and older persons—consume less than ten percent of their daily calories from fat.

Brits always copy whatever Americans do, so the United Kingdom soon adopted similar behaviour.

Despite my preference for low-fat, and despite the head-chaos and bickering between Sister Catherine and Succubus, I was still managing to slowly gain weight. I would eat an entire jar of peanut butter every night in my binge session; a feat which now seems unbelievable to me because other than being incredibly rich and filling, peanut butter makes ones throat and mouth all sticky and therefore is difficult to consume in large quantities. Back in my binge days however, always managed to finish the pot to the point of scraping out every last morsel. To give those reading this an idea of the scale of my binges: consider that a jar of peanut butter acted as an appetizer.

I allowed the night binges to get bigger and bigger because I was desperate to put on weight and I had more or less given up trying to argue with Sister Catherine during daylight hours. I worked out that I could use the binges to my advantage and eat even more and more in that time. In doing so, I was able to gain some more weight. I was unable to control my binge horse, but to an extent I was learning to steer it back towards the stableyard.

I worried constantly that I would be unable to stop binging once I had reached a more normal body weight. I did not know then that once my body had been at a restored weight for a number of months, and once my body could trust that I would eat enough fat and calories on a regular basis, that Succubus would disappear and my binge behaviour would cease. I know that now, because I have not binged in years; in fact, it boggles my mind how it was ever possible for me to eat that much in one go. I know I did it. I know it was horrid. I know that binge eating one's way back to a restored bodyweight is far from ideal; but I am glad it got me there all the same.

One day, around the middle of June, I had to walk through Andover Town Centre to go to the bank and I noticed something about the scenario felt odd. I could not place what it was at the time, and I hurried home as usual. Only on the drive home did I realise that the strangers in the street had not been staring at me like they usually did. I no longer looked sick enough for people to stop what they were doing and gawp at me as I passed.

I was still ill, I promise. This, by the way, leads me onto fact number eight:

You cannot tell if a person has an eating disorder from their appearance.

In my experience, what I looked like on the outside represented about ten percent of my disease. I might have no longer looked as sick as I had done before, but I was still very unwell.

One weekend, towards the end of June, Thierry invited me to help him cook on the barbecue at a party. I remember the half hour drive from my flat in Tidworth to where the party was in the market town of Devizes very clearly because I almost turned home twice. I had not been to a party for a long time. For years, I had stuck to only seeing family and people that I knew had accepted me for the skinny freak that I was. I was scared, but for once I was not scared because I feared rejection.

I did not turn around. I went, and at that party I met a guy. Three years later, that guy and I got married.

Chapter Twenty Six

When I got to the party, thankfully, Thierry put me to work on the barbecue; now I had a job to do rather than loiter on the outskirts of bubbling conversations picking at my nails. I concentrated on flipping burgers. Every now and then, I'd lift my eyes from the pattied meat to talk to someone. It felt obscure to be out at a party and not assume that anyone who set eyes on me was judging my thin appearance. Surreal yet enjoyable. I was so happy just to be there amongst other people; to hear them chatting and laughing and to feel that I was not only welcome, but accepted too. My low weight had always made me the outsider before, the Lucy Tallon of the world. Now I looked similar to other people, and the difference in the way strangers behaved towards me was profound.

The contrariety might have been subtle if observed by someone else, but it screamed at me. It was rather like visiting France or some other foreign country where everything is similar, but remarkably different in an almost inexplicable manner. The very energy directed towards me by others felt so changed that I wondered if I were still me. Perhaps I was dreaming?

The first major contrast was that people looked me in the eye. It felt strange; rather exposing, but not entirely unenjoyable. There is this moment when you look a person in the eye for the very first time. No matter who it is, there is an unmistakable leap of energy. For years I had taught myself to look at the ground, or at the collar of the shirt of the person to whom I was talking. When greeting people, I would look over their shoulder rather than at their face. I did this so that I would not have to see their eyes, and the uncomfortable questioning that those eyes always told of.

Now, for the first time in almost a decade, complete strangers were looking directly at me, and it was okay. The fear, the shock, the accusation that usually accompanied eye contact was absent. It felt wonderful, but took some getting used to.

I was quite happy where I was behind the makeshift-repurposed half-oil drum barbecue: observing, quietly occupied: safe. Then Thierry had to go and mess it all up.

Fuelled with Holsten Pils, he bounced over to me and shouldered me off the grill.

"Here Tabs, I got this . . . take a break . . . get something to eat yourself." Grabbing at my spatula, he set himself to taking care of the burgers I had been minding.

I snatched the spatula back from him.

"It's ok, I'm fine, I don't need a break." I insisted.

I had been more than happy with the "Oh, those burgers look great!" and, "One coming right up!" exchange that I had been enjoying with my fellow partygoers for the last thirty minutes. That had been just perfect for me and I could have worked the barbecue all night and felt adequately fulfilled. I did not need anything more. I did not want to go out *there*.

For God's sake, Thierry, just piss off and leave me alone!

Instead of letting me be, Thierry gave me a stern look and pressed a plate with a burger into my hands. "You need to eat something," he muttered as he softly pushed me out of my comfortable little burger-grilling sanctuary and towards the heaving bustle of people.

He may as well have stripped me naked, because standing there, limply holding a white paper plate with a sad looking burger in the middle of it, naked was how I felt. I considered pretending that I needed the loo and sneaking off to my car.

I could go home?

Thierry would be furious with me if I did that, but it was his own fault; he should have left me behind the grill where I was happy. Like a child being dropped off by its mother on the first day of school, I longingly looked back at him. He motioned at me dramatically with the tongs as if he were swiping me around the back of the head. *Go on.* He nodded towards the party.

Reluctantly, I wandered over to one of the hay bales that had been positioned for seating to the side of the marquee that we were in. I was hungry; I wanted to eat. I knew that I *should* eat, but more recently, Thierry's magic ability to make me eat what he told me to had been wearing thin. The fat drizzled down the side of the burger and glistened on the top. I stared at it. I wanted to hate it. Hate made everything so simple; there was no confusion when hate was present. When I hated fat there was no conflict, no deliberation, only focus. Now I felt muddled, because to my own disgust I wanted to eat that burger, and that realisation in itself shocked me clean out of my trance. I jumped as if I had been burnt and, making sure that Thierry was not watching me, I tipped the jezebel burger off my plate and into a black binliner.

Phew! It was gone. I glanced back to the grill where Thierry was busy chatting up a shapely brunette who was wearing a cute green miniskirt. Distracted by green-miniskirt girl's legs, he had not seen me dispose of my burger. I looked at her wistfully; I had not been able to wear a mini-skirt for over ten years. I looked down at my jeans and wondered if I would ever be able to show my own legs again.

Idiot, you should have just eaten the fucking burger.

I had promised myself I would not skip any more meals.

By binning the burger have I just lost a battle?

I will never get to the cute-green-miniskirt stage unless I keep eating.

Should I go and ask Thierry for another burger?

No, that would be weird. I should find something healthy to eat instead.

I stood up and went over to the salad bar. The table boasted a pretty array of different plates: tuna salads, ham salads, pasta salads, rice salads and baskets of bread. Despite the decorative spread, all I could see in front of me was fat: salads with mayonnaise; salads with cheese; salads with avocado; feta-stuffed tomatoes; and lashings of thick oily dressing. *What could I eat here? Why was it all so bloody fatty? Where was the plainer food? Why was everything always so difficult?* I couldn't think straight; Sister Catherine and Succubus were screaming at one another and all I wanted to do was sit on the floor and wrap my arms around my head.

This is too much, go home!

Just as I had made my decision to give up and leave, I spied a what looked to be a bowl of undressed green salad sitting untouched at the corner of the table. Audibly sighing with relief, I piled my plate with salad leaves and, as a second thought, added a spoonful of salsa.

"Thanks for the burger." Said voice behind me.

Startled, I almost dropped my plate. I looked up to see one of the fellas that I had flipped a burger onto a bun for. I must have served a hundred people burgers, but I distinctly remembered this chap. I wish that I could tell you the reason I remembered him was because he had a cracking smile and the most welcoming eyes I had ever seen, but if I told you that I would be lying. No, I remembered him because he was overweight. It is both sad and hypercritical that I, someone so fearful of being judged by others for my low body weight, only remembered this guy because of his excess. It is, however, the truth. When meeting a new person, appearance has to be registered. In this first impression, the mind's eye uses visual information and categorizes what is seen. *Observing* a person's body weight is unavoidable. However, *judging* them for it is learnt.

He stuck out his hand, "Matt."

Matt was American, chubby, and a smoker. I was not attracted to him in the slightest, but we started talking and he seemed like a nice enough bloke. I liked him instantly; he was both friendly and funny. It turned out that he barely knew anyone at that party either, so we were both in the same boat so to speak. We spent most of the evening discovering that we held a shared passion for British comedy shows and *The Goonies*. During the dreaded, but thankfully short-lived, small talk section of our initial acquaintance, he asked me where I worked. I told him that I was a personal trainer, and that I also taught group fitness classes at the local Leisure Centre in Devizes.

That evening I alternated between helping Thierry at the grill and drinking vodka and diet coke with Matt and a couple of other people to whom he had introduced me. The alcohol loosened me up; I was able to relax, laugh, joke about, and all-in-all I had a great time. The laughter was what had really been key; I love to laugh, and I get a kick out of making other people laugh. I felt refreshed.

I had met a new group of people that night, and the best part was that none of them knew anything about me. Nobody knew that only a couple of months before I had been so painfully thin and suicidal. Nobody was watching my every bite when I sat down and ate. Nobody cared or looked at me with disapproval when I told them I was a cycling instructor. Nobody told me that what I had eaten was not enough and that I needed to eat more. For a couple of hours I had forgotten that I was defined by food and exercise, and it had been wonderful. I had made plans to meet up the following weekend with Matt and a few others, to go out for drinks. As I drove home, I noticed that I was feeling a rather odd, yet familiar emotion. It almost took me the entire thirty minute journey to identify what that emotion was: happiness. I felt happy.

That night, as usual, after eating nothing other than a small salad all evening I returned home and binged on low-fat yoghurts, Special K, cereal bars and anything else I could find in my flat. Happiness might have been the key to me feeling motivated to socialise again, but it could not cure my binge eating.

The following Monday, to my utter disbelief and alarm, Matt showed up in one of my cycling classes. I was at a loss over what to do; somebody as unfit as he was should have started with a gradual exercise program, not just turn up at the gym and join in with the most intense cardio class on the schedule. I tried to suggest that he might want to start a little more gently, and that perhaps he should spend some time on the cardio equipment in the open gym instead. Matt was adamant that he was taking *my* class. I set him up on a bike and advised him to take it easy.

I wagered that he might last through the first five minutes and then leave. To my surprise, he stayed on that bike for the entire sixty-minute session. Struggling, sweating and gasping, he lasted a whole hour class in a room with lycra-clad cyclists. That was impressive; it is one thing for someone who is used to exercising and bike-riding to push through a spin class, but it is quite another thing for someone otherwise unaccustomed to cardiovascular excursion to survive one. I was sure that he must have been utterly exhausted, and as I congratulated him after class I told him that he should still reconsider my advice to gently build up some fitness in the gym before returning to the spin studio.

He didn't. He came back the very next week, and the one after that. Dripping in sweat, within the first couple of pedal strokes Matt would have drenched his clothes, the bike, and the floor surrounding him. It astounded me how he kept on coming back week after week. I admired his commitment; if only my personal training clients had the determination that Matt did.

One week, Matt asked me to join him for a drink after class. I said that I needed to get home to feed Sprout. The truth was that he was making me nervous. Why did he insist on coming to my cycle classes? I knew that he did not live close by, I knew that he was driving an hour and a half in either way and only coming to my classes and not those taught by other instructors. I could not work out what he wanted from me. He was smart and had a wicked sense of humour; one of the nicest people that I had met, which made me all the more suspicious of him. I had never had anyone—other than my parents, and everyone knows that parents don't count— be as kind to me as he was. He seemed to accept everything about me. He made me feel that it was okay just to be me. Even though I was still too skinny. Even though I could often be bad tempered. And even though I worked too much.

I started to look forward to seeing him.

But Matt was overweight, and a smoker; not my type at all.

Matt was also a gentleman; always making sure that everyone was safe and happy. He was generous; always the first to dip his hand into his pocket to buy the first round. He was an easygoing and a dependable friend.

Then, I found out from a friend that apparently Matt had a *thing* for me. I was devastated. I liked him enough as a friend but there was just no way that I wanted anything more than that from him. It was not just him; I did not want that from anyone.

However, his unassuming acceptance of me was a threat to my resilience. No matter what the situation, Matt was there with a smile and something witty to make me laugh. He was one of the only people aside from Thierry who could get me laughing and playful and happy. Unlike Thierry, he never pressured me to eat fatty foods, so there was never the high nor the hangover when I was with him. I could relax and be.

I had no experience whatsoever with guys, but Matt never made fun of me or pressured me. He was so ridiculously pleasant.

Despite having lived in England for so long, Matt was American, and I wondered if it was a cultural thing that he was so sickeningly nice to me. *Or maybe he is just stupid?* Americans have a reputation in the United Kingdom for idiocy; take Joey from the cast of Friends, for example. A nice enough fellow who exists in a blissful state of dumbness.

Realistically, Matt was far too quick witted for this to be the case, so the only supposition left was that the whole friendship was a huge dodgy scam. *Was he after my bank account details?* I considered trying to check up on him, in case he was trying to get close to me because he wanted to hack into my personal funds.

After three or four months, I concluded that even the most elaborate of scams would not invest this far, and it was not like I had much to steal anyway. Despite my innate distrust and scepticism, I began to trust him a little bit, and besides, I'd discovered that I secretly actually enjoyed being treated so well.

That scared the shit out of me.

So, I panicked, and tried to push him away. I made it blatantly obvious that I was not attracted to him; when he called me I would leave it to voicemail and purposefully not call back. I did not want it to come to the point that I had to bluntly tell him that I was not interested.

Matt completely ignored all my attempts at deterrence. He was not phased by my rudeness, my coldness, or my pretense of being too busy to talk to him. Finally, in a desperate and futile attempt to get some advice, I asked my mum what to do:

"Mum, you know that guy that I was telling you about . . . Matt?"

"Yes . . . he is the one that you work with isn't he . . . the French one?"

Sigh. "No Mum, that's Thierry . . . totally different person . .. Matt is the, oh, you know, the . . ." I lowered my voice despite being alone in my flat, ". . . the overweight one."

"Oh yes, the nice one?"

"Yes Mum, the nice one. Well, I think he has a thing for me, and I don't know how to tell him that I am not interested."

"Don't be silly!" Mother interjected, "You are still far too thin for any man to have a *thing* for you!"

Oh Jesus, here we go again.

"Mum, I have put on weight . . . give me a break. Why does everything have to come back to my bloody weight! Just because I don't choose to stuff myself full of burgers and fries!"

And that was how that conversation had gone.

Realising that Mother was probably not the best source of impartial advice on this one, I resolved to asking my sister about it.

"Beth, you know that guy Matt that I am friends with?"

"No." The speed and abruptness of her answer was disconcerting. "I didn't think you had any friends other than Sprout."

"Shut up. I do. Anyway, there is this guy. . . and he's great and everything, really nice . . . kind . . . funny."

"Yeah, yeah, so what's the problem?" Beth, although two years younger than I, was on number boyfriend number five, and much more experienced with the opposite sex (but then again, that was not a particularly high bar). She was currently dating a Welsh Adonis of a rugby player with an uncanny resemblance to a Ken doll. I'd never admit it to her, but this was a topic in which she was much more seasoned than me, and I felt somewhat intimidated; maybe this had been a bad idea.

"Well, he's kind of overweight . . . " I mumbled.

"Fat? You are dating a fat guy!" Beth squawked; this had definitely been a bad idea.

"Beth I never said I was going out with him!"

"Oh My God! This is priceless, you must be like fat and thin . . . little and large! It would be like a stick insect and a tick dating one another!"

"Beth, shut the hell up. Stop laughing!"

I couldn't help but giggle a little bit, too. Truth was, I did not begrudge my little sister's mirth; it was somewhat ironic that in my twenty-six years of living I had never had a boyfriend, and now the only person to show interest in my scrawny self was himself overweight. I also knew that in her laughter was an expression of her relief that I was no

163

longer looking like I was sitting at death's door, and that she was happy that I actually looked healthy enough for anyone, overweight or otherwise, to show an interest in me.

"Honestly though, Tabby, it's about time that you got a boyfriend. Who cares how much he bloody well weighs? If you like him go for it. You can't be frigid your whole life, can you?"

She had a point there, not as eloquently put as I would have liked, but a valid remark all the same. I was lonely. I was bored. I had nothing much to lose.

It seemed that wherever I went, Matt was there. I never minded his presence. For someone who usually much prefers being alone to being among other people, this was a disconcerting fact; *why don't I get sick of him after a couple of hours like I do with everyone else? Why doesn't he have these little habits that irritate me like most other people? Why is he so freaking nice to me?*

We were close friends, that was for sure, but despite Beth's advice, I certainly had no intention of dating him. Nope. None.

Or at least, not until he went away.

Around mid-August, Matt went away to visit relatives in Chicago for a few weeks; to my utter horror, I missed him terribly.

When I missed him, I knew that was it. I had gone and done the one thing that I had promised myself I would never do. The one thing that I knew would make me vulnerable, corrupt my independence and generally fuck things up: I had fallen in love.

Despite this rather shocking turn of personal-life events, life went on as usual. At the gym, clients were still pouring in, and I began working with a woman called Michelle. Michelle was obese; morbidly so. Most of my clients were overweight, but I had never yet worked with anyone as grossly overweight as Michelle; her doctor had told her, like mine had told me, that her weight could potentially kill her. She had to lose weight to save her life, and as a result she called me up one day after asking around for a personal trainer.

"Hello, I am looking for someone called Tabitha, I wanted to talk about personal training?" Her voice was thin and wavering: she was nervous.

"Yes, that's me. How can I help?"

"I need to lose some weight . . . " She trailed off, already sounding deflated.

"Well, I can certainly help you do that!" I was doing my best to come across as upbeat and friendly.

She chuckled somewhat nervously, then cleared her throat.

"Well, maybe, but, you see . . . I have been trying to lose weight for over ten years now, ever since I had my daughter actually, and she's fourteen now, so I guess it's more like fourteen years. Anyway, my health is at risk, and my doctor has told me I have to lose this weight or I am going to have serious problems, but I can't. I just can't do it."

The longer I spoke with Michelle that day, the more attached I became to helping her. We were similar. When she described her behaviour around food to me, the compulsion, the lack of control, I understood; the same behaviours overtook me each and every night when I binged. She told me she was addicted to food, that she binged with regularity and felt the desire to eat all day and night. She told me of her thoughts and dreams around food and eating, and the irrational nature of her own behaviours. The single most defining moment of that conversation for me was when she told me that her son, aged ten, had come to her and begged her to lose weight; apparently he had overheard Michelle and her husband talking about a recent doctor's appointment. The little boy has twigged that there was great concern for his mummy's health, and he was scared Mummy was going to die.

"Kids are smarter than you think," Michelle had revealed to me, "they know the score even when you think they don't. It breaks my heart to know that my little Benny is so worried about me."

I could hear the tears in her eyes when she told me that, and when she spoke also of her husband's fear that her weight would kill her. I got it. I felt the same desperate regret and helplessness when my mother and father had revealed their fears to me; it was just all in reverse: my life was in danger because I had been too thin.

Before we had even met I had dedicated myself to helping Michelle lose weight. I wanted it for her, for her husband, and for her son; but I also wanted it for me.

Michelle, like I, had every motivation in the world to want to change her behaviour around food. She also, like I, faced a mental and physical battle every single day.

My other clients usually only needed a diet plan to stick to and a couple of exercise sessions a month in order to slim down a notch. Michelle needed much more than that. She could not afford to pay the usual fee, so I agreed to train with her for whatever she could give; I had already made a personal commitment to her, so money was irrelevant. I insisted that we train four times a week. She expressed that she felt very uncomfortable exercising in front of other people, so I drove out to her home in order to accommodate her understandable aversion to exercising in public.

I poured my heart into working with Michelle: I called her every day to see how the diet was going; I accompanied her to the grocery store to help her pick out healthier products; and I thought about her more often than appropriate to admit to. I wanted her to succeed; I *needed* her to be able to stop the fear that was escalating from her family.

Unfortunately, Michelle hated me. Not *me* personally: what I represented. I was skinny, and from her point of view, it was *easy* for me to be so. I was telling her not to eat the things that she felt impelled to eat, but I could not tell her *how*. Her frustration screamed silently at me when I told her no more mayonnaise, no more full-fat milk, no more

165

chocolates and certainly no more buttered croissants.

Like Michelle's doctor had done, I gave her reasons, I gave her numbers, and I gave her percentages, but I could not seem to give her what she really needed: the ability to override her desire to eat. The harder I tried, the more she resented me. It were as if *I* was the bad guy; *I* was the person pressuring her to not eat, and *I* was making her feel like a failure when she could not do what I asked. I know that Michelle understood that was my job to try and motivate her and give her goals to achieve. I know that she recognised that I was only doing exactly what she had asked me to do; but, understanding those things did not stop her hating me.

Her husband, a wiry-haired, lofty fellow called Ron, and I communicated regularly. When he was at work, or out of Michelle's earshot, he would confide in me how deeply afraid he was for his wife's life. Her weight, and the health concerns that it brought, affected him greatly; he was scared and confused. Ron struggled to understand the *why*. It should have been so simple, should it not?

Such a simple thing: stop eating chocolate; stop eating cakes and pizza; start eating low-fat foods. "Why can't she do it?" Ron would ask me. "Why can't she do this simple thing that will save her life?"

I did not have the answer to that question, but I knew it was the same question that I had asked myself so many times. The same question that my mother had asked me. The same question that my sisters had asked me. The same question that the eyes of every person I met asked me: why?

Why can't you just eat more food?

Why can't you just eat less food?

Three months into our training regimen and Michelle had not lost a single pound. Never before had I achieved zero results with a client in such a period of time. I was still determined as ever to keep her on schedule. I had to keep trying.

As the weeks went on, Michelle became increasingly apathetic towards our sessions. She would call and make an excuse not to train with me almost every other session. When Ron came home from work early and found out about her missing her training sessions there was a row; I know because he called me afterwards and yelled at me for not tattle-tailing on her: "You have to tell me if she cancels, Tabitha. She can't give up. *We* can't give up on her!"

A couple of days later, an hour before a scheduled training session, Michelle called me. "I can't do this anymore," was all she really said. She cancelled her session that day, and told me she would not be continuing training. When I hung up the phone, I cried. Big angry tears of frustration and sorrow. *How could I have done something more to help her? How could I have kept her motivated?* I had failed Michelle, I had failed Ron and I had failed myself. I pulled on my trainers and went for a run.

166

Chapter Twenty Seven

In the year that followed that barbecue party, my social life returned to levels similar to that which I had enjoyed when I was in my late teens. Matt and I officially began dating in September of 2007. This was an interesting transition for me—someone who had never had a boyfriend before.

By the time that I met Matt, I wanted the old me back, and I wanted to do what I could to get there. However, I understood from my encounters with doctors and family that if put on the spot and directly challenged, I would defend the very facets of my life that I hated so much. Odd as it sounds, I knew that I had to trick myself in order to turn back towards being the person who I once was.

Eating disorders are so tiresome. Anorexia is like living with the most irrational, aggressive and conniving creature imaginable. Sister Catherine and Succubus would converge to work against me regarding anything that had the potential to divert my thoughts away from food and eating. Sister Catherine in particular hated Matt. She feared his ability to distract me. She told me that he would force me to stop exercising. She ordered me to stop spending time with him because doing so was going to make me fat and unhealthy. She warned me that he would diminish my freedom.

What freedom?

Matt never did any of those things. He accommodated me completely. He ignored my strange habits and shifty behaviour around food; in time, this mollified the quarrelling bitches in my head. His apparent accepting of me led to them quieting down; he became less of a threat and they dropped their guard slightly. Soon enough, they were sleeping on post. I was more able to relax. That felt nice.

Regardless of Matt's ability to merge his lifestyle with mine, I was still unapologetically mulish about the food that I ate. Because Matt needed to lose weight, it was easy for me to insist that he be rigid around food and exercise also. This certainly helped me transition into being in a relationship because for the first couple of months at least, I was completely controlling the food and shopping for both of us.

When I told my parents about our relationship, they were thrilled. They had met Matt a couple of times and thought he was a lovely chap. My father, being a Chelsea Football Club supporter, was secretly delighted with the canon fodder that Matt's support of Manchester United provided him. Beth and Candy were happy to hear that I had finally found myself a boyfriend.

My relationship with Candy had been getting less fraught since I had regained a bit of weight; I had become more tolerant of her and she cautiously grew less nervous in my presence. I was getting to know my little sister as an adult, and discovering all sorts of interesting facets to her personality that I had previously remained ignorant to.

When I announced our relationship status to Thierry he was gobsmacked. Not often was Thierry short of an immediate retort, and his silence intrigued me.

"What?" I demanded. I had been nervous about admitting a boyfriend to anyone, especially Thierry. Being in a relationship with Matt was one thing—I felt nervous enough about that—but outwardly admitting to someone felt like some kind of declaration of vulnerability and weakness.

"Well, I, er . . . I just . . . nothing, that's great, he's a really nice chap." He smirked.

Thierry's mirth angered me. I understood exactly what his humour was about: Matt's weight. Simmering on the inside, I kept my tone nonchalant and pushed him for more.

"*But . . .*" I started his next sentence for him in a bid to usher him into actually saying what I suspected him to be hedging on. "Go on," I pressed.

"*But . . .*" Thierry continued, "well, I just never thought he would be your type. You know, he's a bit lardy, Tabs. It doesn't fit. I mean look at you . . . all skin and bone . . . then look at him."

My simmer hit the boil. I was furious at Thierry, him and everyone else who was probably thinking what he had the balls to say out loud to me. *Skinny and Fatty.* That was all people saw. Thierry knew Matt well enough by now, he should have known what a fabulous person he was and been able to see right past his physical appearance. But, no: all Thierry could see was fat.

"Bloody Hell Thierry!" I yelled. "Why does a person's weight have to be indicative of their value, their worth, their *anything*? Why does a person's weight matter so much?"

"Hey, Tabs, chill." He looked abashed. "Sorry, you are right, Matt is a fantastic fellow and if you are happy then I am happy. Ignore me, I'm an idiot."

"Yes you are!"

We left it at that and spoke nothing more of the matter. Despite my vicious protests in reaction to Thierry's observance of our contrasting figures, doubt began to seep. *Was Matt right for me? Did we look ridiculous together? Was I embarrassing myself?*

Questions percolated. I silently considered. It seemed like a decision had to be made; one that, once decided on, would call for absolute commitment on my part. If I wanted to be with Matt I could not allow the opinions of others, silent or otherwise, to affect me. If I could not do that, there was no point in continuing our relationship because this prattle was going to come up, and I could not afford to let it unravel all this doubt when it did. Even the relationship novice that I was knew that I had to let it go or go with it.

I made up my mind: I loved this guy and I had never met anyone whom I could consider spending the rest of my life with. The rest of the world could get bent!

Matt had not known or seen the worst of my food battles, and because of this I had never any reason to fear judgement from him over mealtimes. When we did eat together I worked hard to stay calm and relaxed. I could eat just plain salad if I wanted to and Matt never raised an eyebrow of disapproval. He never pressed me or even acted as if he noticed what I was eating. If this had been any other way I would not have allowed him into my life; anyone who put my eating habits in contention was shut out, and although it was never discussed, I think Matt understood. I was able to feel normal when I ate in his presence. This in itself was very healing and encouraging for me, I slowly began to fear eating in public a little less.

Around the spring of 2008, I had myself up to a much more solid three meals a day of salad plus some lean protein and carbohydrate. I was getting used to eating with someone else in the room, not in the fast, fun and lustful way I had done with Thierry, but in a calmer, more peaceful and sustainable manner. I was still binge eating at night, but compared to where I had been a year earlier, I was making great progress.

Despite being happier and despite being able to eat three meals per day, I was still spending my entire day fighting off the same thought patterns that I had been struggling with for eight years. Every meal presented the same old mental bickering; I was just getting better at standing in defence. I was exhausted from the relentless battle of wills taking place in my head. *Eat this. Don't eat this. Don't eat Fat. Don't sit still.* Then there was the hunger. The gnawing hunger that remained with me no matter how many apples, carrots, salads, and low-fat yoghurts that I ate.

I was still analysing every calorie that I had on a plate; I was just getting better at resisting the compulsion to reduce the calorie count at each mealtime.

I was still fighting the urge to run every hour; I was just very good at hiding the relentless chaos in my mind.

I still had Succubus and Sister Catherine brawling in my head; I had just learnt that I could muffle them if I used enough force.

I thought that this was as good as it could get. I was happier than I had been for years. It was okay; I would have a life of forever counting calories, forever fretting over food, forever wanting to exercise—forever fighting—but it was okay. *Was it?*

Well, no; not now that I know better. Now that I know I can have a life without the thoughts and without the stress I'll happily answer that no, this was not okay, and that no, I should not settle for it. But then, I did not know what I do now; and if you had told me, I doubt I would have believed you.

So I settled a bit, and I maintained the status quo for a while. But it was exhausting; when one is constantly in defence it is inevitable that there will be days when one gets worn down and concedes. On such days my temper would show. On those days, Matt—the person who was around me—would be the person that I snapped at and tried to hurt.

Chapter Twenty Eight

"Do you fancy going out for some food?" Matt looked up from his computer and smiled at me across the room.

The question came at the wrong time at the end of what had been a really hard day battling with Sister Catherine and Succubus. I had taught two cycle classes in the morning, and after struggling to eat lunch and failing to eat all of it I had wanted to go for a run. I felt stressed and tired and I knew that running would make me feel better. Backwards and forwards the argument had gone in my head. *Should I run? Should I not run.* I had settled for going out for a walk, but neither of my internal hellcats were satisfied with that resolution and they continued to prod and poke at me. I was exhausted and fractious.

"Jesus Matt!" I yelled. "Why do you always have to bloody go on about eating!" My temper, needing an excuse to flare, wanted more. I was hankering for a fight. I needed to express some of the unrest inside of me externally. I glowered at him, practically begging him to argue with me, to give me an excuse to explode.

He just looked back at me. Then, he did the worst thing imaginable: he smiled.

"Ok Stroppy," he teased, "we will stay in and fester like cabbages." He grinned at me. It was impossible not to smile back.

Matt seemed pretty decent at knowing the right thing to say to me at the right time. He did not know the origins or the reasons behind my stressed out personality. How could he have: I never told him.

There were so many things that I would have loved to have been able to explain to him simply so that he would know that there was a reason for my apparently cold and cantankerous disposition.

Take being hugged for example: I hated being hugged or held. I think that this dislike stemmed from a fear that anyone who touched me would feel how thin that I was. When Matt hugged me, I would hold my breath and then worm my way out of it. I imagine that this type of reaction from one's partner day in and day out is rather tiresome, and could be seen as something of an insult. Matt never stopped trying to hug me, nor did he ever complain when I pulled away.

He did know about my "exercise addiction". I had told him about it a couple of months in to our relationship. Or at least, I had tried my best to explain it. He worked hard to understand, and was a great support for me when I gave him any insight whatsoever into my daily struggles with simple things such as standing still; sitting in the car; going to the cinema or anywhere else where I would be required to sit for a prolonged period of time. He helped me to challenge these urges to move when I asked him to, but never pressured me if I did not.

My personal training career was flying. I physically cringe when I think of it now. I had done a thorough job of surrounding myself with excuses to exercise and career-based reasons to study nutrition obsessively. Had my personal training career been a flop, it would have been so much easier for me to move on and find a job that was not constantly feeding my eating disorder. Unfortunately, I had a pretty solid client base, and where there's muck, there's brass: I was making a fair few bob.

In fact, I was getting so swamped with weight-loss clients that I had to cut back on my hours at the The Barley. I was making enough dosh with the personal training gig that I could easily afford not to work at nights at all. Now I had Matt, and I wanted to spend time with him in the evening; that really rattled me. What was happening? I actually started to resent working at night and wished instead that I were at home with him. It was disorientating, and I fought it for a couple of months, but one day I thought to myself: *What is the worst that can happen if you stop working nights? You can try it for a couple of weeks, and if it becomes a problem you can take it up again. Be brave!*

I remember how I felt guilty when I allowed myself to relax and not work nights anymore. Sister Catherine and Succubus both hated it.

Who do you think you are?

You are lazy. You should be working.

You are becoming idle just like everyone else.

You will get fat, unfit and you will lose everything that you have worked so hard to achieve.

Matt lost a lot of weight in the first couple of months that we were together. I instigated a very low-fat and restricted diet for him alongside a daily exercise routine. Basically, I fed him nothing but salad, and he was too infatuated with me to complain. Not only would I not do such a thing to Matt—or indeed any other human being now—but I'd not get away with it either. I cannot help but smirk when I write about this time, poor Matt just did what I told him, and I was mean. I was like the food police and he was in my jail; it's no wonder that he lost weight, but is is a wonder that he stuck with me!

Luckily for him, when he reached his target weight I cautiously instructed him to reintroduce meats and some of his old favourite foods back into his diet. Although I struggled so much to eat fat myself, I did understand that most people need it. Plus, I enjoyed cooking for him, and something instinctual was telling me that he needed nourishment other than that which vegetables can provide.

Shame I could not place such good sense on my own self as easily.

What we both learnt from Matt's boot camp was that Matt enjoys exercise, especially biking. After initially losing the bulk of his weight, within a couple of months he

171

had returned to eating like a horse, but remained lean and fit because he had developed a love of the outdoors. I'd actually created something of a monster, and as a result we now live in a house with more bikes than television sets; something which makes me happy right up until I have to fish oily chains out of my kitchen sink.

When we moved in together, living with another person highlighted to me just how uptight I was. Matt had a much more casual attitude towards food than I. Okay, Matt had a more casual attitude towards just about *anything* than I did. I think in those days, my whole world was shown to me through the filter of stress-spectacles—food in particular.

I could cook Matt anything and he would happily eat it. I envied this. I wondered what it would be like to allow another person to cook food for me. I wondered what it could feel like to eat without fretting over the calorie content. My own taste buds were frosted. My frigid nature started and ended with my tongue; the cold numb of my mouth meant that I could not taste, therefore I could not feel, therefore I could not speak warm words either.

I wondered what it would be like to feel that warmth again, and to taste again. I had been there before. Life had once been flavourful. *I* had once been flavourful.

Could I have that back? I doubted that I would ever be able to be—to eat—like that again; but it was inspiring nonetheless. Unwittingly, Matt had given me two people to aspire to: him, as he was now; and me, as I had been before.

"Gosh! Oh my . . . isn't he a handsome one."

We were at a celebration for my godmother's eightieth birthday. My mother and I were talking with a little old lady called Betty. Betty had pearly white hair and was wearing a baby blue beret. Her trouser suit was a primrose colour with white daisies embroidered on the cuffs and between the button holes. She was a scream; Mother and I were in tears of laughter as she told us stories of her first husband. Despite looking like a butter-wouldn't-melt nanna, Betty was sharp as scissors.

She had asked me if I was married and I had told her not yet, but that I had a boyfriend. When she had demanded to know where "this man of yours" was, I had pointed over to Matt who was standing with my dad over by the hors d'oeuvres. It looked like they were casually arguing about something; I assumed they were talking about football.

I had been avoiding the buffet table and was praying that Mother would not pressure me to go over there and eat. I had been mentally struggling with all the standing still and sitting down that this afternoon drinks party demanded and knew that eating anything, especially something from a buffet table, would be way too much pressure.

Hors d'oeuvres are packed with fat, therefore, calories. A deviled egg, for example, is made with mayonnaise. Other things on that table horrified me: sausage rolls; little cheese and ham sandwiches; vol au vonts; all laden with fat. I was much happier staying in the corner with Betty, who was screwing up her face and adjusting her glasses in order to get a better focus on the two men.

172

"Very handsome indeed," she concluded, beaming over at Matt, who was by now shaking his head in despair at whatever my father was saying. It was definitely football.

It shocked me a bit to hear Betty say that she thought Matt was handsome. I had never really noticed. I looked over and realised that she was right, Matt was rather good looking. I hadn't looked at him like *that* before. I had fallen in love with him when he was overweight, and it had never been about physical attraction. Now that Betty had pointed it out, I realised that he had transformed into this fit and handsome fellow. For a moment I felt somewhat shocked.

"You want to make sure that you hold onto a nice looking fellow like that," Betty instructed me. Then, she began telling us how her third husband had been good looking, but very stupid.

My mind wandered from the conversation. I felt strangely happy and secure that I had met and fallen in love with Matt when he had been overweight. There had never been any physical attraction to mar the connection that I felt with him; he was my best friend and the kindest, smartest, funniest person I had ever met. I wondered if things had been different had he not been overweight when we met. Maybe he would never have been single and in a position to ask me out in the first place? Maybe he would have been too surrounded in girls to even notice me at that barbecue?

Had Matt been overlooked by the world because of his bodyweight in the same way that I had?

I felt appreciative towards the fat that he had once been, because had he not been pudgy he might have already been snapped up by someone else by now. I smirked, *their loss is my gain*.

While I adored his new trim physique, it would not have impacted me or our relationship had he stayed pudgy. I loved him either way. I understood then that actually, the physicality of fat was not something that I disliked. I was not scared of being with someone who was fat, of cuddling or touching fat, and I was not opposed to picturing of my own body in the future with fat on it. *Then why am I so fearful of fat in food? Why would I rather place my hand in the fire than eat something with mayonnaise in it? Why is that buffet, laden with fats, shrieking at me across the room?*

My mind had looped back to the food on the far table again, and my eyes followed suit. The conversation between Betty and my mother blended into background interference as my gaze wandered over the plates of sausage rolls and devils on horseback. Everything on the table looked to be contaminated. There was not a single dish that did not have some form of fat in. Nonetheless I was hungry. Of course I was hungry: I was always hungry. *Why was eating so hard?*

Chapter Twenty Nine

November 2007

I sat down after work one evening to do some research. I was agitated with the number of clients that were not taking my dietary recommendations seriously. People would try to keep to the plan, but when they handed me the weekly food diary it would usually display some form of fat related mishap. Pizza, cheese, butter on bread rather than the low-fat *Flora* margarine that I had recommended, and so on and so forth. With the slip ups, there would often be a shameful "sorry" written in next to the entry, as if my clients really felt that they were sticking to the diet that I set for me, rather than for them.

In a way they were. Being an advocate for a low-fat diet was all that I had. Believing in it was believing that thin was healthy; that I was healthy. By choosing the career path of a personal trainer, I could excuse my skinny frame as passable, if not desirable.

Every time a client slipped up I took it personally. I wanted them all to believe, like I did, that low-fat was the way forward. I wanted them to believe that I was as thin as I was by choice. I wanted them to believe that, so that I could believe it.

How can I be of greater influence to those who were partial to fatty distractions? How can I show them, the world, that fat is the enemy?

I had decided to swat up more on the science behind the low-fat recommendations that I was giving. If my word were not convincing enough, surely that of scientists would be.

One of the women that I was training, Susan, was particularly getting to me. She would often comment on my weight, and say things like "Gosh . . . aren't you *lucky* to be so thin!"

Luck had nothing to do with it.

Susan was not the first person to make this naive and misled observation about my slim build, but she was more consistent at it than most. It is very hard to explain to someone that being as thin as I was had nothing to do with good fortune and everything to do with exercising for hours every single day, avoiding foods high in fat and generally being absolutely miserable.

"Do you like being so thin?" she would ask me, week in, week out.

"I'm trying to put on weight," was my curt reply.

"Gosh!" she would snort, "*that* wouldn't be a problem for me. You can have some of mine!" And then she would chortle as if she had just said the funniest and most original thing in her life.

"Why don't you just eat more fat?" she would ask, at which point I would roll my eyes at her in exasperation and mutter something bothersome under my breath.

"Jesus Susan . . . because fat is bad for you, everybody knows that!"

"I don't know," she'd muse. "If fat is so bad for me, why does it taste so good?" At this point I would shut her up by turning the speed up on the treadmill. I would delight in watching her pant and sweat as she tried to keep up with the machine. When she was too out of breath to talk, reluctantly, I'd turn it down again. I often wondered why Susan kept training with me, as I could be quite mean to her.

Susan in particular ticked me off, she was just so annoyingly pleasant. No matter how sharp I was with her she never seemed to get the message and continued to pay me to train with her each week. Not that she was making any progress; each week she came in and her diet diary would show cheese, wine and chocolate. She would draw these infuriating smiley faces next to the dietary slip ups and write "Oops" next to them. As if failing on her diet was some cute little mishap.

I thought about Susan as I sifted through the bundle of research papers that I had borrowed from the local library. I had practically picked up everything I could find relating to fat and diet—maybe I could give her some reading material that would help convince her to actually pay attention to me and cut fat out of her diet like I told her to. One paper fell out of the bunch and onto the floor. It was printed on brownish, old style paper. A sentence on the front page caught my eye:

> "Of all the parasites that affect humanity I do not know of, nor can I imagine, any more distressing than that of Obesity' - William Banting, The Corpulence of Fat. 1863.

Yes! Finally, someone who felt as I did. Someone whose written words proclaimed an actual hatred for fat. I pushed aside the other papers and settled back in my chair to read William Banting's *The Corpulence of Fat*.

Born in London in 1797, William Banting was an upper middle class carpenter. Incidentally, Banting was the very same man who crafted a coffin for the Duke of Wellington; for five generations his family held the royal warrant. He lived long before my time, but his story felt relevant to my interests as it was a hate letter to fat—or at least so I thought—and that appealed to me greatly.

It all started because William was overweight and this distressed him awfully. Upon a visit to the local ear, nose and throat doctor, Banting learnt his obesity was the underlying cause behind the onset his encroaching ear and eye problems; he became determined to lose weight.

The story continued that William Banting did not descend from a line of ancestors that were known for rotund figures, but despite this William found himself struggling with his expanding waistline in his thirties. His doctor, a family friend, had recommended that William take up exercise in a bid to help him shed some pounds.

Exercise. Dammit, I could have told him that.

Now, it would seem that in nineteenth century London, workout gyms were lacking. In fact, despite the word *gym* having been used in England since the 1590's, it was still only really used as an abbreviation for *gymnasium*. Interestingly, the word gymnasium comes from the Greek adjective *gymnos*, which means *naked*, and a gymnasium used to literally mean "to train naked". This is because one would undress in order to exercise, but I have to admit that does get me thinking and wondering what the gym would be like nowadays if we all had to workout in the buff.

Which is also interesting, as the word buff can be used to describe a person who goes to the gym a lot . . .

I digress, back to Banting:

Due to the lack of gyms, and his determination to find a route to a slimmer figure, William took to rowing every morning before work. In the local river. In an actual boat. Imagine how *inconvenient* that must have been; to have to get into an actual boat, probably get all wet, and row. What if the weather were bad?

Despite rowing about in rivers in and around London, William continued to gain weight. In fact, he found that the exercise increased his appetite and he ended up eating even more than before. His doctor, bemused, instructed him to stop exercising because it obviously was not working as intended.

Poor William continued to seek an answer to his big fat problem. The next piece of advice that he was given was to consume only *moderate and light food*, aka: a diet. Apparently, William found that on a restrictive diet, his weight did not plummet; but his spirits did. He, like I was when I was not eating enough, like Hilary when she could not bake pies and puddings, was miserable. He stopped the diet.

William Banting tried very hard: he reported over twenty visits to the hospital over the twenty years that he struggled with his weight. He wrote about going to Leamington Spa and taking hot baths as recommended. He had tried starvation diets and many different forms of exercise. He walked, he swam and he rode horses. He took to the Turkish baths one year at a solid rate of three per week and only managed to lose six pounds. He went to see someone who he described to be "one of the ablest physicians in the land", to only be told that weight gain was a natural part of getting older, and that he should shampoo more, exercise more and take vapor baths as well as medicine.

Poor William. Close to the point of giving in to his fatness, William sought out a consultation with a man named Doctor Harvey who was an ear, nose and throat specialist at the Royal College of Surgeons. Coincidentally, Doctor Harvey had just returned from a trip to Lé Gai Paris, and on this trip, he had attended a seminar by Doctor Claude Bernard—a very renowned physiologist. This lecture had been about a "new" theory which suggested that the liver played a part in the disease of diabetes. Doctor Bernard theorised that the liver did not only secrete bile, but that it also secreted a sugary substance that it made from elements of the blood that passed through it. This presentation inspired Doctor Harvey to think about the roles of the different food elements that went into diabetes, and he began his own research to look at the way that fats, sugars and starches affected the human body.

The timing of all this is important, because it would have been a marker of the era when people, doctors, and physicians began to twig that different macronutrients—fats, sugars and proteins—had different effects on the body. Bearing in mind that news did not travel as fast in the 1700s as it does today as there was no email or internet to speed things along, all these developments took a great deal of time to filter through. Banting did not wake up one morning and check his Facebook feed to see that everyone was suddenly harping on about how fats and carbohydrates have differing effect. Nope, this was the time of s-l-o-w news. And because news was slow, and expensive, and took a lot of effort to retrieve, it was probably more accurate.

Now, when I first read this story I was presuming that this special and revolutionary diet would be one low in fat. I got a little excited about that; I thought I was reading about the first, properly documented low-fat diet. I was wrong.

To my confusion, I read that Doctor Harvey advised William to abstain from all sugar and starch: carbohydrates. This was not a low-fat diet; it was a low-carbohydrate diet. And, to my astonishment, it worked.

In one year, William lost forty-six pounds and over twelve inches from his waist! He then went on to write (rather persistently, and very passionately) about his low-carbohydrate diet.

The first edition of William's *Letter of Corpulence* was published in May 1863 at William Banting's own expense. It went on to be revised and re-published many times. Despite the difficulties of authordom borne by nineteenth century writers, *Letter of Corpulence* did rather well and William Banting's story was widely read.

This scripted self-help book outlined exactly what William ate on a daily basis. I remember feeling disgusted when I read some of the entries; not only was it highly fatty food, but it was also awful offal and a plethora of animal meats:

"For breakfast, at 9.0 A.M., I take five to six ounces of either beef mutton, kidneys, broiled fish, bacon or cold meat of any kind except pork or veal; a large cup of tea or coffee (without milk or sugar), a little biscuit, or one ounce of dry toast; making together six ounces solid, nine liquid."

Remember, this was at a time when I could not bring myself to eat meat easily because I could not bare to see any stringy white lines that might be fat. The thought of such a breakfast was beyond reason and comprehension!

For dinner, at 2.0 P.M., Five or six ounces of any fish except salmon, herrings or eels, any meat except pork or veal, any vegetable except potato, parsnip, beetroot, turnip, or carrot, one ounce of dry toast, fruit out of a pudding not sweetened, any kind of poultry or game, and two or three glasses of good claret, sherry or Madeira—Champagne, port, beer forbidden; making together ten to twelve ounces solid and ten liquid."

William noted that his meal plan led to an excellent night's sleep, which was not altogether surprising to me seeing as he started drinking alcohol prompt at two o'clock in the afternoon. He also described his previous diet:

"My former dietary table was bread and milk for breakfast, or a pint of tea with plenty of milk, sugar, and buttered toast; meat, beer, much bread (of which I was always very fond) and pastry for dinner, the meal of tea similar to that of breakfast, and generally a fruit tart of bread and milk for supper. I had little comfort and far less sleep."

So it would seem that William went from eating a diet high in carbohydrates to one high in fat and protein. William Banting had unwittingly written up the first low-carbohydrate diet book; and to think Atkins took all the credit!

"I am very much better both bodily and mentally and pleased to believe that I hold the reins of health and comfort in my own hands."

Sounds like something Jenny Craig might say; or Ghandi.

Well, *The Corpulence of Fat* had been a big fat let-down. I put down the paper, then, annoyed at it for having wasted half an hour of my time, nudged it into the wastepaper basket. Then I remembered I had to return it to the library and got it back out again. I decided not to let silly Banting's balderdash deter me, and resolved to continue my quest for fat-bashing science.

I turned my attention to the next paper that I had borrowed, *The Western Electric Study*. This paper looked more credible; a proper scientific research study rather than the ramblings of some crazy old carpenter. I hoped it would tell me what I wanted to hear.

It did. The study went as follows: The researchers recruited five thousand and four hundred men whose lifestyles and diet they observed. They recorded what was eaten, who ate it, and what it contained. They then placed said participants into study groups depending on the amount of saturated fat in their diets. Then they watched and recorded what happened and to whom.

The conclusion: lipid consumption of the diet affects serum cholesterol concentration and risk of coronary death in middle-aged American men.

Thank God for that! Clearly this study was saying that what one eats effects one risk of heart disease. I made ample notes so that I would be able to educate Susan on the proven dangers of saturated fats on her next training session. It was due to studies like this that the evidence against fat had begun to accumulate to the point that health authorities would condemn it. These pieces of paper represented everything that I could use to justify my hatred of the nutrient of disease.

The *Western Electric Study* put me in an exceedingly good mood. There is something about being right that is energising and inspiring. Hungry for more evidence against fat, I carried on. It was almost nine o'clock by then, and the angry protests of my stomach were getting harder to ignore. I paused; *I should eat.*

I went into the kitchen and rustled about looking for the apple that I knew was in the fridge somewhere. I caught sight of the low-fat hummus that I had bought yesterday, and could not resist sticking my finger in scooping out some of the grainy chickpea pulp to taste. As I sucked hummus off my finger, I mused on the argument with my mother that purchasing it had incited. She had been cross at me for buying the low-fat version of the chickpea dip.

"Why can't you just buy the regular, Tabby!" She had motioned to the array of different hummus options that Waitrose had to offer and glared at me as I had gingerly dropped the half-fat version into my basket. I had tried to be coy about it. I had hoped that she would not notice, but she did. Oh, she always did. Some days she turned a blind eye. Yesterday, evidently, had not been one of those days.

Truth be told, Mother had held her tongue plenty of times already that day, and the hummus had sat on top of many last-straws. She had not said a word when I had ordered a Diet Coke in the Starbucks cafe that we had visited in Winchester, rather than the original, full-sugar version that she had asked for herself. She had said nothing when I declined the offer of a quarter of the tuna fish and cucumber sandwich that she had ordered. She had kept schtum when I pretended to eat the polo mint that she had offered me in the car. She had pretended not to see me slip it into my jean's pocket so that I could dispose of it later. I know that she had noticed all of these things. I had felt her hold her breath in each instance.

And who could have blamed her, because despite looking better than I had done for a number of years, she and I both knew that was about as far as it went.

Seeing me buy the low-fat hummus in Waitrose had apparently required more restraint than my poor mother could muster in a single day. It all came out then, in the middle of Waitrose. I glared right back at her. A woman in a red knit jumper loitered behind me. Sensing the tension between the two of us in front of her—but also that I was not going to move anytime soon—she was probably weighing up her chances of having her arm bitten off if she ventured too close to the shelf that we were blocking. I didn't care; I was too angry and embarrassed to give her a thought. After a couple of seconds she apologetically ducked around me and hastily grabbed a pot of *Original with Roasted Red Pepper Hummus*, then scarpered.

I held my ground and my silence.

Mother was unperturbed. She had well and truly had enough of me and my ridiculous excuses for healthy eating. She was done with my fibs and fabrications around food. She was hell-bent on making me buy the Original Hummus. She squared her shoulders and lifted her chin a smidgen.

And me? Well, I had spent the afternoon feeling stressed. First of all, I had been agitated about spending time with my mother, because whenever I did that I felt pressure to eat. Second, I had felt guilty about feeling stressed about spending time with my mother, because I loved her very much and know she loves me. *Why couldn't we just have fun together?* Then, I had felt like she was holding a gun to my head in Starbucks when she offered me some tuna sandwich; I was not oblivious to her frown when I asked for a diet coke. I could practically see the teeth marks left on her tongue after she had spent the entire afternoon biting it.

Then when she had said we would stop at Waitrose, I had almost opted to wait in the car, something that I should have done to avoid altercations such as the one that we were now in. But I had been meaning to buy some hummus that day, and for some reason I thought it would be nice for her to see me buy myself food. Wouldn't that put her mind at ease? Wouldn't that please her?

When we had got into the store she tried to put some smoked salmon into my shopping basket next to the carrots and apples. I of course plucked it straight back out again, and returned it to the shelf. Then she had started some prattle about *omega-3 oil* in fish. Whatever. Buying food was still a big deal for me; I did it on a regular basis now, but that is not to say that it had become much easier. I had to psyche myself up for it and approached the cashier feeling tense and nervous. When my mother had shown this dissatisfaction at my choice of hummus I could have imploded with frustration. I felt so misunderstood and wrongly done by. If she had any idea how hard this was for me she would understand that buying anything at all was a victory of sorts.

I'd had enough.

"MOTHER!" I screamed. Red-jumper woman, who was still in the aisle, jumped out of her skin with a startled gasp, then clutched at her basket and scurried around the corner. "Would you just leave me alone and let me buy what the bloody hell I want?"

I stormed up to the checkout, paid for my apples, carrots, and hummus, snatched my change from the teenage cashier at the till, and left the building.

The journey home had been silent other than Mother insisting on putting her *Kenny G* CD on in an attempt to put me "in a better frame of mind." Realistically I was going to need more than listening to a Vidal Sassoon model playing the saxophone to cheer me up, but by the time she dropped me off outside my flat my anger had, as usual, morphed to guilt.

Jesus, why am I always such a bitch!

I wanted to apologise, but not relent. I told her that I was sorry. . . *but* . . . that there was nothing wrong with eating low-fat. I argued gently that even idiots knew that one should eat low-fat versions of things. I explained to her that this was not about my weight, but that it was about my health, and she should be happy that I was choosing healthy foods.

My memory of her unconvinced look as she kissed me goodbye further fuelled my desire for proof beyond any doubt that fat was evil, I went back to my desk with my apple and chomped away at it as I read on.

My next paper was another American science study, *The McGovern Report,* which was started in 1968 and ran until 1977. In early 1977, after years of discussion, scientific review, and debate, the United States Senate Select Committee on Nutrition and Human Needs, led by Senator George McGovern, recommended dietary goals for the people of America—to increase the amount of carbohydrates in their diets and decrease the consumption of total fat, cholesterol and saturated fats.

See Mum!

I was especially happy to read how animal and saturated fats had been specifically pointed at as something to avoid. I had this one client at the time called Thomas who insisted on eating eggs; a couple a day for breakfast. I had recommended that he instead choose a cereal like Bran Flakes and have that with skimmed milk and a banana, but each week his food diary showed omelets for breakfast. As a compromise, I had asked him to remove the yolks as that was the part with the fat in, and he has begun to do so rather reluctantly. The following week he came back whinging that without the yolks, eggs tasted "boring."

I had sighed and suggested that he add some hot chilli sauce to it. Then I gave him fifty burpees to make up for his misdemeanour, and a lecture on his attitude to his health. I had asked him if he thought that a heart attack at forty-nine was worth the presence of a couple of yolks each morning. I looked forward to telling Thomas about the specification that eggs should be avoided from this *McGovern Report* that I was reading.

Despite having eaten an apple my stomach was still rumbling at me. I looked at the clock: half-past nine. I should eat dinner. I returned to the kitchen and put some pasta on the boil. I counted into my hand twenty pieces of pasta and dropped them into the boiling water in my saucepan. Then, I promptly fished three pieces out. Seventeen today, not twenty.

But you need to put on weight, you should eat twenty pieces.

After much deliberation and argument, I put the three pieces of pasta back in the pan. When working as a chef I always add some oil and salt in the pasta as it cooked. I would never consider doing that when I was cooking for myself. No way!

While the pasta was cooking I chopped up a roma tomato and a couple of cloves of garlic, I mixed this up in a bowl with some diced red onion and then tipped my drained pasta on top of it. I swished the bowl a few times to toss the fuselli in with the tomatoes and then returned to my desk to eat.

As I dutifully spooned the rather bland—but healthy, right?— meal into my mouth, I read more into the history of fat.

The next bundle of papers that I had borrowed from the library was clipped together and labelled *The Framingham Heart Study*; so called because it took place in Framingham, Massachusetts. The study began in 1948 with five thousand, two hundred and nine healthy men who were observed by the researchers for health and diet at frequent intervals. Twelve years of watching later, the initial reports were published in the 1960s. These reports showed increased cholesterol as a contributor to the risk factor of heart disease. Another win for the low fat camp!

My pasta bowl sat empty on top of an old edition of *Horse and Hound* to the right of my computer. I glanced at it longingly. I wanted more food. I tried to ignore it, then with Succubus waking up, went back into the kitchen and—after the usual mental battle between her and Sister Catherine—returned with a banana. I chopped my banana up into small pieces in the hope that this would keep me occupied for longer and sat down again to read.

I went on to read about the *Ornish study*, which provided even more proof that saturated fat was a killer. I retained that much information to be sure, but my concentration was waning despite my interest in the papers that I was reading. I felt restless, hungry. The banana all gone, I tried to distract myself by playing around on the new Facebook thing that I had recently signed up for on the internet. I quickly got annoyed with it because it wanted me to "upload a picture" of myself and I did not understand how to do that. Then it wanted me to "add friends," something which I felt was a little bit too much social pressure for that time of night. I turned my computer off.

I got up from my desk and wandered into the kitchen again; within seconds I was feverishly searching through my cupboards. I just needed something else to eat. I started by opening a low-fat strawberry yoghurt. I only intended to eat a couple of spoonfuls; I practically inhaled the entire pot in under a minute.

After that, still unsatisfied, I opened a portion sized package of Special K cereal. I preferred to buy the portioned packets because if there was an open box of cereal in the house I was afraid that I would eat more of it than I should. I ate my measured thirty gram packet of Special K with just a tiny amount of skimmed milk. I ate slowly hoping that my stomach would recognise that it was full. *It must be full! I've eaten so much!*

When that was finished, still hungry, I opened a second single-portion-sized packet and ate that too. Then, I moved on to dried fruits; handfuls of raisins and pitted prunes. The sweetness did nothing to curb my hunger: I still wanted more. Whilst I was cramming handfuls of raisins in my mouth, I knew that a thousand of them would not fill me up. I needed something more than this. Every night I needed more, but I was lost as to what to eat.

I cursed myself for not having better willpower. It reminded me of a conversation that I had with Susan earlier on in the week. She had just given me that week's food diary for my commentary and evaluation.

"What's this!" I snapped at her, she jumped a bit at the sharp tone in my voice as if I had physically pinched her. Good; I wanted her to know I was cross.

"What's what?" Her voice was hesitant; she knew very well what I was referring to.

"*This!*" I pressed my finger hard into the middle of the piece of paper that she had given to me, making it wrinkle and tear slightly, *"choc-o-late* Hob-Nob."

"Oh . . . that." She looked ashamed, like a naughty little girl; so she should.

Susan was paying me sixty quid a week to try and help her lose weight. All she had to do was eat what I told her and stick to my exercise plan and that would happen. As it was, she failed to do so on a daily basis, and quite frankly her lack of willpower was like a personal insult to me. It pissed me off.

"You know how many calories are in a chocolate Hob-Nob?"

"Erm, no . . . maybe fifty?"

That was so typical: my clients always seemed to underestimate the caloric value of the food that they ate.

"No. At least a hundred." I said with confidence. That was also typical: I always overestimated the caloric value of the food that anyone ate.

"Why?" I asked her. "Why did you do that?"

She glumly looked at her feet.

"Do you see chocolate Hob-Nob in the diet plan that I wrote for you?" I pressed. "No. No you do not, because it is not *in there*. It will never be *in there* if you want to lose weight. To lose weight you have to stop eating biscuits. The End."

I crossed my arms and stood staring at her. "Why?" I asked again.

"Well . . . I don't know, I just, my husband had one."

"Don't blame your husband," I interrupted, "I'm not training him, and as far as I am aware he doesn't need to lose weight. This is not about him."

". . . and there was only one left in the tin," she continued cautiously, "you know, I . . ." She smirked a little "I didn't want it to be lonely in there on its own."

"What?" I was flabbergasted.

Where did people get this excuse from? It was not the only time I had heard this Lonely Biscuit Dilemma.

"Susan," I started, "do you have any idea how ridiculous it is that you are attributing feelings of loneliness to a chocolate Hob-Nob?"

She said nothing. She just kept looking at her feet. I felt a little bit guilty for having yelled at her.

"Look, Susan, I know that you want to lose weight, but you really need to try and have a bit more willpower."

"How?" She asked me "How do I get more willpower?"

Good question.

I had never had any problem with willpower. As kids, my sisters and I usually had a competition after Easter to see who could make their stash of Easter chocolate last the longest. I would win that every time, even if I kept that darn Easter egg for three years I would not eat it before they ate theirs.

I had willpower around finances too. As a child, I saved my pocket money, never spending it on frivolous things like penny sweets and hair bows; when I had saved enough for a horse riding lesson, that is where it went. Mother used to call me "My Little Hoarder" as a kid. I guess she was onto something there.

Beth was the opposite of me. Candy and I could always count on her to crack first, so really the chocolate-hoarding competition was strictly between the two of us. Candy was frustratingly good at willpower too.

I did not know how to make Susan have more willpower, but I found her question intriguing and the next day saw me sifting through research studies on the subject. I read a paper titled: *Self-control relies on glucose as a limited energy source: willpower is more than a metaphor,* which explained that willpower was a limited resource. One only has so much of it a day to use, and after that reserve is depleted one is more likely to cave to desire.

I wondered what might be zapping Susan's willpower cache. Children? Husband? Work?

From the daily diet diaries that they gave me, I had noticed that if my clients slipped up with their diets it was usually at night, or after a stressful day. I was still trying to work out how to give my clients greater willpower reserves so that they could stop slipping up.

I only ever binged at night.

I considered my own willpower at that very moment as my body was asking me for more food. Half of the problem was that I did not know which desire was the temptation and which desire was the route of abstinence. I had not eaten very much that day and I was supposed to be trying to put on weight, was eating the correct path? In which case, in eating I was actually not going against my willpower.

The longer I pondered the less that I cared. I was hungry, so bloody hungry.

I caved in and opened a box of ninety-calorie granola bars; the type with the fake yoghurt on the top that looks and tastes like cheap white chocolate. Taking out a single bar I carefully closed over the flaps in the cardboard box with the remaining five in and pushed it right to the back of the cupboard. I would just have one of these tonight. Just one.

Cereal bars: the synthetic sweetness mixed in with some crunchy dried rice puffs and oats give them a taste sensation that I imagined to be similar to what sweetened cardboard might be. *I buy them because they are low fat and calories, not because they taste good.*

As I was eating that first ninety-calorie cardboard bar I regretted that I had ever allowed myself to buy the box. *Resistance is futile.* I knew that my effort of neatly re-closing the packet and hiding it at the back of the cupboard was laughable. I could have stapled the thing shut, wrapped it up in elastic bands and buried it outside in the miserable excuse for a communal garden that all the other residents used as an ashtray-slash-canine-poop-point and I would still go dig it up ten minutes later so that I could binge on its contents. I would have to put myself in a straightjacket if I wanted a shot at not eating that whole box of low-fat artificially-sweetened stick-to-your-teeth sawdust; and even then I would probably work out how to rip open the bars with my teeth. I knew I would eat the whole pack of ten bars that night, and that I would have to keep eating until there was nothing left in the house to eat.

Somewhat pathetically, despite knowing that I would eat the whole box, I crept back and took a single bar at a time. With each one, I kept trying to imagine that this would be the end of my binge, the last—but it never was. With each one, I deliberately re-closed the box and hid it at the back of my cupboard. With each one I discreetly left the kitchen and diligently turned the lights off, as if that was my last visit back to it. With each one, I firmly closed the kitchen door. With each one, I ate laboriously slowly. I savoured every bite of that sickly, nasty, tasteless, cardboard nothingness.

When the tenth one was gone, and the box was empty, there was still an aching hole in my stomach that needed to be filled. I returned to the kitchen; a third portion pack of Special K came out. This time, after allowing a more liberal splash of milk to wet the flakes, I thickly drizzled some runny honey over them. Sweet flakes of air topped with sticky golden sap. I was thankful that I had not allowed myself to buy any peanut butter that day, as had I had a jar in the house I knew I would have been eating it now. Every night would usually end with peanut butter for me. Straight from the jar onto a spoon into my mouth. Only ever last thing at night, right before bedtime, would I cave in to allowing fat to have a place amongst the sweets.

In lieu of peanut butter I spooned honey from the jar to my mouth, and washed it down with skimmed milk. Then I slept.

The next day I went to the library and took out a copy of *The China Study*—a book that was published by a man called T. Colin Campbell with his son. The cover claimed that the book was one of America's best selling books on nutrition. *Anything that sells over a million copies cannot be wrong* I thought to myself.

The China Study examined the relationship between chronic illnesses such as coronary heart disease, diabetes and various cancers. The recommendation was that to avoid these things one should eat a whole food plant based vegan diet, avoiding all animal products including beef, pork, poultry, fish, eggs, milk and cheese. All of this made perfect sense and settled in nicely with what I had already been reading.

The China Study was a bit confusing to me, however, as it proved that protein was bad. The Campbell fellow showed that with laboratory rats, when he fed one group of rats on a high protein diet they developed cancer cells at a faster rate than the rats that were not fed protein. He also recommended that processed carbohydrates should be removed from the diet.

So, this would mean no bread, no Special K, no pasta, and no cardboard cereal bars. I wondered in that case what I was supposed to eat at all? This threw me into all sorts of inner conflict. I had spent the last couple of years trying to convince myself to eat something, anything other than just fruit and vegetables, I had worked myself up to pasta and hummus and was finally able to eat those things in the daylight hours, sometimes even getting close to eating plain bread (or at least thinking about it)—and now the China bloke was telling me that I had been better off before when all I ate in the day was salad.

Ugh. *Had all that stress been for nothing?*

Could I just eat salad and not worry about trying to up my intake of other foods?

Was anything safe to eat?

Should I live my life on cucumbers alone?

Was peanut butter going to give me cancer?

So what do people that live by *The China Study* actually eat? I skipped over to the cookbook section of the library and pulled open a *China Study Recipe* book. I wanted to see what one embarking on this diet would practically do in the kitchen. I was even more confused to find that the recipes featured in the book were mostly salads but with a lot of pasta, breads, soy and tofu.

I thought soy and tofu were processed?

Hmm, well, Doctor Campbell's book did sell over a million copies, anything that sells like that cannot be wrong; I must have just got myself confused. Vegetables are good;

meat is bad. Bread is good; fat is bad. Soy is good; milk is bad. Tofu is good; protein is bad. Pasta is good; carbohydrate is bad.

Got it! Clear as crystal!

My research had led me to the conclusion that I had wanted to see. That a low fat diet was the best form of nutritional advice that I could give as a personal trainer. I felt renewed with my passion for advising my clients and I could rest in the knowledge that my own abhorrence of fat was justified.

Chapter Thirty

October 2010: Boulder, Colorado.

I wandered up and down the aisles of Whole Foods; my pace quickened in annoyance as I continued to fail to find what I was looking for. In front of me, I spotted a man in a beige shirt who looked like a store employee and I made a beeline for him. Hearing my harried footsteps, he lifted his head as I approached. "Can I help you find something ma'am?" he beamed.

I had never been called ma'am before. I had only ever heard the term used to address the Queen of England, and because of this, it crossed my mind that maybe this fellow was being sarcastic. Then I remembered that Americans don't understand sarcasm.

"I'm looking for the tea!" I threw my hands into the air to emphasise my frustration.

I had never had to *look* for tea before. In England, the tea section in a grocery store is practically signposted from the car park. What the hell was going on? Didn't these people drink tea? Having only been in America twenty-four hours, I was at a loss as to how the system worked here. All that I could find were these newfangled, suspicious-looking, herbaceous, fruit-scented abominations.

"Well, come right on with me and I will show you." His demeanor was shockingly pleasant.

In England I was yet to find a grocery aisle employee that did not hate the world and everyone in it. I found it disconcerting that this fellow seemed so happy to be at work, and began to wonder if the store assistants, like the waiting staff in America, required tipping. Regardless, I trailed after him as we weaved our way back through the aisles that I had just come along.

"Here we are . . . tea!" he proudly presented me with an extensive array of floral patterned multi-colored boxes. Herbal teas.

A travesty indeed.

I began to panic. "Nonono, No. You don't understand. PG Tips? Tetley? Yorkshire Tea?"

Please let them have proper tea or I will have murdered someone before the day is out so help me God I swear it!

He scratched his head and began to speak, but I had already turned around in despair; this man could not help me: there was no *tea* in this store. Then, I remembered that I needed to use the loo; I swiveled on my heels to face him again. He flinched a little, as if he expected to receive a blow.

"Is there a loo at least?"

"A what?"

"Oh bloody hell . . . a LOO!"
"Oh . . . do you mean a restroom?"
Whatever.

We had emigrated to Boulder, Colorado, in a quest for sunnier weather for me, and a more promising software career for Matt. I had initiated the move after a typically English summer of torrential rain. Tired of the drizzle, we wanted to try something new.

There were many, many, things that took some getting used to when we moved from England to Colorado. Using the term "restroom" was one of them. I still have no idea why a restroom is called a restroom when the last thing that one would want to do in a loo is take a nap. Despite my dislike for the word, it is one that I have succumbed to using out of necessity; when one needs to spend a penny, it is important that a lav is found, regardless of what one has to call it in order to get there.

When I first moved to America I thought I'd get used to Overly Attentive Shop Assistants. I haven't.

In the United Kingdom, if a shop assistant is conscious, that's an anomaly, and the ones who are will immediately move to the furthest end of the store away from any customers to avoid the possibility of being asked to do anything remotely useful. This is good. This I like.

In America, a visit to the grocery store is rather like sitting next to a pond on a summer's eve without mosquito repellent.

For someone as cantankerous as I, this is enough to deter me from going shopping. Seriously, some days I walk into a store only to turn heel on the first "Can I help you find anything" and flee.

I remember that when I used to go to church, if one did not want to receive communion one would be told to take the service sheet up to the bar as a cue for the vicar to pass you by. Likewise in yoga, if one doesn't want to be assisted there is usually a signal to give the instructor to leave you alone. Can we not make some similar code for American store assistants? A white scarf maybe?

No, I know, a British flag. If I am wearing anything with the Union Jack on it that means do not talk to me.

For petulant people like me, Americans can be rather draining. For the first three weeks at least my face hurt; I was getting smile fatigue by the end of each day. The muscles around my mouth had to work very hard to match the plastered grins of America, and they simply were not used to it. I contemplated developing a facial muscle training programme for cantankerous Brits who need to strengthen their smile muscles to the level of sustainability required in the States; that might just have been my millionaire idea right there.

For the first couple of weeks living in the Rocky Mountains, I was absorbed by the change in culture, trying to find tea, remembering to smile deliriously, and the glorious sunshine. I was not looking too closely at what I was buying—other than to check the fat and calorie content of course. I was pleasantly surprised to find that everything was cheaper. I existed for about three weeks in a state of blissful ignorance as we put all of our focus into finding a truck, and then using it to collect furniture with which to fill our empty two-bed rented townhouse. Driving on the right side of the road, trying to remember not to be too mean to Americans, and distressing over a lack of real tea were my main concerns in that time.

Then, one day, I was shopping, and I was paying close attention to the labels on the milk. In the United Kingdom, the colours of milk cartons do not differ. Skimmed milk is always in a red carton, semi-skimmed is always in a green carton, and whole milk is always blue. This helpful colour-coded system means that regardless of the specific brand of milk that one is buying, one does not have to look very hard in order to make sure the correct type of milk is being selected. America has no reliable system of milk identification other than reading the label. Depending on the brand, any colour can be used for any distinction of milk; it is quite bothersome and can be incredibly confusing.

One day, as I stood peering at the milk labels to make sure that I was actually selecting skimmed milk, I noticed that some of them had the words "No rBGH" on the label, and others did not.

"Can I help you find anything?"

"Good grief! You scared the shi . . . life out of me!" I choked. "Actually yes, I mean no, I mean . . . can you tell me what this rBGH stuff is?"

The shop assistant looked at me blankly; he was just a kid.

I sighed "Never mind . . . go back to sleep, I'll Google it."

I plucked the brand new iPhone thingy that Matt had insisted I swap my Blackberry for out of my pocket. After swearing at the over sensitive touch screen a couple of times, I managed to find the internet button, which opened my eyes to the world of growth hormone.

I was stunned. Baffled. Terrified. *What the hell had I been drinking for the last three weeks?*

I paid an extra dollar for a gallon of organic skimmed milk and scooted out of the store. At home I calmed myself with a cup of tea while I scanned the interwebs and filled my head with information. Firstly, regarding the ghastly rBGH, and then on to other things like high fructose corn syrup, propylene glycol and red food dye number five. I drained my teacup and put the kettle on for another as the Skype on my iPad started buzzing at me. It was Mother.

"Tabby! Tabby! Is that you?" she squawked at her computer screen.

"Hi Mum. So, you managed to work out how to use Skype then?" Before we had left England I had given my mother a lesson on how to use the internet, email and Skype in the hope that being able to stay in touch would stop her worrying about us quite so much. It had ended badly. I was not the most patient of teachers.

"Well no," she admitted, "actually Darling I had to get Daddy to show me again, I don't think I will ever work out this Facebook thingy . . ."

"Skype Mum, you mean Skype, Facebook is the other thing, the one with . . ." I sighed. "Never mind. Listen Mum, you will never guess what I discovered today. They put hormones in the milk and antifreeze in the blueberry yoghurt over here!"

"Don't be silly Tabby. Stop pulling my leg. Why on earth would anyone put hormones in milk? And, why are you taking antifreeze with your yoghurt? Is it some new diet fad of yours?" I rolled my eyes and ignored the question completely.

"Mum they do so! It says so on Google . . . I will send you a link."

"A what?"

"Never mind."

My blissful ignorance had been shattered. The next time I had to go into the store, I sculked cautiously and suspiciously up and down the aisles; the toxic makeup these foods had been wearing had come undone before my eyes and all I saw was shelves laden with ugly chemicals. I trusted nothing.

I started buying organic everything.

We had moved to Boulder because Matt had landed a job there. I, on the other hand, was applying for a spouse visa, and was not allowed to work in the meantime. This was hard for me—someone with workaholic tendencies—but it was a price worth paying to be living somewhere where the sun shone every day. I began volunteering my riding and training services at the local horse rescue. Much to my surprise, it felt lovely to be riding horses again; this time for no money and no pressure. I could feel myself relaxing, the sunshine was obviously doing me good. I smiled more often.

I had landed in heaven; none of the American stereotypes existed in the corner of Colorado in which we lived. In Boulder, people are hikers, bikers, skiers, yogis, and the first thing that I realised when we settled in there was that my days as a personal trainer were over. I was redundant and would be forced into early retirement; nobody in Boulder looked like they needed a personal trainer.

Most Boulderites look like they run a marathon before breakfast. The bike paths are heaving with runners, skaters, cyclists, and newborn babies being pushed along at a racing pace in prams that look more like mini space buggies. On the second day of us arriving there, I saw someone holding a headstand whilst waiting at the bus stop; just because.

In Boulder, the term "Senior Citizen" is code for *spends all day hiking*. Most people over the age of sixty can outpace me on the cyclepath; when one retires it simply means that one has more time for activities. Boulder must be the only place on the planet where coconut water outsells Coca-Cola and kale is in higher demand than Cheetos.

For the first time since the age of twelve, I had no job. Even more alarming was that I had no plan. I had no idea what I would do when my visa finally arrived; all I knew how to do was get people fit, and compared to this crowd I was the slacker.

Much to my distress, everyone in Boulder seemed very into yoga. I had actually been qualified to teach yoga as part of my personal training package, but I had skipped out on most of the practical session and just taken the test at the end; frankly, I did not know my down-dog from my urdhva-mukha-svanasana or my cow-faced-pose from my full-of-shitasana. I had taught the mandatory classes that I had needed to teach for my apprenticeship hours, but other than that I had never had any interest in yoga. I remembered that Susan had asked me about it once:

"Do you think that I should take up yoga too?"

"Yoga! Why would you want to do yoga? "

"Well, my friend Anne-Marie is doing it. She ways it's wonderful!"

I rolled my eyes.

"*She* says it has helped her touch her toes, and other things!" Susan continued, "She even says that her sex life is better because of it!" She lent forward towards me, and motioned for me to lean in also, as if she were going to share something highly confidential. Despite myself, I begrudgingly lowered my nose closer to hers. "She has even got her husband Peter doing it!" Susan's "whisper" was loud enough that the two old fellows who were fifty feet away in the weights room looked over at us.

Enough silliness. I stood back, took a deep breath, and prepared myself for my sermon:

"Susan. Yoga is nothing more than a lazy person's excuse for exercise. It is pointless synchronized stretching and that is all there is to it."

Boulder, Colorado was all over yoga.

Not only was I not the fittest person in town, but I was no longer the thinnest person in the room anymore; this was something that I appreciated. Had I been a couple of years behind in my recovery process I think the influence of a fit and athletic town such as Boulder would have pushed me to exercise further. But, the timing was right for me, and being in Boulder happened to work in my favour.

Best of all (or worst of all), everyone in Boulder seemed to avoid fat, many people were vegan or vegetarian, and most were dairy and gluten free. My eating disorder was camouflaged amongst the wealth of faddy eating habits that this town was riddled with.

After the rBGH incident, when I was not getting thrown about by wild mustangs and unbroken horses at the rescue, I was researching the food scene. One day, I clicked through a link on a *Yummy Organic Mummy's* blog and found myself reading an article on cholesterol. I was stunned; either the person that has written it was stupid, or very misguided. This fellow was claiming that cholesterol was good, and he had some pretty convincing sounding arguments!

I decided to disregard it all as quackery at the time, but could not get that article out of my mind.

The next couple of days, intrigued, I buried myself in online papers on cholesterol and heart disease. My research led me to understand that cholesterol actually comes into play in healing and repair of blood vessels. I had always wondered what cholesterol actually did in the body other than cause problems. It reminded me rather of the time when I was five that I had asked Mother why God had invented spiders if all they did was scare people. My school-child brain just could not understand why anyone, let alone God, would do such a stupid thing! It seemed such a silly waste of time to make a spider; not to mention that it was a rather mean trick to play on those of us that are scared of them! *Why did God invent spiders?*

Why did God invent cholesterol?

Mum had explained that actually the spiders had a very important job: we need them to catch the flies. I had pouted over that. Sure, it made a little more sense if spiders actually had a purpose, but why then did they have to be so ugly looking? What kind of skullduggary was that? I felt somewhat miffed that God had to go and make spiders so scary, it seemed very uncalled for.

Cholesterol, like spiders, apparently has a purpose. It is actually *made*, manufactured and produced in our bodies. It's not just eaten into presence as I had once been led to believe. One of the reasons that our bodies make cholesterol is because it helps to repair stuff. Cholesterol is not just important, it's *bloody* important!

I learnt that my brain is about seventy percent cholesterol; every cell wall in my body contains it. I learnt that my hormones all have a cholesterol base, and my body constantly weighs up the amount that I need to the amount that I eat, then manufacturers the deficit.

Now, one thing that my time spent at university taught me, is that I am blessed with rather limited intelligence. I had just managed to hide my stupidity rather well behind a haughty pony club accent and a good posture. The structure at the University of Edinburgh is that in the first year one takes multiple subjects in order to keep one's options open. Then, in the second year, one narrows things down by deciding on and opting for one major. I actually wanted to major in economics as I had enjoyed it so much at A-level. However, university level brought with it advanced mathematics that my little brain was struggling to grasp. As my tutor advised me at the end of the first year:

"You might do better taking a subject less mentally challenging, one that you brain can manage better . . . like psychology?"

Well, that was a fine idea. I gave up economics in the second year. Psychology, in my opinion, was nothing more than a collection of stories and statistics; I could easily just memorise the essay scripts for the end of term finals. After all, I was stupid wasn't I? So what was the point in trying too hard?

Skipping lectures saved me lots of time. I could do more important things like go to the gym. It was apparent that I had only got as far as I had in economics at A-level because I had found a way of making the abstract concepts more palatable. I would turn the hypothetical ideas of supply and demand into scenarios that made sense to me: like buying and selling horses, or trading tack cleaning for mucking out.

This method of using analogy to better understand concepts which I could not understand, was one that I had actually originally stolen from my primary school teacher; she used to tell us stories about sugar bon-bons and Maltesers in order to help us understand arithmetic. I still use this sort of analogy on a daily basis to help me grasp things like what my husband does for a living. Matt works in computer science and will explain testing to me in terms of recipes or horses: analogies he knows I might have a chance of grasping.

When I was researching about the functions of fats and cholesterol in the human body, and I could feel myself getting confused with all the conflicting information, I knew that I needed to turn cells and body parts into a currency that made easier sense to me. My mind played with the dynamics in the kitchen at The Barley where I had been working years before:

I imagined that the body regulating cholesterol levels was rather like me doing stocktake of the food supply in the kitchen. I would place a food order each week with the wholesaler dependent on how much I had left in the fridge already, and how much demand there was in terms of customers we expected that week.

It would seem that cholesterol is somewhat precious—as if it is not used the body will recycle it back to the liver for storage. One's heart is also involved in all of this cholesterol management, as it communicates with one's liver about the body's need for cholesterol. This is rather like the demand side of the equation.

The liver monitors and manufactures the cholesterol, it tells the carriers—High Density Lipoproteins (HDLs) and Low Density Lipoproteins (LDLs)— where to put it, and communicates with the heart about the overall state of things in the body. In my kitchen scenario, that would make the potwasher, Lucy, the carrier.

Wait a second, would she be both LDL and HDL?

I wondered if they were similar enough, or if I would have to imagine up a second potwasher to play the part of LDL. I would let Lucy be HDL, as other than wearing nail varnish to work she was quite a sweet girl, and everyone knows that LDL cholesterol is the evil one. Maybe Lucy could have an evil twin to play LDL? She would look like Lucy but she would refuse to take off her nail varnish and put her hair up in a ponytail when I asked her to. I scowled at the thought of evil LDL Lucy. Silly brat with a bad attitude. I would probably have fired her on the first day!

I realised that I could not fire Lucy despite her being annoying sometimes because she is part of the whole cholesterol story. And that perplexed me, because why would I have someone in my kitchen that was messing everything up with nail varnish and long dangly hair?

Why would I tolerate the evil twin?

If LDL is bad then why does the body not only keep it, but make it too?

Surely the body is not that dumb?

Even if I was silly enough to hire the evil twin version of Lucy, Thierry would have told her to go, someone at The Barley would have fired her.

Why doe the body continue to manufacture bad cholesterol?

I continued to read, and the answer to this question was that evil Lucy got to stay in the kitchen because she was not really evil at all. She is just a *different* version of Lucy. The only difference between LDL and HDL is the direction that they carry the cholesterol. LDL particles take the cholesterol to the arteries and wherever it is needed, HDL particles take the cholesterol that is not needed back the the liver for storage. This made better sense; both versions of Lucy are the same, they just move in opposite directions.

The HDL twin version of Lucy returns the leftover food to the fridge, and the HDL carriers in the body take unused cholesterol away from the tissues and back to the liver so that it can be recycled. This certainly answered my question before about why the body did not just get rid of the cholesterol by simply carrying it to the kidneys and sending it out. It turns out this is because the body likes cholesterol so much it recycles it. HDL is just carrying the cholesterol about, it is not changing the amount of total cholesterol in the body at all, just re-shuffling it.

In the body, blood vessels have a delicate lining and are at the mercy of turbulent blood flow. Turbulent blood flow is created where blood vessels divide and the blood pressure is high. This turbulence can damage the lining of the blood vessels, and such damage has to be repaired. I imagined the blood vessels to be a bit like my kitchen at work, and on days when we had a high volume of customer's orders running through it at a fast pace, the place is a mess. Pots and pans, food everywhere, usually someone has spilt something, chaos. And I am there yelling at LDL Lucy to hurry up and get me something out of the fridge, then something else, because the orders are coming in fast and I need to cook

195

the food. The busier the shift is, the more that I need the LDL Lucy as she is the one that gets me the stuff that I need.

In the human body, cholesterol repairs the damage done by turbulence. The first sign of repair is a fatty streak, then plaque forms. It is the LDL cholesterol that goes to the tissues and the arteries and gives them what they need. If there is a lot of damage in the body and arteries then there is a lot of LDL cholesterol in the blood. Likewise if things are busy in the kitchen, LDL twin version of Lucy is there more often as I need her to take the ingredients out of the fridge so that I can use them in the meals I am cooking.

I could understand why it was originally thought that a high amount of LDL cholesterol in one's body could be seen as bad: wherever there is LDL, there is chaos and damage. Therefore, at first glance, one might think that it was the LDL cholesterol *causing* the mess. But, really, the LDL is only present because it is needed to *repair* things. That would be like blaming the volume of orders in a busy shift on Lucy the potwasher, just because when you first walk into the scene you see her running all over the place. In truth, Lucy is running all over the place because I, the chef, am telling her to. And I am telling her to because I need her to get me ingredients so that I can manage the amount of work I have to do.

If the chaos is not Lucy's fault, and it's not my fault, whose fault is it?

Whose fault is chaos in one's arteries?

The customers! It's all the bloody customers that come in and order food all at the same bloody time! Take, for example, Sunday lunchtime; that shift would always be utter devastation in the kitchen. We would be running about like lunatics trying to keep up with the volume of orders. Sunday lunchtime always brought so much pressure!

High pressure, and high stress!

Like high blood pressure!

Then I understood: It was the high volume of blood being pushed through one's veins and arteries that was causing the damage, and the LDL cholesterol was just the most obvious thing to measure as it was the more present in a person's body when that person was in a bad state of repair, or had high blood pressure.

And what caused high blood pressure? The same thing that caused me to lose my temper when a million food orders were thrown at me at once: stress.

Stress causes heart disease, not cholesterol and not fat.

Now, we all know that my simple little kitchen analysis of cholesterol is a massive simplification, but I hope that you get that the exact biological science is not really the point here. The point is that I was getting my head around the concept that rather than being the biological boogeyman, cholesterol is actually a vital component to life. And that took some work!

Ever since Ancel Keys had said it was so, everybody thought that cholesterol was bad. This is certainly what I had been conditioned to think; yet now, I was reading that cholesterol is a vital component to every living cell on earth. That feeling was familiar; it reminded me of the time I woke up to find Mother replacing the milk tooth which I had left under my pillow with a pound coin.

There was something even more troubling in the reports and studies that I was reading, something that the very suggestion of made me stiffen. Some researchers were claiming that fat was a good thing, too. Saturated fat at that. I was reading that cell membranes are made up of one-third polyunsaturated fat, one-third saturated fat and one-third cholesterol, and that both cholesterol and saturated fat are essential for life.

That was too much for me to take. I could maybe, after a while, comprehend that cholesterol may not be as bad as I had been led to believe . . . but fat?

No, not fat. My hate of fat was what I had based my whole life on—my job, my passion, my identity! My hate of fat was my justification for the eight years that I had spent thin and alone. My hate of fat was what excused me from feeling guilt about the way that I spoke to my mother should she try and criticize my eating habits. My hate of fat defined who I was.

Could I allow myself to consider that fat was anything other than evil?

Chapter Thirty One

"You will never believe what I read about cholesterol today!" I blurted out to Matt as he came through the front door one evening. He had been mountain biking after work. Sweaty and covered in dust, he gave me a hug and a kiss on the cheek. As usual, I stiffened a little, then wiggled out from his embrace after a couple of seconds. I felt bad about doing that, especially because my neighbour Hannah was always whining to me that she wished her husband, Greg, would be more affectionate.

"What's that then?" Matt mused as he walked over to the sink to pour himself a glass of water.

"Cholesterol is not that bad after all, in fact, it might be good." I could not hide the utter disbelief in my voice.

He looked amused, but said nothing.

"It is so absurd," I continued, "I just can't get my head around it."

"Does that mean that I am having fried chicken for dinner?" He grinned.

The next day I read in an article published by a heart surgeon saying the foods that cause the most inflammation in the body are highly processed carbohydrates—which come from things like sugar and flour. This bloke was blatantly claiming that it was actually the low-fat diet responsible for the inflammation that was causing heart disease, and as I searched around a little more I discovered other voices claiming the same thing.

I was noticing that really, in the world of heart disease, fat and cholesterol, there were more questions than answers.

In the weeks that followed, as the spring-buds in Colorado began opening on the trees, I continued to read. In a nutshell I learnt that there could be a number of reasons for inflammation, and that really, in linking saturated fat to heart disease, most of these other factors had been overlooked. I began to see the difference between acute inflammation, such as that which is felt immediately, and chronic inflammation, such as that which could apparently lead to blocked arteries. Fat, which had been so publicly blamed, might not be the sole, or even the primary, culprit after all.

That is not to say that my diet changed at all; it did not. Not even remotely. There was too much of me, my belief system, my identity— all hooked into my eating disorder— attached to hating fat. I read, studied, researched, and even understood that fat had been mislabelled in Western culture as the bad guy, but I was unable to translate this information so that it affected my behaviours; I simply could not comprehend buying anything other than low-fat products. There was a wall up between my understanding and my ability to embrace it.

Another spanner was that I could not stop my cravings for carbohydrates. I ate cereal for almost every meal, or bread and low-fat peanut butter with reduced-calorie jam or hummus. I'd snack on fruit and low-fat yoghurt during the day, then, without fail, binge at night. I existed within the same routine of meticulous control over what I ate during the day and an oblivion of gluttony at night.

The more that I read, the more I came across differing points of view and conflicting information. Frustrated with all the parody, I was tempted to stop researching and rely on the bliss of ignorance evermore. Before I did that, however, I made one final attempt to convince myself to eat meat. I wondered if part of the reason for my avoidance of it was that I did not trust American meat producers not to put growth hormones and antibiotics in everything, so I contacted some people in the meat industry who claimed to be the "ethical farmers" behind happy cows.

I wrote to a farmer who owned a ranch in Colorado Springs. He was so confident that I would approve of the way that his cows were treated that he invited me down to look in his meat processing plant. I went.

I met the cows; they looked happy.

I met the butchers; they looked happy too.

I met some children that were regulars with their mothers in the farm store; they looked very happy.

I actually looked inside the machine that minces the meat and saw the production process. I bought some meat and took it home for Matt. Seeing happy and healthy cows did nothing for me: I could still not eat meat.

I came to the conclusion that I was bat-shit nuts and utterly hopeless. It seemed that the best thing to do in that case, would be to carry on with life and do my utmost to try and hide my insaneness from the rest of the world.

That summer, still banned from working due to visa delays, I began volunteering at a local organic Community Supported Agriculture farm. There was a huge benefit in that they rewarded my efforts with an abundance of produce. It was wonderful to be able to go out in the mornings and help plant garlic, dig up vegetable beds and pick tomatoes. I delighted in the misshapen carrots and split-ripe tomatoes.

Around October, the first harvest time that I worked with them, Dave, the farmer, showed me how to extract carrots from the ground.

"See! That easy," he said as he demonstrated how to loosen the soil and gently pull the bright orange vegetable from the cold earth. "Try it," he urged, as he handed me one of the carrots he had just pulled up, "there is nothing like it!" And with that he took a bite out of one of the others.

I dusted off the dirt the best that I could and ate that glorious little carrot then and there. It was delicious.

"There is something indescribable about eating a carrot fresh from the earth," Dave mused as he returned to his harvesting, and he was right.

Unbeknown to him, that was a small victory of all sorts for me. I had already eaten my breakfast before venturing onto the farm that morning, and typically this would mean that until I returned home for lunch I had not expected to eat anything. That carrot had not been in the plan, so when Dave suggested that I eat it, Sister Catherine and Succubus squabbled viciously in my head.

Dave could not have known that in asking me to eat a small vegetable at ten o'clock on a sunny Sunday morning, he was challenging stirring up all mothers of mental tantrums. He could not hear the thoughts that rose up and swarmed my head in that moment, so he could never have understood that my squinting eyes and lifted hand were a tactic I had learnt to shield my face when I was dealing with my inner battle, and nothing to do with the sun at all. And in that moment every doubt that I had ever had about myself emerged, in that moment I wanted to run again, I wanted to scream and cry and throw the carrot back at him. He could never have known any of that, because I hid it from him the same way that I hid it from everyone else: really really well. But the bickering died down, and the moment passed.

I looked up at him and smiled as if there was nothing wrong.

That was not a victory of calories or fat, as a carrot contains little to none of either of those things, this was a victory of letting go of my secret but rigorous eating plan. My method of surviving each day by sticking rigidly to my set mealtimes and select pre-planned foods. I got a snippet of freedom that day standing in that field, as if a gate—one that was once firmly locked and guarded—was starting to lean-to.

Alas, as I expected, my disobedience to my own schedule brought with it consequences. Sister Catherine went berserk, and Succubus laughed in delirium.

The usual barrage of mixed emotions—shame, confusion, and regret—quickly followed that first bite of carrot down my throat. On my drive home from the farm, I stopped in at the local gym in order to do some time on the stair-climber. Sister Catherine told me that unplanned eating could only be negated with unplanned exercise. I was tired; obeisance was easier than further disobedience. Two steps forward, one step back.

On the way out, I asked to speak with the manager about teaching cycling classes. I had not taught since I left England, and now, nine months later, my Green Card had arrived and I was able to work again. Maybe it was just a coincidence that today was the day that I chose to step back into the cleated SPDs of a cycling instructor. Maybe.

"So . . ." I hedged. "I got a job at the gym teaching cycling." I tried to keep my tone of voice matter of fact as Matt and I sat down to dinner. For him: a pork chop with sautéed vegetables and potatoes. For me: low-fat hummus and vegetables.

"Um, ok . . . if that's what you want to do, but why?"

200

I had not been expecting Matt to jump for joy at the prospect of me working in a gym again.

I bristled even at a hint of disapproval.

"Because I want to," was my curt reply. I made it clear that we had reached the end of this particular conversation by busying myself tidying plates into the kitchen.

One afternoon, towards the end of autumn, I was reading a report titled *Three Daily Servings of Reduced-Fat Milk: An Evidence-Based Recommendation* on the difference between skimmed and whole milk. The study was questioning the role of milk in the human diet at all, but for me, milk was a necessity because I drank it in my tea. I had heard that one could use soy in tea in the place of cow's milk, but I had also seen that soy milk was actually higher in calories than skimmed milk, so I stuck with skimmed.

As a child, at home, we had used whole milk. I remember the milkman delivering it in glass bottles with the shiny red cap on. That milk had a creamy top to it that was the treat for the lucky person who got to the new bottle first. I would hustle to beat my sisters to it, and the creamy top would taste wonderful mixed in with my tea or even better just drank on its own in a tall glass.

When I was seventeen, when I had dieted so that I could be light enough to exercise those racehorses, I had switched to drinking tea only with skimmed milk in it. That was all that I had allowed myself to drink for years and it had remained so. Now here I was, thirteen years on, reading a paper saying that the organic full fat version of milk contained essential and healthy fats, and was all round a better idea.

Should I start buying whole milk again?

Could I even bring myself to do that?

Maybe I should consider soy after all?

Could I do that even if I wanted to? Would it be worth the stress?

All these fretful thoughts about food surfacing in my head again. I stepped up from my desk to make myself a cup of tea, only to discover that I was, indeed, low on milk.

I walked to the store determined to buy full fat milk. *What harm could it do?* It seemed like another way to challenge my habitual behaviours and I was up for it. I had science on my side, I was feeling feisty that day and I walked through the doors of Whole Foods like a woman on a mission: A Whole-Milk Mission!

My charge lasted almost as far as the dairy fridge. Then, I baulked. *What the hell was I doing? What was I thinking?*

The doubts. Sister Catherine's scolding. Succubus's pitiful laughter.

I reasoned with myself: I should stick to the skimmed milk; *stick to what you know; stick to what is safe. Why change? Why invite change that could damage?*

I paused, conflicted, the fridge door open in my hand.

A woman pushed past me with an apologetic smile and reached into the fridge, she picked up a gallon of skimmed milk and continued on her way.

Skimmed is good enough for her, I reasoned, *so it's good enough for me*. I picked up a half-gallon and headed to the cashier.

No.

This was not about my health anymore, this was about *seeing if* I could buy whole milk instead of skimmed *should I want to*. This was about beating my habits. This was about winning. I returned to the dairy fridge.

I stood in front of it for an embarrassing amount of time. Then, I replaced the skimmed milk, and, proudly, selected a half-gallon of whole. I turned towards that cashier desks at a march, knowing the faster that I paid and got out of that bloody shop, the less chance there would be for further argument. Unluckily, I was greeted with a queue of people. I joined the back of the line and waited.

Don't do it! Don't look.

I looked. The wait had been too long for me to fight off the impulsion to look at the nutrition information panel on the back of the carton. *Shit! There are so many more calories and fat in whole milk!* The doubt came back in.

Too much. It's too much! You cannot possibly drink that!

"Ma'am . . . Hello Ma'am?" I jumped clean out of my skin at the sound of a voice addressing me. It was the cashier, and I was already at the front of the queue. Everyone was looking at me now.

"I err . . . I got the wrong one, sorry!" I explained as I motioned for the person behind me in the line to take my place at the register.

I went back to the dairy fridge.

Holy crap it was hard. I figured that skimmed to whole in one go was too much of a jump, but was determined to come out from that store feeling that I had taken a step forward. What to do?

Semi-skimmed! That's it!

With a half-gallon of semi-skimmed milk in my clutches, I headed back to the cashier again; this time I checked out, got home and made that cup of tea with semi-skimmed milk in it rather than skimmed. I had not won in the way that I had set out to do, but I had taken a step in the right direction and I had done so in a way that I knew was sustainable. I considered that a victory. And blimey had it been a tough one!

Chapter Thirty Two

It was winter in 2011 and the first snow of the year had just covered our driveway. The organic farm had packed up for the season and I was looking for work. I had settled into a couple of horse riding jobs at a few local ranches; the rest of the time I continued researching into the organic food industry and driving myself nuts with my food-related preoccupations and eating rituals. I wanted to change, but things were not going anywhere fast. I'd try really hard for a couple of days and then get complacent. It was proving frustrating and taking a very long time; I'd often wonder if I was making any progress at all.

One afternoon, I answered the phone to my neighbour Hannah.

"Want to come try a yoga class with me at five?" She asked after the mundane small talk that every phone call in America commences with.

"Yoga, seriously? Why?" I could not curb the distaste in my tone.

"It's supposed to be good for stress and breaking habits, and I need to break the habit of saying yes to more stress, " she replied with a laugh.

"Well in that case . . . why not."

I once heard yoga referred to as the "process of undoing", and although I doubted that I would be able to undo the neurological pathways that I had spent eight years creating, I wondered if being able to connect my mind and body better would give me a fighting chance at developing new, less annoying ones. Despite all the bad mouthing that I had given yoga in the years that I had been working as a personal trainer, and granted that I believed Hannah to be an utter nut and that it would be a complete waste of time, I went along to a yoga class with her. I was desperate, and I figured that there was no harm in trying. Off we tottered to the yoga studio that afternoon.

"We are all ... Stardust," the instructor proclaimed.

Oh please, I whispered to myself.

I considered leaving. We were still in downward-facing-dog pose, and had been there for what seemed like donkey's years. This lycra clad hippie with the clichéd deep and swoopy voice was pacing up and down the rows of mats chatting rubbish. The "stardust" comment was just about too much for me to take. I would have left then and there had it not been for Hannah, who was on the mat next to me breathing like an express train as we had been told to do. I wondered if anything more interesting than this dog posture was going to happen all class.

It did.

By quarter-past five I was a conflagration of limbs. My arms and legs were simply all over the place and utterly out of sync with what my brain was telling them to do, which was in turn about three paces behind what the stardust lycra contortionist at the front was instructing the class to do in her melodic, breathy voice.

"Lift your right leg towards the sky. Now, step it through to your left hand and twist your right hand to the ceiling ... *goooood* ... now left leg lifts and wraps around your body until your left pinky toe is up your right nostril . . ."

My fellow students seemed to be in perfect harmony as I wobbled and scurried on my mat at the back. Every posture that we were put in I wanted out of; every posture that we got out of led to another one to be in. Even weirder was that everyone else in the room seemed to be having a fabulous time; the people on the surrounding mats all wore this eerie —and somewhat disconcerting—smile on their faces.

And that was only the first couple of sun salutations. Believe it or not the room got hotter and the postures got harder. The sweat began to tiptoe from my forehead into my eyelashes. Then, something indescribable happened.

Utkatasana.

Utkatasana happened—that's the one where you bend your knees as if squatting over a loo. Our enthusiastic instructor informed us that "utkatasana" was sanskrit for *chair pose*. And I was in it; I was in it for so long that I began to feel like *I was it*. As the seconds meandered past, the sweat that had previously been creeping began to stream into my eyes. We were still in utkatasana; my legs were shaking. We were still in utkatasana: I held my breath. Annoyance turned into hate, hate turned into fury, and finally, fury turned into panic. I was trapped in this body, in this posture, and everything inside me wanted to shout and to scream and to run out the room. But I could not move. We were still in utkatasana. The background noise of the Stardust Woman's continual monologue merged to a blur with the din of my own beating heart. Then, one word jumped out at me from the fray.

"Breathe," Stardust Hippie said, "breathe."

And I did. Because I was desperate; because I had nothing else left to try.

Inhale. Exhale. Inhale. Exhale.

Stillness.

Yoga gave me space. I noticed immediately after class that day that the thoughts in my head were slower; it were as if I could see them coming at me. That space, between thought and reaction, gave me choice. That space between thinking, and *being* the thought, gave me the opportunity to choose not to be that thought after all. That space allowed me to decide, which in turn demonstrated to me how little decision making authority I had held within my own body before.

That space allowed me to really see how utterly fucked up my own thoughts were; for the most part, I discovered that, given the choice, I wanted nothing to do with them.

I came out of that first yoga practice exhausted, broken and crushed. I understood without a doubt that this was what I needed. The class had been an escalation of confusion and discomfort, but in the space at the end—the part where I got to lie on my yoga mat in a puddle of my own sweat—that was the first time in a very long time that I had felt peaceful. Not counting calories, or planning meals, or wanting to do more exercise; I'd been happy to just do nothing.

I felt less irritable, and less rushed. I was able to give Matt a hug when he came in from work without holding my breath and stiffening up. I did not try to wiggle out from between his arms after a couple of seconds. Instead, I stayed; and it was wonderful to be able to do that.

My yoga mat was a revolution: a magic carpet giving me a ride towards a mind body connection. Any thought, behaviour or action was now mine to allow into reality or not. I could feel fear arise at the sight of food but I could choose not to be fearful. I could feel frustration percolate when I wanted to exercise, but choose not to be frustrated. I could feel hate arise when someone offered me food, but choose not to be hateful. I could see my behaviours slowly unfolding before me as if they were moving through honey and, because they were slower, I could reach out and grab them before they came to fruition. I could see my thoughts. Before, they had been bullets flying through the air so fast that they hit me before I ever had a chance to move, but now they were friendly pitches and I was armed with a big old cricket bat to send them flying back in the direction that they had come from. I had the opportunity to choose new paths of actions. And that is exactly what I did.

What that very first class taught me, and what every yoga class after that has continued to teach me, is that in order to stay calm in a stressful situation I have to breathe long slow deep breaths. The postures, like utkatasana, are stressful and difficult. When I was in utkatasana for the first time, I had begun to do what I always do in a difficult situation: freak out. My heart rate had peaked and I had held my breath; my temperature rose and I wanted to scream at stupid Lycra Stardust Yoga Bitch to stop torturing me with her inescapable smile.

And then, I had breathed, just like she had told me to. That was the day that I learnt how to control my nervous system.

It is impossible for one to go into the sympathetic nervous system—that is the place of panic—when one is breathing long slow deep breaths. Try it. Just try and freak out whilst breathing slow and deep: you can't.

When one can stay calm if one is stressed, one can think clearly and make more rational decisions. With this comes the ability to be *within* a stressful situation without *being* stressed.

I went to yoga every single day after that. And, sure enough, things . . . I . . . began to come undone.

I bet you are wondering when I finally realised that I had been suffering from a full-blown eating disorder. When did it actually hit home for me? Well, it was pretty soon after that first yoga class actually, and it was catastrophic.

I had taken myself on a bike ride. I had got on my bicycle because I had been feeling stressed about an upcoming job interview. As I pedalled I felt better, but then came the question, was this too much exercise? Would I lose more weight? And I did not really know, I just knew that I wanted to keep riding my bike that day and I was irked that I had to justify getting some fresh air and exercise in order to make sure that I was not returning to old habits. I was frustrated that using my bike as a stress relief made me feel guilty. I was so fed up with not knowing if my relationship with exercise was a healthy one or not. I was confused around all of this.

Why can't I just go on a bike ride and be happy?

Why was I always thinking about food and exercise?

Why did I have to work so hard to keep my bodyweight up?

I pedalled faster and harder as these questions swirled about in my head.

Why? Why? Why?

Why can't I just be done with all this shit?

The answer came to me that day, and when it did it felt like a double-barrelled horse-kick to the stomach, causing me to slam on the brakes and pull over.

I sat for an unmeasurable amount of time with my bike beside me on the verge of the road experiencing a full spectrum of different qualities of tears. Tears of sympathy for what I had been through. Tears of anger toward my own shame. Tears of confusion as to why this truth had hidden for so long. Tears of understanding as to why I had buried this fact after all. Tears of sorrow regarding the relationships that guarding this truth had caused me to end. Tears of regret about opportunities this illness had caused me to forgo in order to continue to protect its identity. Tears of understanding that this truth had been hidden from me to protect me. A mass of sobbing relief I cried up ten years worth of denial. Every tear that rolled down my face brought out with it some of the truth that I had been stifling, choking down for so long.

Because it never was just an exercise disorder, was it?

That was the truth that had finally surfaced that day. That was the thought that saw me sitting on a grass verge. *Changed.*

That thought, more of a statement than a question, yet the boldest statement that I had ever made. That truth, so accusatory, yet so softly comforting, which caused me to cancel the rest of my plans that day so that I could fully explore it, feel it out and try it on.

Some time later, flooded with understanding, I was able to get back on my bike and ride home. Adding physical movement to the mental circus that I was debuting as the main act in meant that by the time I was parking my bike up at home the tears had dried to battle streaks on my cheeks. The pedal strokes had given an opportunity for my muscles to pace

206

the residual adrenaline to good use. I felt excited. Incredibly excited. Because I knew that was it.

I knew it was over.

Because it wasn't just an exercise disorder, was it? Such a simple and innocent question that had roundhouse-kicked open the door to that room in which my secret hid.

How can one recover from anorexia nervosa if you have deeply hidden its very existence?

One can't. And that was the reason that I had not.

My excitement was this understanding. The reason I continued to struggle to gain weight was that I had not been able to identify the problem. Now that I had done that, I could fight it. In staying hidden from me, my eating disorder had been immune to my advances, but now in full daylight I knew it was over. I had already won.

Anorexia. *I have an eating disorder.*

It took a really, really, long time for me to stop crying, but by the time I did, I was ecstatically excited about what I was about to do. I was about to treat my eating disorder. I was about to get my life back.

That evening, as we relaxed with a glass of wine and a game of cards, I told Matt. I had been mulling all afternoon about how to go about it. I was excited to tell him—about saying it out loud to another person for the first time. I would need to make him understand that this recognition was a *good* thing, this was the beginning of the end for me.

How does one go about that? To tell one's husband that she has had an eating disorder for over ten years and never spoken of it. How does one explain that it was not due to a lack of trust or love but because she did not really know herself? Would he believe me that I had not lied to him on purpose? That was hard enough for me to believe.

After repeatedly starting and restarting the conversation in my head for what seemed like hours, I gave up on waiting for the right moment and just said it:

"I have anorexia. I have had an eating disorder since I was seventeen."

Just like that. I stated it out loud for the first time in my entire life.

"I know."

And that was all.

Of course Matt knew. He had always known. But he had also known that the wall that I had constructed was there for a reason, and he had trusted that when the time was right for me to bring it down, I would.

Chapter Thirty Three

After that little world-wracking episode, I devoted myself to researching and understanding the neurobiological aspects of Anorexia Nervosa.

Due to this study, I was able to understand why I reacted the way that I did around food, eating, and all the behaviours and habits that I had been dealing with as a result of the effect that Anorexia had on my brain. The compassion, respect and love I felt for myself as I continued to learn about my disease was incredible. I had been outstandingly strong to be able to survive despite the continual pressure that I was under; Anorexia has the highest mortality rate of any psychological disorder. Quite understandably, many sufferers—if left untreated—take their own lives. I felt a lot of gratitude. I was lucky to be alive and I understood that the perseverance that it had taken me to re-feed myself without help to this point was commendable.

I understood that I had the activity-based model of Anorexia which had shown itself in the form of my "exercise disorder." Most importantly, I discovered that contrary to popular belief, Anorexia nervosa had nothing to do with a desire to be thin, and that my low body weight was not a result of me trying to control my life as so many teachers and doctors would have had me believe—a rather pseudo-freudian argument that unfortunately is still in circulation.

On the contrary, Anorexia affected every decision that I made, every path that I took in life and occupied every waking thought in my head. I missed parties, I missed holidays, I missed out on four years of university life because I could not eat. I had been literally killing my body and there was nothing that I could do about it. That did not feel like control, it felt like catch-22 in hell.

The reason that the public and many health professionals consider eating disorders to be influenced by a desire for thinness is because those of us that have the right genetic make up for these diseases usually trigger them if we attempt to restrict calories. Remember that little diet that I had embarked on as an attempt to slim down to ride Kit-Kat?

That.

That measly little diet had opened my brain up to the disease that had been patiently waiting for any such a chance to take over.

I also learnt about the brain's reaction to malnutrition. I read studies such as the *Minnesota Starvation Study,* which demonstrated that any person who is malnourished has the tendency to become angry, irritable and aggressive, and more importantly that semi-starved people actually become *resistant* to eating. Anorexia had used my low-resourced state to hide itself from me, as one does not think too clearly when one is starving.

As an adult sufferer, there didn't seem to be much available to me in terms of treatments options—not unless I wanted psychoanalysis, which I didn't. One day I stumbled on the FEAST (Families Empowered and Supporting Treatment of Eating Disorders) website. Here were forums of parents who were using Family Based Therapy (FBT) to refeed their children. I researched FBT and distasteful as it seemed to me or force feed myself, I knew that it made sense. I wished that I had someone to put me through FBT and get me well, but this treatment was only meant for children. It was then that I realised I needed to be my own parent, and that I had to apply FBT to myself.

With continued strength and determination I began to unravel the behavioural and neurological components of my illness. In that year, finally, I gradually began to put on weight again. Being nearly thirty years old, and now living far away from my family in England, I had to be my own eating coach; by that I mean that I had to force feed myself.

I spent a substantial amount of my time researching on treatment options for people with Anorexia. At my age there were inpatient facilities, but I was doubtful about the processes that they used. From what I could tell, many of them touted body-image counselling and trauma therapy as their preferred methods of treatment. I did not feel that these routes were relevant to me and the concepts that they addressed in their treatment policies seemed far too close to the same ideas that my doctors back in England had tried to push on me. It seemed very odd to me: if I could educate myself into understanding that Anorexia is a biologically based mental disorder, then why were so many treatment centres for adults still treating it as a body-image problem suffered by people with low self esteem?

I was interested to discover that for children and young adults, family-based therapy was the treatment method with the best results. This involves the parents in the role of making their ill child eat. "Life stops until you eat" is the motto, and family-based therapy recognises that children with Anorexia are never going to *choose* to eat themselves, that the disorder is a disturbance in the brain which has resulted in a fear of food. I spent months reading blogs and online discussion forums about parents who had been through the hell of refeeding their children. I read about tantrums and screaming fits from kids terrified of eating, and I read the pain that their parents went through as they were forced to choose between insisting that their child eat—and the continual battle that went with that—or watch them starve.

And I read how it worked. How after weight was restored the children became less fearful of food, and the panic attacks at dinner times lessened, and how they gradually turned back into children capable of smiling again.

Each of those stories hit a chord with me. I felt the fear of every one of those children and I knew that despite the onset of Anorexia being much later for me, I had to treat myself as if I was a child and as if I was being given no choice but to eat. I decided one day in mid-June that I was going to eat my way up to the weight that I had been when I was sixteen and I was going to get there no matter what. Life stops until you eat became my motto too.

No more eating only salads in the day. No more avoiding anything high in calories and pretending that I was being healthy. No more leaving part of my meal and pretending that I was full when I knew I was just fearful.

It was hard. I wanted to give up often. Okay, I wanted to give up *daily*. Hell, I wanted to give up with every bloody mouthful. I envied those child sufferers who had a parent there willing to force them to eat; it is painfully difficult to be one's own drill sergeant. I wished I had someone in authority, enforcing the rules that I had set; someone that I could yell at and hate and take some of my frustration out on. I did not. There was just me.

And my yoga practice.

Like the parents on the forum's at FEAST, I saw eating as my medication. Yoga was also in my prescription, because it brought me back to the goal of getting my body well on a daily basis.. With this understanding that to not eat was to allow Anorexia to win, my natural competitive nature kicked in. I started to eat even more during the day. Determination and willpower had really worked against me when I became ill, but now, in recovery, I was learning to use those qualities in my body's favour again. I had a mental tally chart in my head where I kept the score of "wins" that I had over anorexia. I doubled the portion sizes of what I was eating. I was still only eating my "safe" and low-fat foods, but I was eating a lot more of them. For some reason peanut butter was one high-fat food that I could eat without as much resistance than any other, so I made the most of this and set myself a target of getting through a jar of peanut butter every two days.

Skipping a meal would have been considered a lose to me and a win to anorexia, so it ultimately ceased to happen, ever. Even when I had to sit with contention for hours before and after, I would eat my meal. Even if it took me three hours to finish it, I would eat my meal. Even when I felt my eyes stinging with tears and my throat closing in panic, I would fucking eat that meal.

The game became more elaborate. I created additional tasks that I could win at and gain points. I could notch up my score every time I had a thought telling me not to eat something by eating it regardless. I challenged myself every day to eat a food that scared me, and when the panic came I would use my breath and meditation mind to get through it.

I remember the first slice of bread that I ate.

Bread was a big one. The ruckus that kicked up between Succubus and Sister Catherine every time I saw bread was always particularly ugly. Before now, if I have tried to eat some bread, I had usually failed to even get it out of the plastic sleeve that the loaf came in. If I did get as far as taking a piece out of the packet, when it got to my mouth I would have doubts with every chew, rendering the entire experience unfortunate enough for me to give up after a couple of nervous stressed out bites.

I had nibbled at crusts. I had choked down four or five bites once with shaking hands, but I had not eaten a whole slice of bread since I had been that seventeen-year-old girl who could wolf down half a loaf covered in butter and marmite.

That piece of toast was a big marker for me, and that is not to say that it was easy. I had to work for every single bite of it. I had to battle and shake and sweat. But I had sat there until it was gone. Afterwards, I had felt something change in me. Confidence. I had confidence in myself again, if I could do that, I could do anything.

My body changed fast this time, in just a month of focusing on re-feeding myself the differences were noticeable. That first month was the nicest in terms of seeing a result and feeling aligned with it, I saw that my face looked fuller and my breasts went up a cup size. As my thirtieth birthday neared, I began to feel my clothes tighten. I had wondered how this would affect me emotionally when it happened. I knew that there would be stages—markers in my recovery that my eating disorder would use as an excuse to flare up. I had read about such problems in the accounts and diaries that I had found online written by parents of sufferers. I was ready for anorexia to tell me that I was fat, worthless and stupid because for the first time in thirteen years my six-foot frame was out of the "extra smalls".

Matt really helped. I do not think he will ever understand how much he helped. He had always told me that he would love to have more of me to hold, but as I gained weight he showed me how much my recovery meant to him in his admiration of my fuller figure. He quietly urged me to eat more, always applying just enough pressure, not so much that I would baulk, not too little that I would grow complacent.

Another thing that reading the online forums helped me with, was understanding that the eating disorder was not *me*. Anorexia was like a demon that was occupying me. Many of the parents I read about were able to successfully re-feed their children when they separated the eating disorder from the child. When they understood that the illness was killing their child they were able to be firmer in asserting that their children ate.

This worked for me also. Whenever Sister Catherine or Succubus squabbled in my head, which would be thousands of times a day, I taught myself to see those thoughts as something separate from myself; they were not me, they were parasites.

All of these tactics helped a lot, but even so recovery was a meal-by-meal battle.

I had to cut down on my exercise again, too. I quit teaching cycle classes at the gym, as I saw this as an activity that anorexia had chosen for me. That was tremendously difficult. As I handed in my notice I felt as if every cell in my body was torn in separate directions. All of me was screaming silently that I should not do this, that teaching spin was something that I loved and made me happy, and that I would get fat and lazy if I quit. All of me was rejoicing that I would never have to get on one of those bikes again because I truly hated this abusive and intense form of exercise.

In the fourth month I had a blip. I had been unprepared for the "fat stomach" effect of refeeding a body that had been malnourished for so long. I was practically up to a medium dress size now, and that was fine, but it felt as if all my weight was going to my belly. I had this unmistakable pot belly, and my arms and legs were still relatively slim. I could *feel* that fat on me. Sister Catherine went berserk, and because I had been unprepared for this, I almost got sucked into her tantrum.

My clothes touched the top of of my enlarged belly, and whenever I moved I felt my eating-disorder flare up and shout. This was a hard time, and I worried that I might relapse unless I did something. The urge to restrict my food intake was incredible. *Just stop eating as much and this will go away* Sister Catherine told me.

I did what I always do when I am stuck: I researched.

What I found was that this pot belly is a necessary and normal phase in recovery from an eating disorder. This was because my body was sending resources to cover my vital organs initially in order to provide them with insulation and protection. I also read that after a good year at a properly weight-restored weight, I could expect this stomach fat to redistribute itself more evenly over my whole body. I read research papers that proved to me that belly fat was normal for people in recovery from anorexia, and with this I was able to turn my "spare tyre" into a weapon against my eating disorder. I was able to put my fingers on it and love it because its very existence was proof that I was beating the disease that had been trying to kill me.

I continued to throw myself into studying anorexia nervosa, reading daily scientific papers and case studies. I also took a yoga teacher training, and in doing so I discovered my *whispers*: these are voices different than those of Sister Catherine and Succubus—who, thankfully, disappeared almost completely after about a year of being ignored and challenged. Diluted versions of them, however, remained in whispers of insecurity.

Just a note on whispers, as these are not eating disorder relevant, yet I do think that they are human-being relevant:

Everyone has whispers, which I define as thoughts of low self esteem, poor body image, self doubt, anxiety, and a plethora of other insecurities. These whispers often result in those little habits that are used as defense mechanisms. Whispers are the thoughts that repeat themselves over and over: they specialise in "what if" and second guessing. Whispers prod and probe without respite; it is no wonder that so many of us turn to activities which quieten them.

One such activity of mine was running, another was working. I had become accustomed to keeping busy enough to bypass any space, as the whispers love to fill space. Other people shield themselves from their own whispers in myriad ways: hiding their faces in make-up; hiding their bodies in clothes; hiding themselves in solitude, or crowds; eating; drinking—I'm sure you can think of some more.

The whispers are the thoughts that tell you to eat the rest of the cake that is sitting in the refrigerator, or to open another bag of crisps. They justify exactly why you should do that, they tell you that you can eat healthier tomorrow and that you deserve that cake today. They seduce you into eating it and then the second that you've put down your fork they berate you for doing just so. They tell you that you are fat and that you are disgusting and that you are the only person in the world who does things like that. They can be very effective at making you believe that you are alone and different and that you are not worthy of friendship.

The whispers are the thoughts that replay the words in that rejection letter from the last job that you applied for in your head over and over again. They tell you that those words are a polite way of saying that you are stupid and unemployable and that you will never get the job that you want. They package up those words into a neat little bundle that you can take with you to your next interview and tell you that the person who is screening you already thinks that you are a write-off too. They turn those words into bags that you carry around with you and open up every single bloody time you doubt yourself, just so that you can present yourself with some evidence that will make you utterly convinced that you do not deserve an equal place in the world.

The whispers are the thoughts that tell you that your ex dumped you because you have bad taste in clothes, are ugly, boring or all of the above. They buzz around your head like wasps when you try to decide what to wear as you get ready for the first (and the hundredth) date that you have had since that break up. They make you put on more makeup or aftershave than you need so that you can hide yourself better. Then, as you are on the bus on the way to meet your date, they convince you that reason the person across the aisle is staring at you is because you have put far too much makeup or aftershave on, and that you look or smell over the top. Rather than because you are beautiful.

The whispers are the thoughts that cause you to jump onto the defensive anytime you are questioned because they have already primed you for the possibility that you are wrong. The whispers make you feel anger when you should feel compassion because they have convinced you that words and actions of another were intended to hurt you personally; rather than the fact that the other person has just had a bloody bad day and is in need of a hug as badly as you are.

The essence that makes the whispers as powerful as they are is that they are so deafeningly quiet that one can't often identify their presence. Whispers are sneaky; they morph themselves to suit any situation.

Everyone has whispers, voices of doubt, the difference for me was that I also had Anorexia, and Anorexia is a disease which forms the most manipulative, seductive and self deprecating of any whisper that one can imagine. Sister Catherine and Succubus were like whispers with megaphones.

You've probably noticed that I frequently and unapologetically refer to anorexia as a disease. Yes, I consider it a *disease*. It brought my life to a crawl, tampered with my ability to think clearly and resulted in me being very malnourished for a long enough time for me to compromise my health and happiness. Classing anorexia as a disease was very helpful for me as I could hate the disease without hating myself. You also might have noticed that I never once refer to myself as "anorexic". Like I said, I have a disease, that is not to say that I am the disease. I am a person who has anorexia, I am not an anorexic. That would be like calling a person with cancer a "cancerian."

As my recovery continued, I came to notice my eating disorder-related traits and I set up a structure to systematically tackle them one by one. Meditation is like strength training for the brain. Each week I would address a new behaviour in my daily meditation practice. Just for a couple of minutes a few times a day I would take the time to sit, close my eyes, breathe slowly, and imagine what my life would look like if I did not have the tenet that I wanted to be rid of.

When I wanted to break the ceremony of analysing the nutrition-information panel on the back of a food packet for the amount of fat in it, I sat through a meditation where I imagined myself walking into my local store and buying food without doing that. When I wanted to skip the rut of ordering a salad whenever I went out for a meal, I sat in meditation and imagined myself going into a restaurant and ordering something different.

When I wanted to disobey the rule of tiny portions, I meditated that week on filling my plate with food. As my confidence grew I moved on to bigger tasks.

When I wanted to kick the hangup of artificial sweeteners, I meditated on a life where any sweet foods that I ate were made with real sugar; I also meditated on being able to accept the calorie difference: this took longer. I held faith in my practice, and as a consequence, one sunny fall morning in October, I emptied all the cans of diet soda from my fridge into the sink and have not bought one since. I tipped the remainder of a carton of my favoured low-fat yoghurt into the trash can.

When I wanted to stop pre-planning all my meals, I meditated on a life where I allowed other people to cook for me and did not ask them what was on the menu. Then I lived it.

When I wanted to stop eating at night, I sat with a meditation of me enjoying a full breakfast, lunch and dinner so that my body was satisfied enough not to have to. Now, I have to report that this didn't work, and I continued to binge each evening. My body was not ready to let go of this one so quickly, and in hindsight I can see that it had good reason: it needed longer to develop trust in allowing me to feed it. The binges had for over ten years been its primary source of calories, and it would have been foolhardy to place too much faith in my ability to feed myself long term too soon.

Some rituals disappeared easily enough. I simply felt bored by my cookbooks and cook shows: they no longer offered me anything and I lost the will to watch them. I'd stopped noticing food as much as I used to.

One day, when Matt and I were discussing a place that we went out to lunch at, it occurred to me that I had not even clocked what anyone else in the party of people who we were with had eaten. Another day, I noticed that I could not remember what I had eaten the night before. About six months into my daily meditation practice, we went out for a meal. It was not until the end of it that I noticed not only had I chosen what I wanted to eat off the menu rather than whatever the lowest calorie dish was, but that I had *no idea* how many calories I had eaten, and more revolutionary: I did not care. These vicissitudes were both encouraging and enlightening; I knew that my neural processes were changing, down to the smaller details like the stimulus that my brain picked up on.

It is said that when it comes to building neural pathways, the brain cannot tell the difference between what is imagined and what is actually done. This is how meditation worked for me: I imagined that I was what I wanted to be. When I was sitting still and quiet with my eyes closed meditating on how my life could be, I was treading a new dust path for the sheep to walk down.

And the sheep were beginning to follow.

It took about a year for me to begin to feel at home in my newly weight-restored body. I adored the way that my breasts could form a cleavage. I enjoyed that I could roll up and down on my back on my yoga mat without feeling my spine digging into the floor. It was so refreshing to be able to ride a horse in a single pair of jodhpurs and not get sores on my legs. I loved the feel of my body when Matt touched it.

Matt could not get enough of me; if he had been attracted to me when I was skinny, he was even more so now. It felt so nice to be able to relax when he touched me, not to feel like I had to shrink away to protect what I was hiding; I had nothing to hide anymore, no protruding bones to pretend did not exist. No awkwardly prominent hips to try and disguise. Just me.

I did not notice that there was a particular day or moment that my disposition changed. There was not a single event that brought it to my attention that I was laughing more, or that I would stop if I passed someone that I knew in the store for a "hello and how are you doing?" chat. There was not a particular day that stands out as the day I stopped hurrying and rushing all over the place, it all happened gradually in that year that my body weight came back. What did stand out to me was when I overheard one of the ladies that I rode for describe me as laid back and easygoing.

Me? I thought. *Can she really be talking about me?*

I remained a dedicated yogi through my own recovery, and do to this day. Practice is still a medicine to me. As an instructor, I teach with the passion of someone who has lived through struggle; but I never tell my students that they are made of stardust. No, I tell them that they are made of cells; because to me, cells are far more fascinating.

And cells are made of fat: saturated fat.

Whilst the fat on my body did begin to redistribute, and my figure took a more even but much fuller form, eating fat was still a black spot for me. Fat was the last word in the haiku, and I think that what really hindered my ability to overcome my fear of eating it was my confusion caused by the rife medical and cultural consensus that fat was the devil nutrient.

I was confused as to what an alliance with fat should actually be. I ate "good" fats: nuts, seeds, avocados, and the sporadic piece of organic meat; but there was always a remnant presence of stress involved when I did. For this reason I mostly avoided fat. Was this a problem? I was unsure whether my avoidance of fat was a leftover eating disorder trait or just actual common sense.

Everybody knows that fat is bad for you. Right?

Boulder, Colorado, is one of the most health conscious places on earth. Whole Foods is the town's social hotspot, and every restaurant has speciality diet and free-from options. This is a wonderful thing for someone who wants to eat organic foods and look after his or her health. However, it is a minefield for someone recovering from an eating disorder.

My head was being filled with all sort of information: *eat this . . . don't eat this . . . eggs are good . . . eggs are bad . . . fat is bad . . . fat is the devil . . . paleo is the best . . . paleo is the worst . . . high-carb diets are healthy . . . high-protein is the new high carb . . .*

Just about everyone in Boulder has tried vegan or vegetarianism at some point, and many of them stuck with it. Most people are "gluten free", or at least they are in polite public. Lots of Boulder residents have not only pioneered a diet trend, but have written a book about it too. It seems that no matter where one is, the topic of conversation is at some point going to fall to what so-and-so is eating, who is on a juice cleanse, or the latest research on chia seeds.

All I was trying to do was eat without stress, eat well, and give my body what it needed. In a town where everyone is a nutritional expert and nobody is reserved with their opinion on it, trying to do the right thing can be hard. I found myself listening to too many different voices, and I had no idea what was right for me at all.

Ironically, no sooner had I rid myself of Sister Catherine and Succubus, I opened myself up to the external twitterings of diet culture and food tribes. This is the crap that the rest of you—the non-eating disorder population—have to wade through on a daily basis. Even if you are not the type of person who is consciously aggravated and perplexed every time a new dietary fad emerges, I bet that you are influenced on some level. You have to be:

diet culture is everywhere. Even Prime Minister David Cameron admitted to *The Times of London* that he went low-carb to lose weight; probably in order to be a more attractive political figure. As a culture, we are so deep in diet shit that we barely even see it anymore.

I found it particularly difficult to separate my eating disorder from healthy eating and diet fads. For ten years I had been rejecting any attempts that my body made to tell me what it needed, and now when I was finally *trying* to listen to it again I found it impossible to hear anything; it was as if I had utterly severed that connection. One thing I did know for certain was that my diet as it was was not really working for me. I knew that because I was still binging at night, and when I did it felt ghastly. Despite the yoga, despite the meditation and the good intentions, I was still ramming food into my face every evening, and because of this I knew I had some exploring to do.

Chapter Thirty Four

People in Boulder are interesting. Most of them are very fit and smart: intelligent high achievers. They are, quite frankly, not at all what I had been led to believe that Americans are like. Boulder is known of as "The Bubble", and indeed it is. When Matt and I first moved here in 2010, we made friends fast because we had so much in common with everyone. We like to hike, to bike, and to be outside; we got a couple of dogs and I, missing Sprout—whom I had left behind in England with my parents—also got a cat.

By Spring 2011, I felt well and truly settled in. That was around the time that I started regularly taking yoga classes, and those exposed me to a whole new tribe: the yoga people.

I had a friend called Lisa whom I met in a yoga class; it turned out that we lived close to one another. We started walking the dogs together and did so for a number of years before her husband's work commitments meant that they moved out of town. Lisa was vegan, and she was the first vegan whom I had got to know well. She apparently thrived on a plant-based diet and had not eaten any meat or dairy for over twenty years. She did, however, wear leather shoes.

Apparently, Lisa decided that she wanted to be vegan when she was just twelve years old when she informed her parents that she no longer wanted to eat anything that caused animals suffering. This was an independent decision, and not one that was supported by her family, who, according to Lisa, tried to persuade her to consume meat when she was a teenager, and still nagged her about it as an adult. She was very strict with her diet and had never, ever, strayed to as much as a rasher of bacon. Her husband, whom I'd not met, was also vegan—and even more of a stickler than she.

Lisa boldly judged anyone who ate meat, and for this reason I avoided the topic of food with her if I could help it. Should food and diet come up in conversation, she always made me feel that because I ate meat and dairy, I was a big contributor to the problem that the meat industry posed—even if it was all organic and locally sourced. She had done a lot of research in her time, and would tell me about all these studies that apparently proved that humans are actually not designed to eat meat. According to Lisa, we can, and should, live vegan. "In fact, lots of vegans are ultramarathon runners," she would often remind me.

One morning, in the spring of 2012, a headline popped up on my Facebook feed about a pair of vegan parents who had been charged with child endangerment because their baby had been exclusively fed breast milk, and died. It reminded me about the research that I had done years earlier into the fat content of breastmilk when I had been working as a personal trainer. I wondered what vegans did about breastfeeding, as if a mother is not eating animal fats, how does the child receive all the fat and cholesterol that is needed to form its central nervous system properly?

Lisa had two children, and the following day, as we walked the dogs, I asked her. She told me that she had indeed breastfed her babies, but she needed to use supplements and formulas so that they could get the level of fats and nutrients that they needed.

"I had to supplement them with B12," she told me, "It's actually even better for the baby."

Interesting. Intriguing that Lisa, someone so *into* natural living, thought that a man-made substitute for vitamin B12 was just as good, if not better, than her children getting it from her milk.

Can't say that I agreed with her then; nor do I now. But that is *my own* opinion, and remember what I told you earlier: never take nutritional advice from someone who has an eating disorder.

Come to think of it, maybe to take nutritional advice from anyone at all is foolhardy. I mean honestly, humans, what the hell do we know?

The trouble with nutritional discussion is that people tend to always find something to support their point of view. I did it myself all the time when I spouted studies proving that a low-fat diet was superior. In the case of the neglect trial in which the baby died, the non-vegan tribe were claiming that the vegan lifestyle was a danger to children; the vegan tribe countered that this was utter tripe and that, in fact, a baby could grow up very healthy and strong with man-made supplements. When it comes to nutrition, everyone is an expert.

Everyone, that is, apart from mother nature. Mother nature is well out of fashion.

Back to the neglected baby case: I read in the news that the autopsy showed the infant had been low in vitamins A and B12. As I understood vitamin A to be a fat soluble vitamin, I asked Lisa what she thought about this. Surely, in order for fat-soluble vitamins to be passed from mother to baby in milk, a mother has to herself be eating enough fat? How could a low-fat vegan diet support this?

"That is not proof that the baby died of malnutrition," Lisa pointed out. "They just made up a load of hype about the fact that the parents were vegan."

I kept quiet. As I got to know Boulder better, I noticed that most people were on some form of specialised eating plan. There are the vegetarians, the vegans, the paleos, the gluten-frees, the dairy-frees, the cleansers, the raws, the biohackers, and the non-GMO crowd. Each group holds its own set of values. People's diets are so much more than just food: they are a way of life. A way of being. And often a subject of heated debate.

This is because food is an emotional talking point. It ranks right up there with politics and religion as subjects to steer well away from unless one is looking for a barny. I did not have to wait long for Lisa to elaborate on her point.

"Jeez, I mean, my mom didn't talk to me for almost a year because of that."

"Sorry?" I was confused. "Because of what?"

"The breastfeeding thing," she explained. "My mom is not vegan . . . and she hates that I am. She was furious that I did not eat meat or dairy when I was breastfeeding, we had a huge row over the phone one day and did not talk for a long time after . . . things are better now . . . but you know . . . she hates it that I have raised the boys to be vegan. I won't let them go and stay with her because I know that if I do she will try and get them to eat some meat." She shook her head in annoyance at the thought of that.

I said nothing. I thought that it must be very difficult to be a parent having firm beliefs in a way of being, a way of eating, and come under criticism for them regarding the upbringing of her children. I imagine that, in a town like Boulder, the school-gate gossip runs more along the lines of who is feeding their children what than it does who is voting for which political party:

"That's Jane Dow's kid . . . did you hear that she feeds him meat?"

"No!"

"Yes, yes she does . . . and it's not certified organic or grass-fed either . . ."

I feel sympathy toward any parent trying to make sense of the ever-changing nutritional environment. Being a parent looks like hard work. Even for those mothers who are not vegan or speciality-diet focused, the information on correct nutrition seems so . . . flighty. One minute whole milk is good, then the next it is bad. Then one day soy milk is healthy, and the next day it's not. For every piece of information that one receives about food and nutrition there are ten to prove it wrong. I've found life hard enough just making decisions for *my own* health, let alone having to be responsible for that *of children*. It's this sort of thing that makes me thankful that Matt and I mutually agreed never to have sprogs of our own.

The thing is, if you raise a child within a religious or political belief that you hold, you only set yourself up to mess him or her up psychologically. Not the case with food. With bad nutrition, there is proper physical damage that can be done—as well as the mental hangups. Everything ranging from diabetes when parents feed too much sugar, to anaemia and nutritional deficits when parents subject their kids to vegan, raw or fruitarian regimes.

At least as an adult I can only damage myself.

And oh the irony, because one thing that I've noticed from observing other people's children is that the kids themselves don't seem to care. At least, not before they are old enough to adopt their parent's food stress. I bet Lisa's kids wouldn't have minded if she'd have eaten animal fat when she breast fed them.

Children get it easy. Babies don't fret about the latest science around food, or if they should be taking probiotics or prebiotics. It's true: when I was a kid, I just drank milk; I did not care that it was high in fat. I just drank it. Boom. Down the hatch. No thought.

When I was a child, there was no agenda behind my consumption. My relationship with food had been pure. I was not drinking milk because I was feeling depressed or because I had read in some magazine that it was the latest superfood. I was not concerned about the quality of what I was consuming. I did not have to worry about my bread being GMO-free or manufactured in a factory that contained gluten. I did not have to fret about the lives of some fluffy baby animals that may or may not have been ethically treated. I did not need to think about the mercury levels in the sea or the pesticides on the soil. I did not have to consider the hygiene standards of the process, or how long the tofu had been sitting outside of the fridge. I did not have to worry about the price of organic dairy or if drinking soy milk was fashionable.

I just drank and ate and thought nothing of it.

Not like that anymore, is it?

Welcome to being an adult.

Some days I am not sure why I got promoted to grown-up.

I decided to break the news of my veganness to Matt over a game of cards and a glass of wine.

"So, I um, I might, I think I am going to . . . I'm going vegan." I mumbled, half hoping that he might not have heard me and wondering if I should save this conversation for another time—like when he was asleep.

"What?" Matt gave me a blank stare.

"Well I don't eat much meat anyway," I was treading water.

"What?" Blank stare. Obviously he was unimpressed with my justification thus far.

"And I could use soy milk in my tea."

"What?" Blank stare. Still not convinced.

"And everyone knows that saturated fat is bad for you, so this just means I will eat more healthy fats instead."

"Who are you trying to convince? You or me?" He asked.

Good question.

Lisa seemed to do very well on her vegan diet, and I had to admit that a part of me found this lifestyle attractive. Now, considering I was only a couple of years into my recovery from Anorexia, I bet you can guess what part of me that was.

Yes: my eating disorder loved the thought of me being vegan.

If I were vegan, I would have the *ultimate* excuse not to eat fat. All that stress that still came up for me regarding high fat foods would be eliminated if I went vegan. Yeah, I was aware that this could be construed as a cop-out on my part; rather than overcoming my fear of fat I was adopting a lifestyle that excused my avoidance of it. But . . . whatever. How did I know that Lisa was not correct? How did I know that humans were not actually designed to live life on a plant based diet? After all, according to her, there are studies to prove it.

According to her.

There are also studies that disprove it. And there is common sense. Look at the herbivores of the world. Look at the carnivores. Look at the omnivorous. Now, what do you think you would rather be? A cow or a tiger?

Would the human race have evolved as superior if we had not eaten meat?

I'm tiger. I've always been tiger. Nothing against cows of course, but I am at the top of the food chain.

Apart from when I was vegan.

Other than the not-so-convincing arguments that humans are not supposed to eat meat. There was another factor I had weighed into my decision: cost. Organic meat and dairy is expensive. *Blah, blah, blah.* Let's face it, I had a plethora of excuses behind my decision to "go vegan," but, I was aware of my underlying motivation: eating vegan is a great way to avoid eating saturated fat.

Was I making this decision? Or was Anorexia making one last bid to control my diet?

Saturated fat was certainly easier to avoid as a vegan because my options were more limited. No cheese, dairy, or meat. I could eat beans and legumes; these contain a whole lot of carbohydrates and protein, but very little fat. I could eat avocados and nuts; these were the fattiest foods in my diet now. Basically everything else I ate was low in fat, and high in carbohydrate.

The nicest thing about being vegan was the reduction in decision fatigue. No choices to be made: if it is animal, I can't have it. Vegan gave me a category. Vegan gave me a clan. Vegan gave me an excuse to eat low-fat.

You know what else vegan got me: relapse.

Yes. My eating disorder had deviously worked its way back into my eating habits via restriction. Being vegan is the ultimate in restriction just because it is, by nature, so restrictive. The best part, as far as my eating disorder was concerned, was that being vegan was socially acceptable, even considered healthy; therefore, it had a chance of long-term survival. Anorexia could hide under a vegan cloak. Sure, it was not the star of the show like it had been before; but at least it had managed to weasel its way out of the gutter and into my eating behaviours again.

Truth was that I really loved being vegan. No, strike that: Anorexia really loved me being vegan. I had the perfect excuse to pass on cheese, and chocolate, and cream. The best part was being able to order a latte with soy milk and not have to deal with the whispers that would argue over whole milk or skimmed. Life was easier.

Anorexia liked me having that label. A single word to tell someone at a party when I was offered some food. "No thanks, I'm vegan," is so much easier than, "No thanks, I'm recovering from an eating disorder, so piss off."

Yeah: Anorexia loved vegan.

Shame my body disagreed. My body wanted to be the tiger, not the cow.

For many people, eating vegan seems to work a treat. I am sure that if you are vegan, that your motivations for being so are much purer than mine were. (let's face it, that would not be difficult). I know people who have found energy that they never thought they had upon turning vegan, and some people genuinely seem to thrive on a plant-based diet. But not me.

I don't like soy and neither does my tiger-stomach, so I lived off beans, nuts and avocado for fat and protein. The other eighty percent of my diet was carbohydrates: oatmeal, bread, pasta, vegan sweets, and lots of home-baked oatmeal squares. I would need a mound of pasta or rice in order to feel satisfied, which made me feel bloated and heavy. It was incredible how much I could eat, yet still feel empty.

Granola was my staple; I would go through a couple of boxes a week, because, guess what I was eating at night: bowls and bowls of cereal. The peanut butter jar continued to take a battering every evening with my binge eating in a spoon-to-mouth fashion. If anything, I noticed with dismay that my night eating was getting worse rather than better; I consoled myself with the thought that at least it was healthier foods that I was eating: vegan chocolates, protein bars, sugar glazed nuts, chocolate almond milk and handfuls of dates or dried fruits.

One day I went to Costco and came out with a huge tub of vegan protein powder and a forty-eight-bar box of protein bars. The first day I ate one bar and had one shake. The second day I ate two bars. By the third day I was on three bars and two shakes. My sweet tooth was having a party with all the chocolate-flavored protein supplements I was on.

It's okay, vegan is healthy, right?

Bull. Shit.

Most pre-made vegan goods are very highly processed and full of sugar. One can make one's own vegan snacks, of course. But it's so much bother! I'm not against eating unhealthy foods, quite the opposite—I think there is a place for everything, and that includes the odd deep-fried Mars bar—but it gets my goat when faddish diet products market themselves as healthy when all they really are is a Snickers in a fancy suit.

Unfortunately, when I was vegan, I was eating a ton of what is marketed as "health foods," and yes, I was being clannish about my food, but one thing that was really encouraging, was my nonchalant attitude to the calorie intake from eating all these high-protein bars. Surely that showed some kind of progress that I was making in terms of being able to eat high-calorie foods? That, however, is pretty much all I can say in favour of my vegan stint. And by the way, gluten-free, dairy-free, plant-based protein bars retail at a much higher mark than Hershey's or Cadbury, so my argument that being vegan was more economical was null. Basically, I had wound up spending as much money on highly-processed, carbohydrate-heavy "health" foods as I would have done on organic meat and dairy.

When I became one, I was interested to find out how veganism actually started, so I did some research: The vegetarian diet was first documented by a bloke called Sylvester Graham who lived from 1794 to 1851. He actually invented this diet in order to preserve chastity and deter lust; his theory was that cutting meat out of one's diet helps one become more resistant to sexual desire. He believed—and was very adamant—that excessive sexual activity caused disease.

No comment.

Actually: Yes comment.

I agree with Graham. My sex drive decreased when I stopped eating meat and dairy. But is that a good thing? Is that human? Is it natural?

Probably not. Nowadays, when faced with overpopulation, the human race does not need to expand at the rate that it is used to—but that is not to say that the desire to reproduce is not a fundamental part of being human. This all harps back to the days of Catherine of Siena and those who starved themselves in the name of God—who were, incidentally, also fond of taking the vow of chastity—and I cannot help but see a correlation between restrictive diets and that holier-than-thou attitude even now. It shows up differently, but there is still an air of superciliousness detectable in those who restrict food categories. I should know, because I've been the haughtiest diet-pusher of them all. And now that I am not, I still experience it from others on a daily basis.

Like the disdainful vegetarian, whom I had the misfortune of sitting next to at a wedding reception, who told me that those of us who had ordered the meat option were consuming fear.

Like the uppity paleo woman demoing ostrich jerky in Whole Foods who told me that the peanut butter I was just about to purchase would undoubtedly inflame my bowel.

Like the despising fruitarian, whom I met beside Boulder creek, who told me that even picking an apple off a tree—rather than allowing it to fall when it was ready—was an act of murder.

Like the scornful raw foodist, whom I worked next door to for a summer, who told ,e that he could hear vegetables screaming while they are being cooked.

Like the proud biohacker, a colleague at a yoga studio, who would ask me if I had any idea how much more spiritual my life would be if I would only optimize myself.

Not to mention the army of gluten-free evangelists who hide behind corners ready to jump out and scream "IT'S THE GLUTEN" whenever I feel a little tired, or my skin is dryer than usual, or I have a hangover, or I don't win the lottery, or my cat pukes on the floor.

I think that there is a reason that people find a food tribe or a speciality diet and stick to it religiously, and that is because it hits the same chords as religion. Food and sex are both things deep wired into the survival part of the human brain. Why is it that restricting these things is often thought of as superior and pure?

Anyway, enough of what I think, let's get back to the facts:

Soon after Graham, there was John Harvey Kellogg (1852-1943), who too thought that a whole-grain and high-fibre vegetarian diet would curb lustful urges; additionally, and quite conveniently, he also believed that a plant-based diet could cure constipation. This Kellogg fellow thought that any sexual activity was a sin—even if it were between married couples.

In 1944, a chap called Donald Watson co-founded the British Vegan Society: a group of people who abstained from all dairy and eating meat. His doctrine was that man should live without exploiting animals. I'd like to say that I agree with him, but I am not sure that I believe eating animals is the same as exploiting them. Can one eat meat without disrespecting the animal from which it came? Or drink dairy, eat eggs, or even wear leather? I have to admit that I did ponder these questions, but even when I was vegan, I never considered myself an *ethical* vegan. I believe that humans are designed to eat animals, but that is not to say that I think that the way we currently go about it is by any means right.

It's not cheaper, it's not about the animals, why are you vegan then?
I guess that it's still all about the fat, isn't it?

Oh, it's always about the fat. And that's not just me!

Living in America, it is difficult to shut out the obesity crisis; fat, that rebel macronutrient, is still causing a lot of upset in the world. When I was vegan, I felt justified in my avoidance of fat because just about every media source told me that I was. I had included some of what I considered at that time to be "good" fats in my diet: avocados, nuts, seeds, more nuts, guacamole, peanut butter, noix, le beurre d'arachide . . . and, did I mention nuts? I knew that I was eating healthily, and for the most part I was eating without concern. In comparison to a year or so earlier, my mental state around food was so much better than I could have ever imagined or hoped for.

But why was the night binging getting worse? Since I had been vegan, my night binges, which had begun to wane in quantity somewhat in the months prior, had exploded back to a hideous episode of uncontrollable face-stuffing. This was perplexing; things were supposed to get easier, not harder.

I asked a friend—who was a fellow yoga instructor and "cleanse guru"—about the binge eating one day. She, unsurprisingly, recommended that I go on a cleanse. She pointed out that all the junk food must be leaving my liver and colon in a bad state, and that the best thing for that would be to cleanse-detox it all out. And guess what else: she could sell me the cleanse product in order to help me do just that.

Now, just hold on a second, I thought, *how exactly does cleansing help my liver?*

So I asked her, and I was told that by cleansing, and removing the pressure of digesting foods from the body, the organs are given a "rest" of sorts.

Skeptical, I looked into that a little. Okay, extensively; I looked into it extensively.

With the authority of someone who really wanted to be convinced that cleanses are a good idea, but who bothered to fully understand the mechanisms of the liver just to check, I can tell you that cleansing in order to detoxify the liver is a crock of shit.

The liver cleanses the blood in a multistage process, and the primary stage utilizes a group of enzymes called the P450 group. These enzymes need a number of things, but a couple of these things are fat-soluble vitamins. The skinny on that, without boring your pants off, is that removing fats and protein from the diet does not help the liver, nor does it "rest" it. In fact, abstaining from food for any prolonged length of time arguably stresses the liver, as it depletes the nutrients that it needs. Cleanse products are snake oil; if you really want to do something kind to your liver, back off processed foods and down some bone broth. Bone broth is excellent for delivering just the sort of fuel that your hard-working liver needs.

Needless to say, when I was vegan, I was not drinking bone broth; but I'm proud to say that cleansing was one diet fad that I managed to debunk early enough to avoid getting sucked into.

Despite never having cleansed myself, the cleanse culture that I am surrounded by is something that I find particularly vexing. Mostly, I think it annoys me that people are stupid enough to believe the marketing that surrounds the products they buy. Alongside this, through, runs a deeper unrest. You see, in order for marketing to work, there has to be a hole that the product fills—be it imaginary or real, in order for something to sell there has to be a demand.

Why is there such a demand for cleanse products?

I believe that it ties in with the same reason that chastity and dietary restriction appeal—and back to religion. Why do people feel that they were born a sinner and need to repent?

Why do people feel that they are innately dirty and need to cleanse?

Why can't people just leave their bloody livers alone to do their jobs?

Ironically, the type of person to go on a cleanse is not the fellow who starts every day with a McDonald's McMuffin and ends it with a six-pack of Coors and a 12" from Pizza Hut. Nope, the cleansers—and the people to whom those marketing cleanse products focus on—are those who are already super-conscious over what they eat; the health-fanatics of the world.

(I'd like to stress *every day* for the McMuffin fellow, because his main problem is that his diet of fast-food is unbalanced. I do not have a problem with fast food and believe that it can be incorporated in a healthy, balanced diet.)

I digress; back to vegan.

About six months into my vegan stint I began to notice things: I felt tired, weak, and lackluster. I wondered if this was a hormonal thing, or a passing phase. I toned down my exercise, opting for more restorative yoga classes instead of the challenging and active vinyasa. Still, the fatigue continued.

My teeth felt weak and oddly sensitive. A visit to the dentist revealed some cavities. I felt frail. I tried a different protein powder to see if that would help buck me up a bit.

For the first time in my life I began to feel the need to supplement. I got myself some B vitamins, calcium and iron. After a couple of weeks of feeling below-par, I was up for trying anything that would make me feel a little sparkier.

"I'm so tired all the time," I told Lisa one day as we walked the dogs, "I can't work out why."

"Are you eating enough protein?" she asked.

"I think so."

"What about supplements? Are you taking B12?"

"Uh-huh."

"And iron?"

"Every day."

"Hmm . . . you know, I felt a lot more energetic when I went gluten-free. Maybe you are intolerant?"

So, that was when I went gluten-free. Sorry.

The thing about gluten is that it makes everything taste better. The word *gluten* comes from the latin for *glue*. Without gluten present, foods lose their chewy texture and become crumbly and dry. Gluten-free bread, for example, is no match for a soft and chewy white loaf. To be frank, gluten-free baked goods taste like crap; I gave up on those pretty fast and, instead, simply ate less carbohydrates.

As a result, I was hungry. I ate a lot of rice; and even more gluten-free, plant-based, organic protein bars, and peanut butter.

I still felt tired, but now I also felt depressed. I had only just about got myself to a point where I could eat food without the severe stress associated with an eating disorder, and now there were barely any foods I could eat again.

But everyone knows that gluten is bad for you, right?

Wrong. Unless a person is Celiac (and less than one percent of the population are), there is a lot of emerging evidence to suggest that opting for a gluten-free diet can be meddlesome for the digestion process and alter the microbiota in the gut. That is true of any sudden dietary shift.

Many of the whole-grain foods that contain gluten carry with them a whole host of beneficial vitamins and minerals. As of right now, in 2015, nearly twenty million people believe that they have a gluten sensitivity—something which was practically unheard of at the turn of the century. What's more, the gluten-free fad is still gaining, as sales of gluten-free products in America are forecasted to exceed fifteen billion dollars by 2016, twice the amount of what they were five years earlier when I was testing the waters myself.

For many people, it seems that being gluten-free is much more than a dietary choice—it is a life choice. You can go to a gluten-free restaurant, drink gluten-free beers and wines, attend a gluten-free meet-up group, go on a gluten-free vacation or a gluten-free yoga retreat. Hell, you can even purchase gluten-free treats for your dog and find a gluten-free date on a gluten-free dating site.

Some people believe that the wheat itself has changed; morphed into a version that is no good for us any more. I've looked into that a little too, and a study published in the *Journal of Agricultural and Food Chemistry* found no evidence that a change in wheat-breeding practices might have led to an increase in the incidence of Celiac Disease.

While there is little reliable scientific data to support claims that after thousands of years of eating wheat humans should suddenly stop, there is a lot of evidence to show that self-diagnosed dietary intolerances are quite often incorrect. I tried gluten-free for a couple of weeks, and I felt even crappier.

Bemused as to why I felt so dull, I became a frequent shopper in the supplements section of the grocery store—hoping to find the missing ingredient that would have me feeling more vital again. After weeks of supplements and protein shakes, however, I still felt as if I was failing.

Why was this not working for me like it did for my vegan friends?

Why could I never seem to stop this incessant eating at night?

Why was knowing how to eat still so bloody difficult for me?

I took the question to my meditation practice one afternoon. I sat, took a couple of deep breaths closed my eyes. Once I felt connected to myself I just put the question *What is wrong?* to my body. I knew the answer immediately.

You need milk and eggs.

I knew it. I knew it right away. I don't know why, finally, the inner guidance that I had been hoping for had come to me that day, but it had. And it was not a whisper. No, it was a big booming unmistakable bellow.

Eggs!

Eggs, which I had continued to avoid despite all my cholesterol reprieving research. Eggs, which I had not eaten for years. Eggs, which are full of protein, cholesterol and fat.

Eggs? Why did my body want eggs?!

Then the doubt, the whispers.

Eggs, there is tons of fat in the yolk, and cholesterol is bad.

I rarely ate eggs even *before* I was vegan; and if I did it was the whites only without the yolk as that contains all the fat. How could my body just suddenly decide that I should start to eat eggs and go against all that I had believed and acted on in the last decade?

It occurred to me that this mind-body lark might be overrated. I didn't like being told what to do by anyone, or anything. My body wasn't just suggesting that I eat eggs, it was down-right demanding! Maybe things had been easier when it refused to talk to me.

But, like it or not, I was getting messages loud and clear. Messages that neither asked my opinion or consulted my anxieties. Eggs. Plain and simple: just eat some fucking eggs.

I have to admit that I did have a mini tantrum in my mind that day. I liked being vegan. I liked that I had a viable excuse not to eat fatty foods and meat in public. I liked that I could relax and hide behind my vegan label.

Why can't I just be vegan and be happy?

Why is my relationship with food always so hard?

Why can't I be the way that I was when I was a child, when I could eat eggs and cheese and butter and love every moment of it?

And then I realized that was my answer. I could. If I really wanted to change, I could.

And that makes it sound easier than it is. Because change of any kind is difficult, all I could assume was that now, finally, I was truly ready to make that change; the complete change. My intuition, which I had been begging to come forth but had so far stayed quiet, had finally shown up, and when it did there was no more argument to be had because intuition does not negotiate.

My body was telling me to get the hell off this vegan diet, and to do it fast. *My* body did not care that I had friends that have been vegan for over twenty years. My body did not care that vegan was fashionable in Boulder. My body did not care that other people's bodies are fine and happy being vegan. My body was telling me plain and clear.

You need animal fat.

I mourned my vegan diet that afternoon, and then I sulked a bit. Sulking is pretty tiresome, so that only really lasted half an hour before I rolled out my yoga mat. As I moved my body with my breath I understood that this lesson had been meant for me. I had to have tried the vegan option to fully understand that, for me, meat and dairy are essential. If I had never tried the vegan diet I would never have got to the point of desperation where I was finally actually able to shut up my head and listen to what my intuition had to say; to what my body had to say. Everything happens for a reason, and that afternoon I understood my lesson:

Eat with your gut, not with your head.

I'm not here to tell anyone how they should eat. I have no authority to do so and don't like to pretend that I do. I mean, I almost died of Anorexia for Christ's sake, so who am I to talk about how to eat. I'm just telling my story and how I had to learn to trust my body over my brain when it came to eating.

But what the hell, I'll say it anyway. In my humble opinion, if you are vegan you are the definition of eating with your head and not your stomach. You are thinking about it too much, and you are not allowing your body to dictate your diet. We can argue back and forth about science and history, about how the meat industry has got out of control and this and that, but guess what: arguing about food only proves my point exactly, as that is a cognitive process. When we argue about food and diet, we are *thinking*.

What bugs me most about vegan culture is that those in it consider it to be the diet that is the most in touch with nature. Seriously? You want to get in touch with your more natural self and I will show you exactly what that looks like; believe me, it is not soy beans and nuts. If you really and truly let your body decide what to eat, it would choose the fattest, meatiest food it could get its digits into, because that is where the nutrients are.

And if the thought of eating some fatty meat disgusts you, then that really shows you how very distant you are from your body. The body is a meat eater. It always has been. It is programmed to like meat in the same way it likes sex. Get in touch with what it really means to be a human being and understand that allowing your human body to have animal fat is being kind to it.

Now answer me this: What would your inner beast have chosen, a tofu salad or a chicken leg?

Once upon a time, many years ago, before things like convenience stores, iPhones and online shopping, in order to survive, humans had to be pretty darn feisty. One could not afford to um and ar over dinner and be prissy about where it came from. That only started happening when we moved into spending more time in our heads than in our bodies.

That is not to say that without a good deal of intervention and supplements that nowadays a person cannot survive without meat: you can. But when your periods stop, or your bones get brittle, or your teeth become more sensitive . . . just consider listening to what your *body* is telling you.

Chapter Thirty Five

You see, the thing about fat is that it is nutrient dense. Sure, it is calorie dense too, but when one is able to stop fearing calories, one realises that—as any carnivorous animal would tell you—the fat is the best bit.

Failing so epically at being vegan was the best thing that happened to me; because that short six months that I stuck with it really seemed to mess my body up good and proper. And because I'd messed it up, I had to mend it.

Why did being vegan have such a negative impact? One would think for a body that had stood up to twelve years of Anorexia and semi-starvation, six months of being vegan would be a piece of (plant-based and gluten-free) cake.

The answer to that I do not know. Maybe this long-suffering body of mine saw veganism as the last insult to follow a lifetime of nutritional abuse. Whatever the reason, the result was undeniable and unmistakable: I hurt. My muscles ached, my joints were sore, and weirdest of all: my teeth smarted.

When I had first started being vegan, I admit that I had read somewhere that the diet is not particularly good for the health of teeth and bones, but I had chosen not to pay any attention to that at the time. In fact, I had googled a report that told me the opposite to make myself feel better. That's the great thing about science: one can find a report to suit one's preferred point of view. It's very easy to believe everything that you read when you have your blinkers nicely fitted to the side of your face.

When I was eight, I used to ride a pony called Blinkers. Blinkers was called Blinkers because he wore blinkers on his bridle. I asked my riding instructor one day why Blinkers wore blinkers.

"The blinkers stop him from spooking at scary things in the hedges and making you fall off," she answered very matter of factly. Riding instructors are often rather concise people.

"What would happen if we took them off?"

"You would fall off." She nodded at me to look where I was going and not at her. Conversation over.

When I began researching into the *benefits* of dietary saturated fat, it was as if my blinkers had been removed. For twelve years, I had been dutifully marching along with the low-fat tribe. Strike that; I had been at the front, leading the march and banging the drum!

Google is a minefield when you do not have your blinkers safely positioned on your search engine. The day I decided to eat eggs and animal fat again I googled "Teeth cavities vegan". Then I began to sift through the results.

I read a lot that afternoon; everything from vegan-bloggers claiming that, actually, being vegan can be very beneficial for teeth, to paleo sites shouting just the opposite. I found one article telling me that I had to eat butter. The thought of it sent an excited shiver up my spine. *Imagine eating butter again!*

I was both terrified and thrilled at the prospect of this. I had not eaten butter since I was seventeen. Butter is the epitome of everything anorexia despises and hates: it is fat, really high calorie, but additionally it is calories from *saturated animal fat*. Butter is the Norman Bates of the eating disorder world. I'm sure I heard those piercing strings for the *Psycho* shower scene whenever I pulled the lid off the butter dish.

Anorexia ruined my life, and I hated anorexia with a passion, so if anorexia hated butter I wanted to love butter. I was going to do anything that anorexia did not want me to do. I was motivated by a hate for the disorder that had held me hostage for so long; I wanted every trace of it out of my life, and it seemed beautifully fitting that I should eat it into oblivion.

I meditated then and there on butter; on not fearing butter; on healing my body with butter. I focused on the butter that I used to eat as a child—butter on bread or butter on a potato. I remembered how I used to love the way that butter would curl up and over a knife running along the top of a block of it.

I kept repeating the word in my head: butter, butter, butter, butter, butter, butter.

Later that evening, I fiddled around on the interwebs some more whilst sitting on the sofa watching a film with Matt. I found a study titled *Food Choices and Coronary Heart Disease: A Population Based Cohort Study of Rural Swedish Men with 12 Years of Follow-up,* that concluded that the beta carotene found in carrots was better converted into vitamin A if the carrots were cooked and eaten with butter, because vitamin A is fat soluble. The authors went on to say that a person's daily fruit and vegetable consumption were associated with a lower risk of coronary heart disease only when combined with a high intake of dairy fat. Conversely—and controversially—if a person had a low intake of dairy fat, and ate a diet mostly consisting of what would be thought of as "healthy" food, they did not show the same heart benefits. Wow!

As I scoured the net, I stumbled across the website of a "fruitarian" who utterly slammed anyone who might consider eating fat, animals or even killing a plant for vegetables. I could feel frustration building again, as when it comes to diet there are so many different points of view—all of which when argued with enough venom seemed plausible; I really wished that everyone would shut the hell up, because maybe then I would have a chance of actually eating with my body rather than my brain.

I was going to have to get better at keeping my own focus, and not latching onto whatever dietary tangents the rest of the world was on. What I needed to figure out was what would be best for *my body*, not anyone else's; because I was going to have to live the rest of my life in *my body* so really, *my body* should be my greatest resource.

I remembered the jacket potatoes that I used to eat as a child; how I loved the slow Aga baked potatoes with the soft fluffy insides, and how I had loved to eat them with butter.

The golden curls that one could transfer into the middle of a steaming hot baked potato. The way that the melting butter would turn the white flesh of the potato a primrose yellow colour.

My frustration subsided and exhilaration grew. I could do this!

I was going to eat butter again.

I looked over at Matt, "I need to eat butter!" I declared.

"Yeah, you do!" He looked over at me with an amused tone to his eyes. "What made you decide that though . . . do vegans eat butter?"

I jabbed him playfully in the ribs. He knew very well that vegans do not eat butter, but I could hardly blame him for mocking my absurd and unexpected 360-degree dietary turn. I didn't care: It felt right. Finally, I had made a dietary decision that *felt* right!

I'd also noticed something: Most of the foods that I had loved as a child were the very same that I was scared as shit to eat as an adult. Butter, whole milk, Greek yoghurt, cheese (oh cheese!), the crispy skin off chicken, bread.

Not once, not once when Mother had asked me what I wanted to eat before I was seventeen, would I have asked for kale and tofu.

I needed to eat like a child again. I had to find the inner guidance around food that I'd had before my brain had gone and pissed on my parade.

I looked over at Matt again, who was still smirking at me with a kind disbelief on his face.

Later that evening, he asked me why. Why had I suddenly felt able, willing and determined to eat fat? An understandable question. After all, Matt had observed my struggles with food for a number of years. I bet even he had not seen that one coming! And to be honest, neither had I. I told him that I did not really know why, but that it just felt like the right thing to do.

And at the time, I was not sure how and why either. Why butter? Why eggs? Why fat?

Nowadays, I would be much better equipped to answer that question. Now, I could explain to him that butter contains many nutrients that actually protect against heart disease —such as vitamin A, which is good for the health of my thyroid and adrenal glands as well as being a strong antioxidant with fantastic immune system strengthening properties. I could have also told him that vitamin A is needed by my body in order to absorb calcium, and that if my body absorbed more calcium—as I had been attempting to make it do by chewing on calcium supplements for the past couple of months—my teeth and bones might feel a little stronger.

I could explain to him that the reason I should eat butter is *because* of its high fat content, and that this is relevant because vitamin A (like vitamins D, E and K) is fat soluble, so even though it was present in all the vegetables that I had been eating, without the fat to transport it my body could not make good use of it. And, that vitamin A is more easily absorbed from butter than any other food.

I could tell him that it was highly probable that the reason I had been popping both pill form and droplets of vitamin B12 after a couple of months on a vegan diet was because I had been feeling fatigued and lacking in mojo, and that B12 can naturally be found in animal products because it is made with the bacteria found in manure fertilized soil from which the grass grows that animals eat.

I could explain that another fat soluble vitamin, vitamin D, is also needed for the calcium to be absorbed into my body, and this too would be a wonderful thing for my teeth and bones.

I could tell him that all the low-fat protein bars and shakes that I had been eating and drinking were possibly causing my body to release acids into my bloodstream as I metabolised them. And that this acid, should it be there, would most likely be being neutralised by calcium that my body was drawing out of my bones. I could show him the studies that I had read that evening. The *Protein consumption and bone fractures in women* study, for example, where women who ate more than ninety grams of low fat protein a day were twenty percent more likely to have broken a wrist over a twelve-year period when compared to those who ate an average amount of protein (less than seventy grams a day).

I could remind him that saturated fatty acids are what my cells are made of, and for this reason it should be considered to be an inherently good substance—rather than inherently bad. I'd go as far to say now, that hating fat is classed as a form of self-abuse in my book, because we *are* fat, our cells are built from fat, and fat is an essential part of what it is to be a human body.

Nowadays, if answering that question why, I could reason to both science and philosophy in defense of fat. But then if I did that, for fairness sake I should also give credit and consideration to all the studies quoted by those that were living a healthy and happy vegan life. I should also show him the Olympic vegan athletes that got strong without saturated animal fats. And for good measure I should show him *The Framingham Osteoporosis Study* in which high-protein diets were associated with increased bone mineral density.

In fact, the more popular and widely accepted view still holds that animal fats are bad. But, to be honest, I am sick and tired of researching, reading, and taking in the opinions of other people, friends, health gurus and the like. I have been exhausted by thinking about food, worrying if I was eating the right thing, listening to all these different opinions and points of view. Trying to understand the advanced scientific reasoning behind why one should eat this and why one should not eat that.

The day that I decided to eat butter again was the day that I shut down everyone else's opinions on my diet. It seemed that everything—my reading, my experiences, my vegan fail—had been leading me up to this moment of final and complete understanding. Not cognitive understanding: bodily understanding. My body was talking to me again. After what had seemed like months of meditation and yoga, soul searching and down right begging, my body was talking to me, and it was telling me I needed butter.

Milk, cheese, butter, and eggs were the foods that I could feel myself longing for. Not lusting for, but *longing* for. Food lust feels uncomfortable—like the binge-feeling that I would get at night when I devoured sugar-laden sweets and baked goods. Longing for dairy felt different: nostalgic and comforting.

It's hard enough, bombarded with media as we are, for any person to really avoid influence and listen to his or her body when it comes to nutrition. I'd suffered an additional complication in that I had Anorexia, and therefore I had to work my way through my eating disorder to a weight restored state: that had been stage one for me. Most people don't have Anorexia to contend with, just society and culture.

Stage one involved getting to a point where Anorexia was no longer killing me. That is no easy task, as anyone who has ever dealt with an eating disorder will know.

"Your heart will not be able to sustain you at this body weight," my doctor had very clearly told me on a number of occasions. I understood what she was saying to me, but Anorexia had me powerless and irrational. Eating disorders do not like rationality. Anorexia spits prudence out.

Stage one was getting past that. Stage two was getting past society's hate of fat, which I had allowed to fuel my own.

I had spent years relying on science and fashion to feed me. I had looked to others for guidance about something that should have been all about me and only about me. I had been eating off every plate other than my own.

Once I had made that decision, I could not get to the shops fast enough. I wanted butter. Nowadays, I am pleased to say that I use butter over anything else in the kitchen. I spread it, I fry with it, I bake with it and I roast with it. Now, nutritional science aside, I use butter because it makes everything taste fabulous, but . . . interestingly, butter from grass-fed cows in particular, is a great source of vitamins. Specifically, grass-fed cow's butter is high in the fat-soluble vitamin K, which actually comes from green plants.

There are two types of vitamin K, aptly named K1 and K2. K1 is available in leafy green vegetables—spinach, kale and broccoli. Unfortunately, due to the low-fat fad, many people prefer to eat them without salad dressing or fat, and without fat, it is hard to absorb fat soluble vitamin K.

In my fat dodging days, I would have told you that I prefer salad undressed. That is a bloody lie. Have you ever tried eating undressed leaves such as lettuce or kale? They taste like leaves. Unless you are a cow or a horse, leaves taste pretty horrid. Now, go put some fat on those leaves in the form of dressing and suddenly they taste like something worth eating. The body knows that fat allows it to absorb more vitamins, so it gears one's taste buds to like the taste of fat. That is, until we allow our brains to get in the way and mess up our perception of what is healthy and what not. Low-fat salad dressing is a nutritional travesty.

Vitamin K2, on the other hand, is the product of fermentation in the gut, which usually needs intestinal bacteria in order to happen. This is one of those mechanisms that knocks me for six in terms of respect for nature. The story goes that the cows out in the pasture eat the grass that has vitamin K2 in, then we humans can access that form of vitamin K when we consume meat and milk from grass-fed cows.

The moral of the story: be nice to cows. Cows given a pleasurable life out on a pasture in the sun are going to absorb into their bodies the very things that we need to eat in the meat and dairy that they give us. A cow that has been shut in a tiny stall and fed on only grain for its whole life can certainly be processed for meat, and it can certainly be eaten. But there is a catch: the meat is less nutritionally useful to us humans.

I guess nature wants us to do things her way.

Every time I think of cows now, and consider how much better their meat is when they are happy, I think of Lucy Tallon. "Fat Cow" is what the schoolyard bullies called her. Ironically, the Fat Cow is the happiest, most abundant and nurturing creature that could roam the earth.

And on that note, I can also tell you that after a couple of weeks of eating an adequate amount of animal fat with my daytime meals, the binge eating that had plagued me for so many years began to subside. Gradually my night binges waned in quantity, until one day I woke up having slept through without waking up to eat.

Apparently, what cured me of binge eating at night was eating enough saturated fat during the day.

Bloody simple when you put it like that; such a shame it took me so long.

I bet you are thinking that after rejecting my veganhood and returning to the dark side of fat, everything worked out for me and I lived happily ever after. Almost. There was just one more thing I had to go through first: paleo.

Chapter Thirty Six

Well, I'm only human. You know the deal with us homosapiens: two steps forward, one back:.

My friend Sandra had decided that she was paleo, which sort of instigated the whole thing.

"I feel so much better and my skin has cleared up . . . I just have more energy."

"Interesting, I guess it's really just eating lots of meat and vegetables?"

"Yes! Totally! It's a much more *natural* way of eating. I mean, I'm basically eating like a caveman . . . things like rice and bread are not natural, we would not have eaten them thousands of years ago, would we?"

"No . . . I guess not." I had to admit, that seemed to make sense, but there was something about it that was bugging me. "But . . . we wouldn't have shopped at Whole Foods thousands of years ago either . . . would we?"

I'd like to add, that since then, in 2014, there was a study released that showed that not only did cavemen not shop at Whole Foods, but they did not eat anything close to what the Paleo diet predicts. It was titled *Blood, Bulbs, and Bunodonts: On Evolutionary Ecology and the Diets of Ardipithecus, Australopithecus, and Early Homo,* and the researchers concluded that the amount of meat eaten by our ancestors on a daily basis would not have been as high as paleo advocates believe as a result of the caveman's poor hunting skills.

The paleo diet was initially popularised by a bloke called Walter Voegtin in the 1970s. And yes, it was based on the theory that those living in the Paleolithic era would not have eaten processed grains and McDonalds. One of the most controversial aspects of the paleo diet, in my opinion, is the preference adopted by some writers to capitalize the "P." That really annoys me. Seeing paleo diet written "Paleo diet" annoys me almost as much as seeing a hyphen in place of an em dash.

Yeah, yeah, I know what you are thinking, part of me was thinking it too. *What the hell Tabs? Why do you feel that you need to adopt yet another dietary trend?*

The thing was, without my vegan label, I was feeling a bit naked, and paleo appealed. I was seduced by the thought of having a food identity again. I went for it.

I broke the news to my poor, long-suffering and ever faithful husband:

"So . . . er . . . I decided that I am paleo."

He looked at me blankly.

"Well . . . Sandra was telling me."

He raised his eyebrows. "Sandra is paleo now?"

I shrugged.

"Eat more meat I agree with," he encouraged, "but don't you need carbohydrates too?"

"I can eat potatoes and vegetables," I responded with authority. "and anyway, it's not as if eating paleo will be very different from how I eat already."

Except that it was.

Unfortunately, paleo is not dairy friendly, so soon after I had been enjoying Greek yoghurt, butter, and of course full-fat milk, I was back to restricting it again. I also, naturally, consumed less carbohydrates. No bread. *Jesus Christ.* (That's not blasphemy: he ate bread.)

I had not appreciated how many grains that I ate until I was no longer able to eat them. No oats for breakfast? Fine, because I prefer eggs anyway. Eggs on what? Not toast; the sourdough bread that I had been enjoying with my morning eggs was certainly out now that I was paleo. For some reason, a fried egg on top of a pile of vegetables is not quite as satisfying as it is on hot buttered toast.

Bread is a truly wonderful thing. It is a great vehicle of transportation for fats and proteins; eggs, butter, cheese, peanut butter, are my personal favourites. Also, for me—someone who was unable to eat bread for over ten years due to Anorexia—bread still feels like a victory food, so I really did feel at a loss when my paleo diet meant I could not have it.

Then there was the dairy. I scouted about for some coconut yoghurt instead of the full-fat Greek that I had been enjoying. It was nice enough, but lacked that satisfying creaminess that accompanies dairy yoghurt. I have to admit that, even then, it struck me that it was strange that coconut yoghurt is considered paleo as I struggled to imagine that cavemen had eaten it. Plus, it is a processed food.

About a week in, I was told that true paleo calls for non-starchy vegetables, so in a strict sense potatoes were out. I thoroughly missed eating potatoes, and often found myself hungry for more carbohydrates. There were times where I felt full enough and happy, then for no apparent reason there would be the odd day that my body just seemed to be calling for some starch. This brought up dissonance within me. Should I listen to my body or listen to my dietary label?

"Are you sure you don't want some of my toast?"

Matt and I had gone out to brunch at a local restaurant called Tangerine. He had ordered the full monty of eggs and bacon, beans, sausages, hash browns and toast. I had poached eggs and a salad. True paleo says sausages are a no because of the processing and additives, and so was just about everything else on the menu.

"No. I'm fine." My words did not sound convincing, even to my own ears.

"You sure?" He waved a piece of buttered toast in front of my nose. This irritated me, probably because I was still hungry. I'm always fractious when I'm hungry.

"Stop it!" I brushed the offending toast-baring hand away from my face, "I'm fine, I've enough to eat."

My heart sank as I said that. It sounded horribly familiar.

True paleo cannot eat beans either, so hummus was out, as were many of the Mexican dishes that I had been enjoying. I was in food déjà-vu again and wondered if this was another sneak on behalf of Anorexia. I might be eating, I might be a good weight . . . hell, I was even eating fat . . . but, something about any form of dietary restriction—even if it was the fat-loving paleo type—stank of relapse. After six weeks, I ditched paleo too.

Truth is, any diet that restricts has the potential to ruin me. Restriction is my nemesis. Rules and games are what my eating disorder wants me to be governed by.

Why was I vegan? Was it because I believed that it was the right way to be, or was it because in being so I had an excuse to restrict?

Why was I paleo? Was it because I really believed that one should eat like a caveman, or was it because in being so I had an opportunity to restrict?

Why did I feel the need to go gluten-free? Was it because I thought my gut was faulty, or was it because doing so proved an opportunity to restrict?

In truth telling, I often find that it is not the answer that I want that is the answer that I know is the truth, the real truth and nothing but the truth. In truth telling, it is usually the answer that I don't want that is the truth. The one that makes me cringe. In truth telling, I find it is often the answer that I am rejecting that actually is the truth.

In truth telling, any diet for me is about restriction. My mind has the ability to pollute even the most sane and saintly of eating plans. I cannot diet. I cannot restrict. Ever.

For some people, an adopted eating system or "diet" has a benefit in that it stops them over indulging. For other people, a specific diet is needed due to their individual digestion requirements or metabolism. For most people, it is a load of carefully-marketed bullshit that makes them think it is *normal* to have a "food identity."

Take, for example, gluten free. The vast majority of people who purchase gluten-free food products do not do so because they have a medical condition that dictates they do so. The number one ranking reason for eating gluten free is "because it's healthier." Isn't it?

If you are Celiac, sure.

Like I said, most gluten-free customers are not Celiac, they are just confused.

Ask Doctor Daniel A. Leffler, director of clinical research at the Celiac Center at Beth Israel Deaconess Medical Center in Boston:

"People who are sensitive to gluten may feel better, but a larger portion will derive no significant benefit from the practice. They'll simply waste their money, because these products are expensive," says Leffler, who is also an assistant professor of medicine at Harvard Medical School.

That's Leffler's opinion, and there are a thousand others that I could quote who argue just the opposite. I could dedicate a whole book—no, a whole series of books—just to the back and forth science and opinion behind the question of gluten. But, I'm not going to because I am over it. I am over it *all*.

Gluten-free, dairy-free, soy-free, low-GI, paleo, vegan, vegetarian, sugar-free and —most of all—fat-free. I am *so* over it.

Just shut the hell up and let me eat my bloody dinner.

Thank Elvis for Fat and Gluten!

I made that decision then, and did not look back. I love food. I love eating. My stomach can handle anything, and there is no excuse—other than those generated in my head—for me to not eat anything. Except cottage cheese. I hate low-fat cottage cheese. I also hate tofu. And quinoa.

There are not many foods that I do not like, but those that hit that category are usually foods like cottage cheese and tofu; foods that I made myself eat for years because they are low-fat and—apparently—healthy. In my opinion, anyone who claims to actually enjoy eating low-fat cottage cheese, tofu and quinoa more than full-fat cheddar, chicken and bread is a dirty rotten liar.

That's a harsh statement, but it is one I stand by. Humans are at the top of the food chain, and we did not get there by eating coagulated bean curd. In the same way that I think not voting in political elections is an insult to the women who fought for my vote, claiming that humans are supposed to be on a low-fat diet is disrespectful to my early ancestors who grew their brains enough to get me out of a cave and into a house with all the luxuries that human-invention has allowed me. Humans are many things—not all of them good—but nobody can deny that we aren't smarter than your average cow. So with that in mind, some of us still need to stop eating like an intellectually inferior species.

I like vegetables, but I don't enjoy them in the same way that I do fatty foods. I have never woken up in the morning and felt excited at the prospect of eating broccoli, but I often wake up and jump out of bed at the thought of eggs on toast. When I am hungry, I don't crave carrot sticks and salsa, but the idea of a pulled pork sandwich is enough to see me sprinting towards the nearest place where I can get some barbecue.

I ditched "healthy eating" in favour of a truly balanced diet (i.e. one that contains a mix of all nutrients—including a nice amount of saturated fat) and so far, all I have seen is positive mental and physical effect. I feel good, but most of all I feel *happy*. If I am influenced by anyone at all when it comes to what I eat now, it is the child version of myself to whom I look.

What would I have wanted when I was ten?
What would I have eaten before my brain started to get in the way?

Usually, the answer is cheese.

The Thank You Page

Before I wrote this book, I'd always assumed that the "Thank You" page in books was just one of those places where authors suck up to their publishers and agents. I don't have either of those things, so why do I have a page such as this?

Honestly, it is because upon finishing this book I feel immense gratitude towards certain people. It looks like I am getting soft in my old age after all!

First of all my parents, for never giving up on me. And in the same vein my two sisters, who really suffered the blunt end of my temper when I was sick. They all stuck with me through thin and thinner—and we all survived to see me get better.

Then there are all the people in the eating disorder advocacy world who have helped me do something with all the things that I learned the hard way. The people who make up International Eating Disorder Action (IEDA), but especially Jennifer Denise, Amy Cunningham, and Jenny Haken (Jenny: I owe you one!).

There are plenty of others who deserve my thanks, but I'll cut it short with one more person: my wonderful Matt. I don't know how I landed the most loving, kind, and patient man on the planet, but I did (sorry ladies, he's taken!). Thank you Darling.

A note for 2016

First off, thank you for reading my book. When I wrote and published I was not prepared for how it would feel to know that people actually read my book. Thank you to those of you who have taken the time to email me. It has been fabulous to get to know you.

In this book I mention that I used the principles of Family-Based Therapy as typically used on children and adolescents with eating disorders and applied them to myself. A couple of readers contacted me and asked me to elaborate. So I will, here is how that all worked out:

So I start Googling eating disorders. And I come across this F.E.A.S.T website that is a resource for parents of children with EDs. On that website is a forum, and I create a username and start reading.

The stuff on that site… . You've got parents who are terrified and watching their own children starve to death. You've got parents who have lost children to ED. You have parents who have successfully used Family-Based Therapy to treat a child with an ED, and you have everything in between.

The anonymous nature of the forum means that this is a place where parents don't need to hold back. They can openly grieve, rage, and unleash their frustration at their child's illness. It's raw.

I read a lot. Initially when I read about FBT and the process of practically force feeding children who are at risk of starving to death my own eating disorder had a fit. It told me that was cruel. But a part of me knew it wasn't. A part of me knew it was the only thing that was going to help these children in the long run. As I continued to read about the horrific mealtime tantrums that these parents were dealing with six times a day every day I could see both sides: I was the child, but I was also the adult wanting the child to get better. Those days reading FEAST taught me the following:

1. **I understood that a parent could love their child but simultaneously hate their child's eating disorder.**

2. **You can force feed something (myself in my case) as an act of love.**

3. **Learning about how FBT is used to treat children I was able to take the framework and apply it to my own self.**

Life stops until you eat. I would make myself sit at the table and tell myself you are not leaving until you have eaten it all. Even if it takes hours. No matter what else

243

you had planned to do today, you don't get to do any of it until you have eaten this meal.

Was it easy? Hell no!

Many a time I slammed my chair back and left that table with food still on my plate, but I only got a couple of feet out of the kitchen before the "FBT voice" said: *If you leave that food Anorexia has won. I hate Anorexia right, so that thought of letting it win would send me straight back to the table to eat the rest.*

4. Food is medicine.

FEAST drummed this into me. I think that it's tattooed onto some part of my brain somewhere. I still think it every day for good measure. I made that my motto. I made it my mantra. I repeated it over and over to drown out the ED voice telling me to obsess over calories or exercise.

5. After some time, I turned that into "Fat is Medicine" in an attempt to help myself redefine my more feared nutrient in my head — and that is what lead me to the book that I wrote: *Love Fat*.

CPSIA information can be obtained
at www.ICGtesting.com
Printed in the USA
BVHW040730180421
605242BV00030B/1071